ADVANCES IN LIBRARY ADMINISTRATION AND ORGANIZATION

ADVANCES IN LIBRARY ADMINISTRATION AND ORGANIZATION

Series Editors: Edward D. Garten and
Delmus E. Williams

Recent Volumes:

ADVANCES IN LIBRARY ADMINISTRATION
AND ORGANIZATION   VOLUME 19

ADVANCES IN LIBRARY ADMINISTRATION AND ORGANIZATION

EDITED BY

EDWARD D. GARTEN

Dean of Libraries and Information Technologies,
University of Dayton, OH, USA

DELMUS E. WILLIAMS

Dean of University Libraries, University of Akron,
OH, USA

2002

JAI
An Imprint of Elsevier Science

Amsterdam – Boston – London – New York – Oxford – Paris
San Diego – San Francisco – Singapore – Sydney – Tokyo

ELSEVIER SCIENCE Ltd
The Boulevard, Langford Lane
Kidlington, Oxford OX5 1GB, UK

First edition 2002

Library of Congress Cataloging in Publication Data
A catalog record from the Library of Congress has been applied for.

British Library Cataloguing in Publication Data
A catalogue record from the British Library has been applied for.

ISBN: 0-7623-0868-0
ISSN: 0732-0671 (Series)

⊚ The paper used in this publication meets the requirements of ANSI/NISO Z39.48-1992 (Permanence of Paper).
Printed in The Netherlands.

CONTENTS

INTRODUCTION

As we enter 2002, it is no surprise that the challenges facing library managers are many and varied. As always, they reflect a gradual evolution in our profession and include both the familiar and the unfamiliar. In addressing them, the approaches we take as leaders include both innovative and time-tested techniques. In Volume 19 of *Advances in Library Administration and Organization*, Ed Garten and I again offer an array of articles addressing some of those management issues. As usual in this series, the subjects treated vary widely, and the introduction of three articles by authors working outside of the United States offers a more international flavor to the selections. But the matters addressed represent areas of common interest within our profession and reflect a universal understanding that the problems managers face are more alike than different no matter where we live.

The lead article comes from Australia and was developed as a result of the work of Mark Brogan, Philip Hingston and Vicky Wilson in developing a curriculum on knowledge management to be introduced into Library and Information Science and IT programs in February 2002. The importance of this work is two fold. First, it provides an opening salvo in curricular discussions, but, to those of us more interested in practice than in pedagogy, it also offers an in depth definition of what is meant when the term knowledge manager is used. While individuals may argue with the authors' definition and the sub-disciplines included in their curriculum, the article provided me with the clearest statement I have yet found of what the term knowledge management means and what is required to make it a viable part of my program.

Bill Dworczyk follows this with an excellent case study of the application of Stufflebeam's CIPP model for change management at Southern Methodist University. Change is not new, and articles about how people are addressing the need to transition their organizations to meet changing environments are also not new. But Bill's analysis of what worked and did not work as this model was applied provides an insight into the ramifications of putting a technique into practice and the lessons learned that do not appear in textbooks. This kind of "after action report" is too rare in our literature and well worth the time taken to read it.

Roger Durbin, James Nalen, Diana Chlebek and Nancy Pitre are up next with an article about how one library is working to develop a policy for acquiring eBooks and integrating them into their collection. While much has been written about the technology and economics of eBooks, and many people constantly tell us that they will become an important part of our future, little guidance is available in the literature about how one creates an eBook collection in aggregate and how that fits into the collection policies of University Libraries. Durbin and his colleagues synthesize the literature that is available relating to eBooks and then integrates that into a thoughtful presentation about where eBooks fit into our lives. Again, one may differ with the authors' approach, but their work lays a foundation for a discussion among collection managers that must soon begin.

Elizabeth Buchanan then offers a piece on ethical issues relating to the use of the Internet for research. This new medium offers the social scientist excellent opportunities to collect all kinds of data, but Ms. Buchanan encourages us to make sure that, as we use this tool, that we protect human subjects and assure ethical research conduct.

Diana Kingston is another Australian who has taken it upon herself to look carefully at what effective managers actually do as opposed to either what they say they do or what other say they should do. As a pragmatist, I have been drawn to this kind of study ever since I discovered Henry Mintzberg more than twenty years ago, and am pleased to offer Kingston's work as a worthy addition to this literature.

Jean Mulhern's interest is in quality assessment in higher education in general and in academic libraries in particularly. She talks at length about emerging trends in accreditation and related assessment programs and offers a solid update on changes that are taking place in this area. Given the emphasis that most institutions in and outside of higher education are placing on assessment and the rapidity with which new approaches to it are emerging, this is a "must read" for any manager.

Anne Pierce offers a short piece on research by undergraduates using the Internet, the impact that this new source of information has and the challenge it presents to both librarians and classroom instructors. It is a thought provoking piece that should be a call to arms for us all as we attempt to encourage our students to use this resource wisely.

Finally, the volume closes with two articles on library networks. Kathy Schulz has done a fine job explaining how participation in OhioLINK, the state network in Ohio, has affected her work at Wittenberg, and then proceeds from there to look at how that network has impacted the work of librarians working in liberal arts colleges throughout the state. Schulz has done a good job in explaining the challenges and opportunities presented when small colleges join consortia. This is followed by a descriptive article developed by Hao-Ren Ke about the national information network being developed in Taiwan. His emphasis is on the special challenges that present themselves when library directors working outside of the United States and Europe work to develop a national information network. While some of these challenges are familiar to anyone working in a network, others are not. Dr. Ke offers interesting insights into how a national cooperative can develop within a unique culture and in spite of problems created by distance from information providers and other elements.

As you can see, the topics treated are both varied and interesting, and we commend this work to you as important additions to the literature of librarianship and information services. We hope you will find them informative and that the insights provided are of help as you the library leader and manager do your work.

Delmus E. Williams
Co-editor

A RICH STOREHOUSE FOR THE RELIEF OF MAN'S ESTATE: EDUCATION FOR KNOWLEDGE MANAGEMENT

Mark Brogan, Philip Hingston and Vicky Wilson

INTRODUCTION

Knowledge is a rich storehouse, for the glory of the creator and the relief of man's estate

(Francis Bacon)

Thinkers and writers from Ancient Greece to the present day acknowledge the fundamental importance of knowledge to the furtherance of human society. Debates on the nature of knowledge have occupied philosophers from Aristotle to Hegel, but discussion about the best way to 'manage' knowledge is of fairly recent origin.

Education systems are under constant pressure to adapt to changes in society. Some believe that our societies are undergoing a transformation as important as the industrial revolution and that knowledge is the core element in the emerging mode of production, with learning as the most important process. Our understanding of what knowledge is and of how knowledge is created, transferred, managed and used remains partial, superficial and partitioned in various scientific disciplines, with the result that 'the basic concepts of knowledge are defined and interpreted in different ways' (CERI, 2000).

Advances in Library Administration and Organization, Volume 19, pages 1–26.
© **2002 Published by Elsevier Science Ltd.**
ISBN: 0-7623-0868-0

Knowledge Management (KM) has been practiced and reported on for a number of years. As early as 1988, Peter Drucker called attention to the primacy of 'knowledge assets' in the future success of companies. By 1994, many articles addressed the importance of the individual employee's knowledge as opposed to the company's databases and reports (Ruth, Theobald & Frizzell, 1999). As the early enthusiasm for the concept subsides in the current management literature, KM is becoming part of the corporate culture of large complex organizations, especially those that operate in a multinational environment. Early insubstantial applications of KM theory and practice have given way to broadly focused initiatives that are transforming the way organizations work (Davenport, 2000). Despite this integration of KM theory and practice into the core operations of organizations worldwide, very few universities have taken up the challenge of offering full courses in this discipline area. One of the reasons for this is the difficulty of determining the intellectual territory to be covered by any viable and practical KM course (Ruth, Theobold & Frizzell, 1999). Consequently, there is a tendency among university educators to offer units of instruction on KM as parts of other awards, but to see the development of a fully-fledged and integrated KM course as just too hard.

FRAMING KNOWLEDGE MANAGEMENT

Researchers and practitioners in the fields of computer science and information systems have equated KM with the management of information, that is the management of objects that can be identified and handled in information systems. The information-processing view of KM has been prevalent in practice and research for a number of decades. This view of KM has been characterised by 'technology-intensive, optimisation-driven, efficiency-seeking organizational change' (Malhotra, 2000, p. 4) The paradigm makes simplistic assumptions about storing past knowledge of individuals in the forms of 'routinized' rules-of-thumb and 'best practices' for guiding future action. There has been little, if any, emphasis on business model innovation and the assumption has been made that the adaptive functioning of the organisation could be based on 'explicit knowledge archived in corporate databases and technology-based knowledge repositories' (Malhotra, 2000, p. 4).

Such views, which are still prevalent today in the information systems industry, are based primarily on a static and syntactic notion of knowledge and have ignored the human dimension of organisational knowledge creation. The paradigm has a place, in that systems designed from this viewpoint often provide the preferred solutions to well-structured problem situations that occur in stable and predictable organisational environments (Malhotra, 2000, pp. 4–5).

The information processing view of KM has, however, propagated some dangerous myths about KM. Malhotra identifies these as:

(1) KM technologies can deliver the 'right information' to the 'right person' at the 'right time';
(2) KM technologies can store human intelligence and experience;
(3) KM technologies can distribute human intelligence (Malhotra, 2000, pp. 7–8).

Malhotra calls for a greater emphasis on the human aspects of knowledge creation and knowledge renewal that are difficult – if not impossible – to replace completely with knowledge management technologies. He calls these aspects the 'sense-making' model of KM and identifies the particular aspects as:

• Imagination and creativity latent in human minds;
• Untapped tacit dimensions of knowledge creation;
• Subjective and meaning-making basis of knowledge;
• Constructive aspects of knowledge creation and renewal (Malhotra, 2000, p. 11).

He proposes a model for business model innovation that provides a guiding framework for KM, and hence for any KM curriculum. It is based on equal weight being given to both the information processing and the sense-making models of KM so that the optimisation driven and efficiency oriented benefits of the information processing model can be effectively combined with the knowledge creation and knowledge renewal aspects of the sense-making model. This framework offers the organisation 'the best of both worlds' – a combination of flexibility and agility while ensuring the efficiencies of the current technology architecture (Malhotra, 2000).

Malhotra is by no means the only commentator to recognise the importance of the human element in any KM system. For example, Collison and Parcell (2001, p. 18) conceptualise knowledge management as a 'hybrid' discipline in which the role of people is vital. The elements of a successful knowledge management program include:

• a common reliable *technology* infrastructure to facilitate sharing;
• connecting the *people* who know, and the behaviours to ask, listen and share; and
• some *processes* to simplify sharing, validation, distillation.

They argue that organizations seeking to emphasise technology at the expense of human factors may be disappointed since "without the people aspect, there is a strong risk that any effort to make change will generate resistance" (ibid).

Survey of the literature shows that the human aspects of knowledge creation are widely recognised as being critical for sustaining knowledge management systems that facilitate inquiry based on divergence of meanings and perspectives. The human nature of knowledge creation seems more pertinent now than ever before, given an increasingly 'wicked' working environment characterised 'by discontinuous change and a *"wide range of potential surprise"* ' (Malholtra, 1997). Nor is that discontinuous change and potential surprise restricted solely to the business environment. Recent events in the U.S. have caused comment on the tragic consequences of an over-reliance on technology to control terrorist activity and the importance of detailed attention to the human aspect of the problem (Eccleston, 2001).

Those that have been educated in the disciplines of philosophy, psychology, sociology and/or business and management have long equated KM with the management of people. They believe that knowledge managers are primarily involved with assessing, changing and improving individual human skills and behaviour and that knowledge is a series of processes, a complex set of dynamic skills and expertise that is constantly changing. Proponents of this school tend to discount the importance of the information-processing paradigm (Sveiby, 2000). Malhotra's contribution is to recognise that both aspects are of equal importance in the KM framework and it is our assertion that an effective and relevant KM course would be incomplete without equal attention being given to both of these paradigms.

The two groups also view 'knowledge' quite differently. The IT-focused group views knowledge as "objects" to be documented, classified, stored, retrieved, analysed and otherwise manipulated for useful applications. New developments in information sciences such as artificial intelligence, fuzzy logic and simulation modelling provide fertile ground for experimentation and development of KM systems based on this 'information-processing' paradigm. The people-focused group views knowledge as primarily tacit, largely embodied in the skill of experts, embedded in processes intimately linked with people, and often difficult to codify (Talison, 2001).

Hansen, Nohria and Tierney (Hansen, Nohria & Tierney, 1999) conducted a major study for the *Harvard Business Review* in 1999 in which they observed the KM needs of knowledge-based services firms (e.g. consulting firms, health care providers, IT services, etc.). They found that the needs of these companies fall somewhere between the two extremes.

The first of these extremes are knowledge-based services companies that offer repetitive, similar or modularized services and whose competitive strength lies in delivering such services quickly, cheaply and reliably. These companies create value by large-scale re-use of knowledge applied to similar recurring types of service. They need to codify and store such knowledge for easy and efficient retrieval, and so invest in sophisticated knowledge databases accessible via the company intranet, especially if the company has numerous branches all over the world. Once a project has developed an effective new approach, work processes and templates, these are captured into documents and stored electronically for use in later similar projects. Efficient people- to-document (e.g. process documentation, taxonomy) and document-to-people (e.g. tracking, intelligent search engines) processes become crucial for delivering their kind of service. For companies of this type, an IT-focused, information-processing KM strategy is most appropriate (Hansen et al., 1999).

At the other extreme are companies that offer one-of-a-kind or custom services and whose competitive strength lies in their high level of expertise, tailor-fit quality and personalized customer relationship. They create value by high-level expert service tailored to particular client's needs. Every engagement is unique and every solution requires fresh research. Service delivery requires accurate assessment of client needs, and the design of a responsive solution. Such services require knowledge with high tacit content, people-to-people transfer of knowledge, effective teamwork in cross-functional teams, innovation or improvisation, and excellent people skills. Investment in IT hardware and software tends to be moderate but hiring of senior professional staff is a crucial and elaborate affair. For companies of this type, a people-focused KM strategy is most appropriate. Hansen calls the approach of the first type, "codification strategy" and that of the second type, "personalization strategy." A company can practice both: the codification strategy in those projects where frequent reuse of knowledge is encountered, and the personalization strategy in other projects where highly tacit and person-centred skills and expertise are important (Hansen et al., 1999; Talison, 2001).

There seems to be agreement that, no matter what the enterprise, KM must deal with both approaches. It follows that most companies will require any 'knowledge managers' that they employ to have skills and expertise in both 'codification' and 'personalization'. KM education should therefore be made up of both the hard technical discussions of knowledge storage, retrieval and dissemination and a whole range of softer issues that involves fostering an environment in which knowledge and information are shared and new knowledge is created (CERI, 2000; Bukowitz & Williams, 2001). Peter Drucker, writing about KM in 1999, argued that:

> What we call the Information Revolution is actually a Knowledge Revolution. What has made it possible to routinize processes is not machinery; the computer is only the trigger. Software is the reorganization of traditional work, based on centuries of experience, through the application of knowledge and especially of systematic, logical analysis. The key is not electronics; it is cognitive science (Drucker, 1999).

Given that we accept the need for both technological and human aspects to be addressed in any KM course, what other issues should be addressed by the curriculum? To provide an answer to this question, it is worthwhile to examine the nature of knowledge and information from a variety of perspectives.

The economic point of view is that knowledge and information appear in two different contexts. The fundamental assumption of standard microeconomics is based on rational choices made by individual agents. In this model, how much and what kind of information agents have about the world in which they operate and their ability to effectively process that information are crucial issues. This perspective on knowledge puts the focus on a transformation process whereby data (the actual state of the world) can be transformed into information (indicators that are accessible to the agents representing the state of the world) and then into knowledge (through the processing of the information in analytical models by agents) (CERI, 2000, p. 12).

The other major perspective is one in which knowledge is regarded as an asset. Here knowledge may appear both as an input (competence) and output (innovation) in the production process. Under certain circumstances, it can be privately owned and/or bought and sold on the market as a commodity. The economics of knowledge is to a high degree about specifying the conditions for knowledge to appear as a normal commodity. Innovation theory and competence-based theories of the firm address how knowledge can be produced, mediated and used in the market economy (CERI, 2000, p. 13).

It is latter perspective that gets closest to the concerns of educators designing a KM course. It raises the issues of how knowledge is used and is helpful in making distinctions between generic and specific knowledge and between different forms of learning. It begins to determine the role of the knowledge manager in building the conditions for knowledge to appear as a normal commodity in the economy.

Further clues as to what should be included in the KM curriculum can be found in the debate about knowledge as a private or public good. While these two perspectives are seemingly opposed in their contrasting emphasis on protection and sharing of knowledge, they raise some fundamental questions about how knowledge is transferred classified and mediated – in other words, on how it is used. These questions are predicated on the characteristics of knowledge as: facts of information; principles that explain; and competence and skills that may need to the shared more among companies to produce a more composite, networked knowledge base. Technology makes is easier to disseminate some knowledge, but human networks remain crucial in accessing information and also in disseminating theoretical knowledge (CERI, 2000, pp. 14–16). The KM curriculum needs to expose its students to debate on these questions and to provide guidance in how to design the required networks and infrastructure.

Further evidence as to the breadth of the curriculum required for a KM course can be garnered from a discussion of the present research agenda in the area. The Centre for Educational Research and Innovation at the OECD has identified a broad range of research questions associated with knowledge management in the learning society and has organized these into five areas:

(1) The Management of Knowledge and Learning.
(2) Towards New Measurements of Knowledge and Learning.
(3) Policies of Innovation in Education.
(4) The New Challenges for Educational R&D Systems.
(5) Towards and New Research Agenda for the Learning Sciences.

Of these, the specific research questions raised under the first two areas provide a starting point for our discussion. They are:

1. *The Management of Knowledge and Learning*:

(a) How can organizations use knowledge more efficiently?
(b) What are the differences in KM between the public and private sectors?
(c) How do different professions manage knowledge?
(d) What are the characteristics of a learning organization?
(e) How can schools and other educational institutions develop a commitment to KM?
(f) What are the costs and benefits of knowledge transfer in education?
(g) Can educational institutions be given incentives to promote knowledge management and learning organizations?

2. *Towards New Measurements of Knowledge and Learning*:

(a) Can indicators of tacit knowledge be established?
(b) Can we get a better grasp of which kinds of learning are important for which kinds of innovation?
(c) How can we measure the performance of learning organizations?
(d) Can indicators be developed which show the role of social capital in the promotion of economic development including learning and innovation?

The cross-disciplinary nature of these research questions, taken together with input from the range of disciplines that make a contribution to Malhotra's KM model, dictate a cross-disciplinary approach to any KM course design. The broad and far-reaching nature of these research questions suggest that the 'territory' for KM study is far from decided; that any course will need to be agile and flexible as the 'map' of the territory changes and that it will need to provide for 'continuous construction and reconstruction . . . as a dynamic and ongoing process' (Malhotra, 2000, p. 15).

THE KNOWLEDGE MANAGEMENT CURRICULUM

In summary, it would seem from our examination of the discussions relating to Knowledge Management that the KM curriculum must encompass two fundamental aspects, each of which is of equal importance to the development of 'knowledge managers' with the right mix of skills and abilities to perform useful work in the knowledge economy. On the one hand they must be skilled at understanding and exploiting a wide range of information-processing technologies. On the other, they must be skilled at understanding and exploiting the human aspects of knowledge creation and knowledge renewal. In addition to these two fundamental requirements, they may require a broad understanding of wider social issues such as the nature of the overall knowledge economy and of the role of social capital in the promotion of economic development across industry sectors. Two questions emerge for the course designer:

(1) How do you encompass all of these requirements in a single course without diluting the student's exposure to the concepts to the point of triviality?
(2) Given the wide range of possible sectors in the knowledge economy in which the student may practice, how do you ensure that the skills and expertise developed in this future knowledge manager match the needs of their anticipated sector of operation?

As researchers and practitioners in the field of computer and information science, we have skills and expertise in the field of information management. The topics covered by this discipline area are now well defined and there is general agreement that they make a substantial contribution to knowledge management. However, as can be seen from the preceding discussion, it is a severe mistake to assume that they encompass the whole of KM theory and practice.

Much of what has been said so far about the framing of KM emphasizes its essentially multi-disciplinary nature, or what Collison and Parcell (2001) refer to as its 'hybrid' character. Collison and Parcell (2001, p. 18) diagrammatically conceptualize this hybrid notion of KM as an area of boolean intersection of the three core concerns of people, technology and process (see Fig. 1).

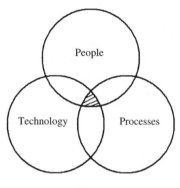

Fig. 1.

In the section that follows we have attempted to chart the history and the development of the technology dimension of KM- something which has grown out of the information-processing paradigm and that we choose to call 'knowledge computing'. Our goal is to show how it has contributed and will continue to contribute to the overall theoretical base of KM, subject to the qualifier that it does not encompass KM in totality. It is our view that a major issue all educators must face in course design, concerns *Knowledge Management's* relationship with what we call *Knowledge Computing*.

KNOWLEDGE COMPUTING FOR KNOWLEDGE MANAGEMENT

Knowledge Computing is about the construction of Knowledge Management *Systems* informed by a body of discipline knowledge inherited from information science and computer science. The current interest in knowledge computing is sustained by factors such as globalisation, down-sizing and of course, the Web, an increasingly important delivery vehicle for knowledge management solutions.

The Web began life as a hypermedia document delivery system, but has since become established as a computer-based knowledge-sharing tool. The runaway success of the Internet speaks eloquently for the power of a system that makes it easy for users located anywhere to contribute knowledge and to access knowledge contributed by others. This model has been adopted and adapted to create intranets, improving knowledge management for all kinds of enterprises.

The key part played by Web technology has made other computing technologies more relevant and brought about renewed interest in some old ideas. Among existing technologies that are being incorporated into computer-based knowledge management solutions are expert systems, intelligent agents, decision-support systems, natural language processing, information retrieval and electronic document management. In the left hand side shows some knowledge management tasks making up a knowledge cycle, while the right hand side shows some information systems and computing technologies that can be used to support these tasks (see Fig. 2).

For information and information technology professionals, such a model has the advantage of enabling activity within one professional domain to be straightforwardly mapped to corresponding activity in the other complementary domain.

Knowledge computing is entering an era of excitement and innovation centred around the technologies of next generation Internet and the idea of a 'Semantic' Web, introduced by Tim Berners-Lee, one of the creators of the original Web (Berners-Lee, 1998). In a recent article in Scientific American, he describes it thus:

> The Semantic Web is not a separate Web, but an extension of the current one, in which information is given well-defined meaning, better enabling computers and people to work in cooperation (Berners-Lee et al., 2001).

The first requirement for the Semantic Web is a universal knowledge representation system, to provide a common language allowing knowledge from disparate sources to be understood, combined and manipulated. Knowledge representation has long been studied in the field of artificial intelligence, and at least the taxonomy aspect of it has been well studied in LIS. But the Semantic Web requires a decentralised knowledge representation scheme.

This is where knowledge representation systems from artificial intelligence, classification schemes from LIS and mark-up languages from electronic publishing converge to provide the solutions. eXtensible Markup Language (XML) lets us include structured information in documents, and Resource Description Framework (RDF) provides the way to associate agreed meaning to this information, using Universal Resource Identifier (URIs) to refer to concepts defined in ontology pages on the Web.

How these ideas come together and their relationship with long standing ideas in information science such as classification and taxonomies can be powerfully demonstrated through consideration of some simple illustrations. For example, let's suppose that our goal is to create an intelligent system to assist family historians. To make automated reasoning possible in this knowledge domain we require two things:

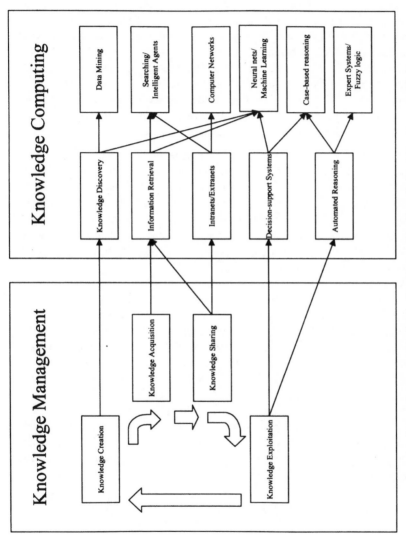

Fig. 2. Some Computing Technologies Supporting Knowledge Managements Tasks.

- Firstly, a knowledge representation framework describing entities in the domain (such as mothers, fathers, sons, daughters, aunts, uncles) and relations between them – in other words an *ontology*. This may seem like common sense, but unless the properties inherited by a male child from its father or the rules that make someone an aunt or uncle are defined, automated reasoning is impossible. An ontology is typically captured in RDF and commonly represented in an XML schema;
- Secondly, we need a way of identifying each instance of an entity in the database of family members. Where Molly is an aunt to Mark, we can apply XML markup to capture these values e.g. <aunt>Molly</aunt>, <nephew>Mark</nephew> in the data. In this way, XML gives structure to the data, another condition for automated reasoning.

Once we have a knowledge representation scheme, we can enable its re-use by others through a Universal Resource Identifier, an idea already familiar to us from the most common form of URI, the Uniform Resource Locator or URL.

Ontologies are long familiar to library and information science practitioners, who are adopting RDF and RDF Schema as implementation languages for defining metadata. Ontologies can contain inference rules as well as data, allowing sufficiently capable tools to carry out intelligent searches, reason about answers to user queries etc.

Agent technology, another established field of study in artificial intelligence, has also received a boost from the rise of Web technology, particularly with regard to applications in e-commerce. Agents and the Semantic Web are made for each other. The Semantic Web provides an ideal nourishing environment for "softbots", software agents that can roam the Web, accessing knowledge from Web pages, exchanging knowledge with other agents, carrying out information retrieval (or should that be knowledge retrieval?) tasks or otherwise acting on behalf of their human or corporate masters.

As this discussion suggests, knowledge computing exercises a good deal of influence over the trajectory of knowledge management, something likely to persist into the future. This influence is currently so profound that the study of knowledge computing must be 'a given' in any valid knowledge management program of study.

WHAT ELSE MAY BE NEEDED?
THE ECU KM SURVEY

While it is important to examine the literature and to take note of the opinions of experts and researchers as to the nature and structure of a KM course, it is also important to undertake some market research as to the viability of such a course and to survey the opinions of those who are likely to undertake it – or potentially employ – the graduates. To that end we developed a short questionnaire that was intended to elicit information on the course content, the likely market for the course and the employment opportunities for graduates.

Prior to finalising our design, we held focus group sessions with academics and industry practitioners and conducted research into what should be included in a relevant and useful course. In addition, we examined the range of units and courses in KM offered by other universities both in Australia and internationally. The resulting questionnaire was distributed to practitioners in the library, information management, records management and computing industry sectors. The survey questionnaire was also published as a HTML/CGI form on the World Wide Web.

On the basis of the results of the survey and from our other research, we developed a model for a course that we believe will meet an identified need in the marketplace for study and teaching in this area. The remainder of this paper discusses the results of our survey and the process of developing the course structure, as well as other related developments within the School relating to information and knowledge management.

THE SURVEY INSTRUMENT

The survey instrument was designed to measure preferences in terms of course content, course options (professional development, program of study in an existing award or dedicated award), industry demand for KM qualified personnel and attitudes toward knowledge management. The survey population comprised information technology professionals, librarians, records managers and fellow educators. Whether respondents were positively or negatively disposed towards KM was measured using a Likert scale. Statements focussed on three key dimensions of attitude toward KM, denoting expectations, identification or belonging and perceived value. Dimensions were operationalized with statements that invited respondents to say whether they:

- regarded KM as durable;
- saw themselves as Knowledge Managers;
- could see career benefits in learning more about KM.

LIMITATIONS OF THE SURVEY

At the time of writing, data gathering has not been completed to our satisfaction, as time and cost restraints restricted our initial survey population to local (Western Australian) respondents involved in IT-related industries. This meant that the number of respondents was small and the limited industry sectors surveyed introduced some bias into the results that we obtained. It is our intention to regard this initial survey as a pilot and to try to gather further responses through our survey website. We are also exploring options for administering the survey to a more randomised national, and possibly international sample. Updates of analysis outcomes will be posted on the survey web site: (http://www.scis.ecu.edu.au/research/KM/survey.htm) as they become available.

Another limitation on what we have done so far is the reliability of the data gathered from the Internet. Well-known sources of unreliability from Internet surveys include the possible adoption of alternate personae by users and multiple submissions of the survey instrument. While the number of Internet responses at this stage are small and we are fairly confident that they are valid, these potential problems cannot be ruled out altogether and are likely to cause us problems in the future, if we attempt to use the Internet for more randomised international sampling.

While a detailed discussion of Internet market research is beyond the scope of this paper, we would direct the reader to a useful account of the advantages and limitations of such methods that can be found in Tanya Cheyne and Frank Ritter's (2001) *Targeting Audiences on the Internet*.

DATA ANALYSIS

The following are the outcomes based on analysis of the original survey data in SPSS. The total number of responses received was 66, of which 21 were completed online using the web-based version of the questionnaire.

Sample Population Characteristics

By position, the survey respondent population was weighted in favour of Technical or Subject Experts, Line Mgr/Team Leaders and Management (see Fig. 3).

Distribution by industry/sector showed greater representation in education, services and public administration (see Fig. 4).

Knowledge management training needs (Course content)

Strong support was evident for knowledge management foundations (Knowledge Taxonomies, Knowledge Maps, Intellectual Capital and KM Roles) (69.2%

Job Position

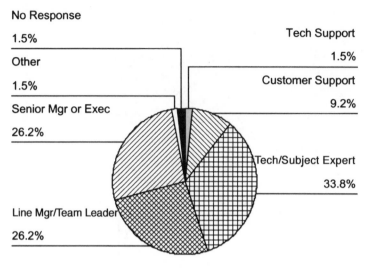

No Response
1.5%

Other
1.5%

Senior Mgr or Exec
26.2%

Line Mgr/Team Leader
26.2%

Tech Support
1.5%

Customer Support
9.2%

Tech/Subject Expert
33.8%

Fig. 3.

Industry

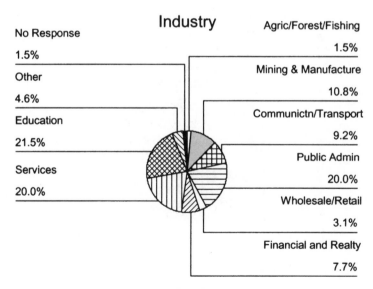

No Response
1.5%

Other
4.6%

Education
21.5%

Services
20.0%

Agric/Forest/Fishing
1.5%

Mining & Manufacture
10.8%

Communictn/Transport
9.2%

Public Admin
20.0%

Wholesale/Retail
3.1%

Financial and Realty
7.7%

Fig. 4.

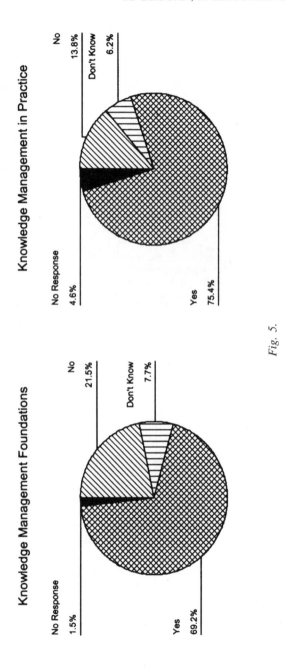

Fig. 5.

'Yes') and Knowledge Management in Practice (Organizational behaviour, Change management, Project Management, Teams) (75.4% 'Yes'). These results were anticipated (See Fig. 5).

Trends in information technologies across the sample were more interesting. Distribution for and against Internet technology (49.2% 'Yes', 44.6% 'No') was approximately equal. Web application development (52.3% 'Yes', 41.5% 'No'), Intranets/Extranets (52.3% 'Yes', 40.0% 'No') and Image Management (43.1% 'Yes', 35.4% 'No') all received strong support. Groupware and workflow was even more decisive (69.2% 'Yes', 18.5% 'No'). A majority of respondents did not want Electronic Commerce (40.0% 'Yes', 44.6% 'No').

Knowledge-based Systems

Decision support systems, Intelligent Systems and Agents and Artificial intelligence form recognized taxonomies of knowledge based systems. Measured support was highest for decision support systems (56.9% 'Yes', 26.2% 'No'), followed by intelligent systems and agents (47.7% 'Yes', 33.8% 'No') with artificial intelligence recording a somewhat ambivalent result (41.5% 'Yes', 38.5% 'No').

Database

Enthusiasm for data warehousing isn't evident in this sample with respondents for and against evenly divided (47.7%, 'Yes' 43.1% 'No'). Data mining and knowledge discovery were more popular with respondents (63.1% 'Yes', 30.8% 'No') (see Fig. 6).

Information Science

Preferences for Information Organization, Information Retrieval, Electronic Document Management (grouped with Electronic Recordkeeping) and Information Services Management were tested. Ambivalence was observed with Information Organization (47.7% 'Yes', 41.5% 'No') and Information Retrieval (43.1% 'Yes', 44.6% 'No'). Strong preference was shown for Electronic Document Management & Recordkeeping and also for Information Services Management (see Fig. 7).

Course Options

Far and away the most popular KM course option was the intensive short course

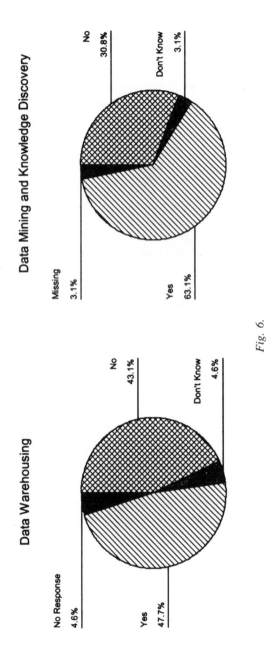

Fig. 6.

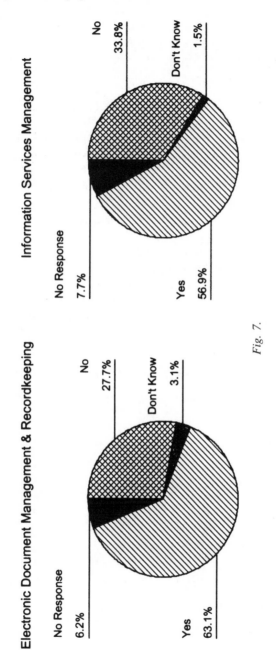

Fig. 7.

(90.8% 'Yes', 6.2% 'No'). The majority of respondents voted against the idea of KM as a minor in another award program (43.3% 'Yes', 56.7% 'No'). More support was evident for KM as an award program of study in its own right (see Fig. 8).

Employability

The data displayed a strong preference for employing KM trained personnel. A total of 75.4% of respondents said that they would consider employing a KM award graduate. Similar levels of support were measured across course of study and professional development (short course) trained personnel (see Fig. 9).

Attitudes Toward KM

A panel of judges was used to weight statements on the Likert scale. A data subject sympathetic to knowledge management recorded a cumulative score across the scale greater than 0. Taken as a group, respondents were on the whole positively disposed toward KM (Mean = 0.91 Std Deviation = 0.62). A total of 87.7% of respondents regard the meaning of KM as unclear, a survey outcome containing an important message for the proponents of KM and how

Dedicated Award Training Option

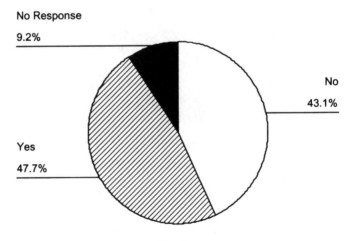

Fig. 8.

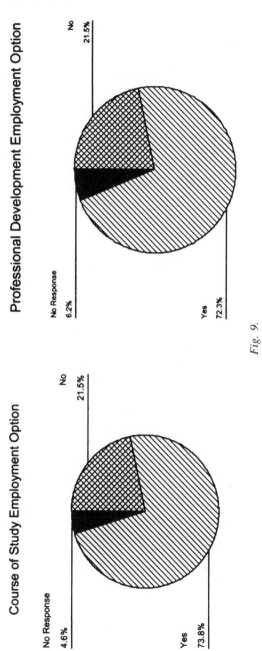

Fig. 9.

KM is being communicated to the industry. Echoing the positive sentiment across the sample, 65% of respondents thought that their careers would benefit from KM studies. More than half (55%) of respondents see themselves as a knowledge manager and 80% consider KM will be important in the future.

INTERPRETATION

As previously stated, data gathering and analysis has not yet been completed to our satisfaction for the ECU KM survey. The number of respondents is currently too small and cross tabulation is required to provide a more objective picture of market segmentation. The sample is disproportionately weighted towards information and computing professionals and therefore furnishes no guide to wider market preferences. Subject to these limitations what can be asserted about the market for KM courses?

Course Content Preferences

In terms of course content preferences:

- The demand for what we have defined as Knowledge Computing is strong in the sample with Internet technologies, Knowledge based systems and database all recording strong levels of support. Groupware and workflow were strongly supported, with Intranets/Extranets and Web development receiving endorsement from a majority of respondents. Strong support was also shown for Electronic Document Management and Recordkeeping;
- There is strong support for the inclusion of Knowledge Management Foundations (Knowledge Taxonomies, Knowledge Maps, Intellectual Capital and KM Roles) and Knowledge Management Practice (Organizational behaviour, Change management, Project Management, Teams) in knowledge management training;
- Electronic commerce is not thought suitable for inclusion by a majority of respondents, despite its place as a major factor in the knowledge economy;
- In Information Science, respondents were ambivalent towards the inclusion of classical Information Organization (cataloguing, classification, indexing) and traditional Information Retrieval skills.

Course Delivery

Intensive short courses are strongly supported by this group, with a small majority of respondents favouring a dedicated award. This may support the impression of the researchers that there is still considerable confusion in the IT-related industries as to the nature of KM and its likely impact on their working lives and future careers. This is further supported by respondents' reaction to the attitudinal question on the meaning on KM later in the survey (Attachment 1). It can be speculated that by strongly supporting the holding of short courses, respondents were thinking more of their own immediate professional development needs than the future development of formally qualified knowledge managers. We will attempt to test this supposition in later surveys.

Another tentative message to course designers that could be drawn from these results is that flexibility is required in terms of exit points, course delivery options and course duration, so that practitioners can, if required, participate in cost-effective continuing education while working full-time.

Employment

Strong support exists in the sample in terms of the employability of KM trained personnel across all three course of study options (professional development, minor studies and dedicated award). This is heartening to us as course designers as it points to unmet demand in the marketplace for these types of skills and expertise.

Attitudes toward KM

This sample of information professionals (librarians, information technology professionals, records managers) is positively disposed toward KM – a result expected given the social desirability factor presumed to be at work in a population of information and computing professionals. Responses to data items concerning the durability of KM, perceptions of the significance of KM studies to career advancement and personal identification with KM are all very positive suggesting good market potential for KM studies. Around two thirds of respondents consider that their career would benefit from KM study and more than half see themselves as 'knowledge managers'. Generalizability of this sentiment to the industry cannot yet be confirmed, but such indicators do suggest that these industry sectors are embracing KM.

THE KM COURSE MODEL

The literature review, discussion groups and survey provided us with the basic parameters for course construction. As time is of the essence in these matters, we have moved quickly to establish a course here at ECU based on the findings reported in this paper. To that end, our post-graduate studies model:

- operationalizes the critically important content areas revealed in the literature review and survey data in the program core and creates a wide range of choices in a stream/elective structure, allowing students flexibility in constructing their academic program;
- reflects the cross-disciplinary nature of the KM 'universe' and its rapidly changing nature by prescribing the minimum number of 'core' units and offering electives selected (at present) from 4 different schools at ECU, arranged in three streams of study (see Fig. 10). The elective structure allows students maximum flexibility while ensuring that the lists that can be rapidly updated and modified as the field matures and grows. As online learning opportunities and cross-institutional cooperation increases, this will also allow the students the opportunity to undertake units from other institutions within this course structure.
- reflects the strong content preferences expressed in the survey for Knowledge Computing, Knowledge Management Foundations and Knowledge Management Practice;
- takes into account the aversion shown by respondents towards classic information retrieval but recognises the importance of current developments in information retrieval theory and its relationship to document management by combining both topics in one of the six core units in the full Master's structure.
- allows for multiple exit points corresponding to award type and full time equivalent studies from one to three semesters in duration (Attachment 2).

The role of the course coordinator is crucial to ensuring that the student selects the focus most appropriate to their future career aspirations. In addition, to ensure that the graduates have the maturity and experience to undertake a course of this nature, students cannot enter directly after obtaining their undergraduate award. A prerequisite of entry is at least one year's full time industry experience.

In Fig. 10, the six core units are shown in the centre and the focus stream units are shown in the three intersecting circles. The first two core units are required for students undertaking certificate or diploma level awards.

CONCLUSION

The process that we have undertaken to develop this course in the School of Computer and Information Science at ECU has been arduous but rewarding.

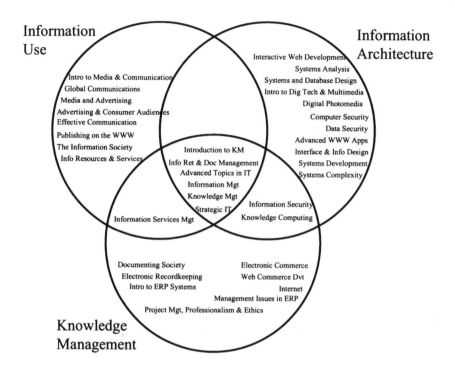

Information Use

Information Architecture

Intro to Media & Communication
Global Communications
Media and Advertising
Advertising & Consumer Audiences
Effective Communication
Publishing on the WWW
The Information Society
Info Resources & Services

Interactive Web Development
Systems Analysis
Systems and Database Design
Intro to Dig Tech & Multimedia
Digital Photomedia
Computer Security
Data Security
Advanced WWW Apps
Interface & Info Design
Systems Development
Systems Complexity

Introduction to KM
Info Ret & Doc Management
Advanced Topics in IT
Information Mgt
Knowledge Mgt
Strategic IT

Information Security
Knowledge Computing

Information Services Mgt

Documenting Society
Electronic Recordkeeping
Intro to ERP Systems

Electronic Commerce
Web Commerce Dvt
Internet
Management Issues in ERP
Project Mgt, Professionalism & Ethics

Knowledge Management

Fig. 10. Units Composing the Master of Information and Knowledge Management.

We now have a flexible and responsive framework in which to continue to develop the KM suite of courses as our understanding and experience of the field grows and matures. In addition, as a consequence of our activities in this area, we have formed an Information and Knowledge Management Research Group within the School that will lead and inform both staff and students involved in teaching and learning in this subject area. We already have a number of students actively researching on issues as diverse as the indexing of images to knowledge management in Australian schools and are in the process of developing a website to showcase our research efforts. We would welcome the opportunity to discuss developing education in this field further and to explore areas where, as educators, we can cooperate to improve the quality of courses that we offer our students.

ACKNOWLEDGMENT

Special thanks to Carol Muir for her toil with SPSS!

REFERENCES

Berners-Lee, T., Hendler, J., & Lassila, O. (2001). The Semantic Web: A new form of Web content that is meaningful to computers and will unleash a revolution of new possibilities. *Scientific American*, No. 501, May 2001. Available: http://www.sciam.com/2001/0501issue/ 0501berners-lee.html [2001, 1 October].

Bukowitz, W., & Williams, R. (2001). Ask the expert. *CIO magazine*. Available: http://www.cio.com/ archive/071500_expert.html [2001, 21st May 2001].

CERI (2000). *Knowledge management in the learning society: education and skills*. Organisation for Economic Cooperation and Development.

Collison, C., & Parcell, G. (2001). *Learning to Fly: Critical lessons from one of the world's leading knowledge companies*. Oxford. Capstone Publishing.

Davenport, T. (2000). The Last Big Thing (November 1 2000). *CIO magazine*. Available: http://www.cio.com/archive/110100_davenport.html [2001, 21st May 2001].

Drucker, P. (1999). *Beyond the information revolution*. The Atlantic ONline. Available: http://www.theatlantic.com/issues/99oct/9910drucker.htm [2001, 21st may 2001].

Eccleston, R. (2001). Bush's War. *The Weekend Australian*, p. 22.

Hansen, M. T., Nohria, N., & Tierney, T. (1999). What's your strategy for managing knowledge? *Harvard Business Review*, 77(2), 106.

Malholtra, Y. (1997). *Knowledge Management in Inquiring Organisations*. @Brint.com. Available: http://www.cio.com/archive/enterprise/091599_ic.html [2001, 21st May 2001].

Malhotra, Y. (2000). Knowledge management and new organization forms: a framework for business innovation. In: Y. Maholtra (Ed.), *Knoweldge Management and Virtual Organisations*. Hershey Pennsylvania: Idea Group Publishing.

Ruth, S., Theobold, J., & Frizzell, V. (1999). *A University-based Approach to the Diffusion of Knowledge Management Concepts and Practice*. SIGCPR '99. Available: www.icasit.org/ finalkmpaper.htm [2001, March 2001].

Sveiby, K.-E. (2000, April 2000). *What is Knowledge Management*. Available: www.sveiby.com.au/ KnowledgeManagement.html [2001, 22nd May 2001].

Talison, S. D. (2001). Knowledge and People: KM strategies 1: IT-focus or people-focus? *Businessworld*.

ASSESSING A CHANGE EFFORT IN A DIVISION OF A UNIVERSITY LIBRARY

William J. Dworaczyk

As educational institutions experience pressures for greater accountability as well as financial constraints, the need to evaluate organizational structures in order to make them more efficient and improve operations is growing. This trend began in the eighties in the for-profit sector, moved to the healthcare industry, and is currently underway in many divisions within higher education institutions. Among colleges and universities, this need to improve efficiency and to be more responsive to changing environments may be more prevalent in libraries than in other units within these institutions.

At Southern Methodist University, the Central University Libraries began to review their operations and to develop a strategic plan for the future. One result of this strategic plan was to make staff aware of change management issues and the need to critically review organizational structures in order to successfully implement program initiatives. With this entree into the possibility of organizational change, the three library managers of the Processing Services Division of the Central University Libraries began to look at the work flow processes within the division in early 1996. They became aware of inefficiencies and duplication, as well as a lack of unity in the division. After discussions with an organizational development specialist and the library director, the managers received permission to undergo a reorganizational effort in order to alleviate these problems.

The purpose of this study was to describe and assess this organizational change effort from the initial stages to the final implementation of the newly

Advances in Library Administration and Organization, Volume 19, pages 27–58.
Copyright © 2002 by Elsevier Science Ltd.
All rights of reproduction in any form reserved.
ISBN: 0-7623-0868-0

designed division. The evolution of the process from beginning to end was described to identify the actions taken by the design team and the results of those actions on the overall reorganization plan. The process was assessed by an examination of the factors that constrained the process, those that kept the process moving toward the goal, and those that were not foreseen by the design team. The results of this examination were expected to help determine what affect the change strategy had on the division in terms of the evolution of the plan, the implementation of the change process itself, and the outcome of the plan.

As more institutions are undergoing change or reorganization efforts, it is important that these efforts be evaluated to determine what variables might be identified as contributing to successful implementation and what variables might be identified as constraints to successful implementation. While there are numerous models applied to higher education units or services few of them are being evaluated in depth from a case study perspective in order to determine what worked and what did not work. The general overview of the process undertaken at this institution will be presented and the specific actions within each phase will be documented. By assessing the process through an analysis of the problems as well as the successes of the design team in this study, this change effort can be evaluated to determine its effectiveness, and the insights gained can provide lessons for other organizations and a model that they might use. It is hoped that implementation of future change efforts at both this institution and at others may be made easier as a result.

REVIEW OF THE LITERATURE

The literature on change within organizations is filled with myriad terms that attempt to capture the various dimensions of change. Planned organizational change, total quality management, continuous quality improvement, re-engineering, learning organizations, chaos theory, change management and diffusion of innovations are the most common theories and organizing frameworks described in the change literature. All of these come with their own principles, models, frameworks or concepts. Denton (1996), in reflecting on the many concepts and specific activities described in the organizational change literature, goes so far as to say that "Improvement initiatives such as quality circles, activity-based accounting, TQM [total quality management], horizontal management and reengineering are all the same. They all involve big changes in the way we work" (p. 76). While Denton mixes specific activity-based strategies with broad organizing principles in making such a statement, he reflects nonetheless a perception that these terms often incorporate similar underlying concepts and strategies that make it difficult to know which strategy to apply when a change effort is desired.

The literature on planned organizational change, quality improvement, and learning organizations was reviewed as well as the literature on change and quality improvement in higher education and libraries. In the end, Stufflebeam's CIPP (Context, Input, Process, Product) model was used to evaluate the change effort in this study, and it will be described.

Organizational Change

While there are numerous models for change activities in vogue today, one of the first fundamental models of planned change was developed by the sociologist Kurt Lewin. Lewin (1951) believed that there were two sets of forces active in any organization – those that maintain the status quo and those that favor change. In order for change to occur, one of two things must happen to these forces – either the forces pushing for change must be increased or the forces advocating the status quo must be diminished. Lewin's contention was that less tension and resistance is created by modifying the forces for the status quo than by increasing the forces for change. As a result, he contends that this approach is a more effective strategy when introducing change. He viewed the process of change as consisting of the three phases or steps – unfreezing, moving, and refreezing. From this broad framework for change, many models have been developed which elaborate on Lewin's system.

There are at present numerous reasons for a dramatic shift to a new management paradigm today. These range from the need for greater efficiency in operations to the need for a system wide reorganization. Change management is the term used in the human resource profession for managing these change efforts. The American Management Association (AMA) defines change management as "the developing discipline of planning, organizing, and controlling organizational change to better solve present and future business problems" (quoted in Laabs, 1996, p. 54). These change efforts range on a continuum from the more incremental evolutionary approach to the more dramatic revolutionary approach. No matter where they lie on the continuum, however, these change efforts require a new organizational management structure to be successful. In describing this new organizational paradigm, Kanter, Stein, and Jick (1992) state:

> This model describes more flexible organizations, adaptable to change, with relatively few levels of formal hierarchy and loose boundaries among functions and units, sensitive and responsive to the environment; concerned with stakeholders of all sorts – employees,

communities, customers, suppliers, and shareholders. These organizations empower people to take action and be entrepreneurial, reward them for contributions and help them gain in skill and "employability." Overall, these are global organizations characterized by internal and external relationships, including joint ventures, alliances, consortia, and partnerships (p. 3).

The new organization must be able and willing to change to remain viable and competitive. It must be willing to embrace change as a natural process in its evolution. It is important, however, to know why an organization or company desires to undergo change. As one senior human resource professional stated, "The two most important questions every company must ask are: Why do we need to change? And, what is the value proposition for everyone involved in the change process? Each company must be able to clearly state the need for change to each stakeholder group, including employees, shareowners, neighbors, customers, and if applicable, regulators" (in Laabs, 1996, p. 62). Clack (1995) refers to change as ongoing, constant, and occurring at an unprecedented rate, as a process, not an event and both intensely personal and at the same time systemic. She summarizes the organizational landscape in which change occurs as a holistic environment in which information is shared widely and new strategies are allowed to emerge, participation is encouraged, staff is motivated by shared values, and management is busy "coping with" rather than controlling.

Seymour (1994), in addressing change from a quality improvement perspective proposes a performance improvement framework for institutions and those who work within them which requires them to think more harmoniously about quality improvement and productivity. He believes that this framework helps answer the brain teaser "How can we do more with less and do it better?" He offers five components for this framework:

(1) Direction setting
(2) Process design and management
(3) Feedback
(4) Enablers
(5) Personal involvement

The first three components are linked together in an organizational learning cycle. Direction setting entails an aim – a vision of where an institution or a program wants to go. This aim is often based on a fundamental paradigm shift, not just on eliminating symptoms. The process design and management component provides some effective methods for implementing the aim. Weak processes can leave individuals in the organization feeling frustrated, even betrayed, when visions and goals remain neatly bound on the shelf. Feedback then allows performance measures and feedback loops to check on the processes to see that they do not degrade over time. Seymour believes when these three components work together, the result is organizational learning.

Kovel-Jarboe (1996) identifies five general bodies of literature on change, to include planned organizational change, diffusion of innovations, quality-specific strategies, chaos theory, and the theory of learning organizations. Denton (1996) identifies nine methods for creating an atmosphere conducive to change, to include:

(1) Create dissatisfaction with the status quo
(2) Reduce the fear of change
(3) Describe the benefits of change
(4) Build support for change
(5) Define specific change objectives
(6) Tie compensation to change
(7) Concentrate on measurable improvements
(8) Approach change incrementally
(9) Plan training to coincide with change

In Laabs' (1996) interviews with change agents and professionals, several strategies and guiding principles were identified to enhance the success of change efforts. One change management consultant noted that it was important to understand the 20-50-30 rule before embarking on a change effort. This rules states that approximately 20% of the people in the organization will be change friendly, 50% will be neutral, and 30% will resist or even attempt to make the effort fail. One of the toughest challenges is to get the entire organization involved and engaged in the change process. According to a human resource director, "It's absolutely critical that everyone moves toward a certain level of involvement and engagement in the change process. Otherwise, a wide divergence of focus concerning the reasons for the change can slow or derail the entire process" (Laabs, p. 56). Many of those interviewed stressed the importance of trust in managing change. Steven Covey, for example, identified what he calls 360-degree trust which means trust of not only the customer, but all those who may have a stake in the success of an operation. This might include staff, suppliers, the community, dealers, owners, or the media. He says that if you build trust with customers only and violate the staff in the organization, you will gradually kill the goose that lays the golden egg. He goes on to stress the importance of aligning work systems, information systems, and other organizational components with the values of cooperation, interdependency and 360-degree trust among all stakeholders. One human resource manager said that employees should trust that those controlling the change effort are sincere about their efforts to make improvements that add to the quality of the company or organization (Laabs, 1996). That trust is built on people seeing action or results based on what they are telling management. Once that trust is established, people are more likely to offer ideas about making improvements in the workplace.

Schneider, Brief, and Guzzo (1996) stress the importance of creating a change effort that affects multiple levels of an organization simultaneously. They propose a perspective for change they call Total Organizational Changes (TOC). TOC is designed to effect multiple policies, procedures, and rewards across multiple units and levels of an organization; it affects the psychology of all employees in an organization. They emphasize the need to affect both the climate and the culture of an organization in any change effort, claiming that TOC is in sharp contrast with the "silver bullet" approach. TOC combines any number of focused, singular strategies such as new training programs, new compensation programs, or team building. As they state:

> By failing to attend to a wide variety of issues, the silver bullet strategies never get implemented completely, much less sustained, because the attempt is too narrow in perspective. This narrowness fails to generate sufficient momentum to redirect people's energies and competencies, so workers persist in past behaviors that are familiar and comfortable. It is not surprising, therefore, to find that the initial positive effects of many silver bullets quickly fade with the passage of time (p. 12).

Learning Organizations

The concept of the learning organization goes back to the earlier works of Argyris (1977) and Argyris and Schon (1978). Senge resurrected their ideas and popularized them with the publication of the *Fifth Discipline: The Art and Practice of the Learning Organization* (Senge, 1990). Senge organized the practices of effective organizational learning and developed a holistic theory based on participative management and individual growth. He identifies five core disciplines which are the principles of his theory of the learning organization.

- Personal Mastery – Senge believes this discipline to be the cornerstone of the learning organization because organizations learn only when individuals learn. Personal mastery entails a continual process of clarifying and deepening one's personal vision and learning to see reality objectively. When individuals obtain a high level of personal mastery they are able to understand what matters most to them and they become committed to lifelong learning. He contends this discipline has its roots in both Eastern and Western spiritual traditions, and, as such, it is "the learning organization's spiritual foundation" (p. 7).

- Mental Models – These are deeply held convictions, assumptions, and generalizations of how people view the world and how they should act. People need to be aware of their mental models to look objectively at themselves and understand how their view of the world and its people affect their behaviors. When people expose their own thinking effectively, they become more open to looking objectively at their work environment and allow for the creation of institutional learning.
- Shared Vision – Without a shared vision of the future, institutions have no direction and are more likely to wander aimlessly looking for their niche in the marketplace. Building a shared vision involves fostering "genuine commitment and enrollment rather than compliance" (p. 9). Individuals should learn and excel in their work environment because they have a desire to rather than because they are told to do so.
- Team Learning – This discipline attempts to answer the paradox of how individually intelligent, committed managers can make poor decisions. Senge believes that team learning begins with " 'dialogue' – the capacity of members of a team to suspend assumptions and enter into a genuine 'thinking together' " (p. 10). Through this free-flowing exchange of ideas, groups are able to develop insights that would not be attained individually. Through this type of dialogue within and among teams, organizations can recognize those barriers that undermine effectiveness and learning. Senge believes that "teams, not individuals, are the fundamental learning unit in modern organizations" and goes on to state that "unless teams can learn, the organization cannot learn" (p. 10).
- System Thinking – Senge believes that all disciplines must develop together within a holistic perspective and not be viewed individually. Thus, systems thinking is the fifth discipline. Members of the organization must learn to see the connectedness of their interactions. They must understand how their actions are connected to the organization as a whole, rather than viewing them as separate acts.

McGill, Slocum and Lei (1992) describe generative learning as essential for a learning organization. This learning places an emphasis on continuous experimentation and feedback where organizations are constantly examining the ways in which the organization defines and solves problems. They claim that "Managers in these companies demonstrate behaviors of openness, systemic thinking, creativity, self-efficacy, and empathy" (p. 5). They contrast generative learning with adaptive learning where organizations focus on solving problems in the present or on incremental improvements in their services.

The learning organization implies consideration of radical new approaches to solving problems. Traditional methods of dealing with complex issues within organizations often prevent these organizations from seeing the larger picture. People within the organization tend to break problems down into smaller units to make them more manageable. However, this reductionist type of thinking assumes that the parts equal the whole (Solomon, 1994). Solving a problem at only one level may not address the underlying cause for the original problem. A systemic view of the organization usually reveals a much more complex web of interactions and reactions that prevents problems from being solved only at one level. Thus the interrelationships must be analyzed from the context of the larger picture.

Worrell (1995) identifies ways that libraries can apply the principles of the learning organization. She indicates the importance of data gathering to make informed decisions about adding new services or resources, for example. Qualitative data can also be valuable in making decisions about reorganization efforts where information about processes and relationships are paramount. She also notes that ongoing programs of experimentation occur regularly in libraries such as pilot projects on document delivery or changing staffing patterns on a trial basis.

Kramlinger (1991) believes that the learning organization must incorporate eight basic assumptions into its policies, procedures, and practices. These are that:

- Everyone can be a source of useful ideas.
- The people closest to the problem usually have the best ideas about solutions.
- Learning flows up as well as down in the organization.
- Nothing is sacred except the governing vision and values. Employees need to remain open to new ideas.
- The process of open dialogue improves ideas. Open dialogue is defined as the sharing of information and ideas without fears, insecurities, or concerns over status or turf. Ground rules may be established for open dialogue, disagreements provide an opportunity for learning, and blame is avoided.
- The more information people can access the better.
- New ideas are valuable and can be generated by activities such as brainstorming, focus groups, or suggestion boxes.
- A mistake is simply an opportunity to learn. New ideas should be encouraged and mistakes are accepted as a part of the innovation process.

Organizational Change in Higher Education

Applying principles of organizational change to institutions of higher education has been more difficult and slower in coming than change efforts undertaken in the for-profit sector. In general, the use of the term "customers" in the academic setting is still somewhat disturbing to faculty as well as to some in administration. Obtaining feedback from those customers is seen as even more problematic. Nevertheless, higher education is increasingly undergoing change efforts. Sometimes these change efforts take the form of quality improvement to make processes more efficient or cost effective. However, some change efforts are also beginning to take shape in what has been termed restructuring in the education arena. While restructuring seems to imply a more systematic global change effort, it too is based on a need to improve operations.

Despite the lack of consensus about quality efforts and how they can be integrated systematically, many institutions are joining the quality bandwagon. Tuttle (1994) says that institutions are embracing quality improvement for the same reasons that government and industry have done so: The management systems in existence today are outmoded, unable to create successful outcomes in a more competitive world. A survey of institutions by the American Society of Quality Control describes the level of quality-based activities in 139 universities and 46 community colleges. Its findings indicate that 78% of universities and 70% of community colleges reported that they were in the early stages of TQM. Approximately half of the universities and 41% of the community colleges reporting had quality councils, officers, or centers with responsibility to coordinate TQM activities (Horine, Hailey & Rubach, 1993, reported in Seymour, 1994).

Organizational Change in Libraries

Libraries, like most divisions or programs within colleges and universities, have historically been based on a hierarchical management structure. Most advocates of the new management philosophy believe that such a structure is too cumbersome to deal with the rapid rate of change prevalent in most organizations today. Within higher education this kind of rapid change may be more prevalent in libraries than in any other unit due to their dependence on technology and its related systems. Shaughnessy (1995) states that "The most important reason for restructuring, however, is also the most abstract, namely, that libraries must be organized to deal with the extraordinary changes that are occurring in their environment. It is not simply the complexity of the changes . . . but also the accelerated pace of change" (p. 252). While change may be an abstract concept, its effects are quite real. He notes that staff in libraries are experiencing "mental and physical exhaustion, burnout, frustration, low morale, and other symptoms of stress" (p. 252). He adds that the library's bureaucratic structure adds to this stress, because it embodies a system with slow response time and an inability to solve problems cross-functionally.

Goble and Brown (1996), in comparing change management differences in profit and non-profit sectors, conclude that academic libraries, because they operate in stable environments in which faculty and students are captive clients, provide few rewards for risk-taking and offer little money to support new initiatives. Because this environment has become less stable due to decreases in funding and greater user expectations, libraries must consider changing the ways in which they operate and manage people. They go on to state that "Librarians must consider the 'participative structure' that enables all levels of staff to engage in the evolution of change. This will require the sharing of power, active listening, encouragement, and at times, conflict resolution" (p. 199).

Kovel-Jarboe (1996) has identified four approaches to change on a continuum ranging from revolutionary to evolutionary models. The first is the "big bang" or top-down model which emphasizes speed in implementing change throughout an organization at the same time. It involves heavy involvement from top management and usually only entails short-term losses in productivity. The second approach is called "managed change" where the change effort targets specific areas or activities, often as pilot projects. In this approach there is less likelihood for major losses in productivity and the length of time for implementation is much longer. The third approach, "small wins," is opportunity-driven where top management may or may not be involved and the change is implemented in an area or division that is more likely to accept change. This approach is more experimental and the risk is that the changes effected may not be adopted throughout an organization. Kovel-Jarboe calls the fourth approach "back door" or bottom up because it almost never involves top management and is usually not visible within the organization. This approach is one in which a unit within an organization implements a change effort on its own initiative because it sees the benefits that are possible.

Kovel-Jarboe then goes on to explain under which conditions each approach is most likely to be successful in libraries. The "big bang" is most likely to work best when there is strong external pressure for change, strong staff and management support for change, experience in using teams, a good communication structure, and the necessary resources to offset a temporary loss of productivity. She adds that few libraries are equipped for such a change effort today. The "managed change" approach requires many of the same conditions, but is more likely to work when these conditions are not as well established or when one or more of them is missing. An example might be a library in which team management is not well entrenched and yet a particular division requires significant improvement in its operations. The "small wins" approach is best used when there is uneven support and commitment within the library and many important conditions are not in place. Support from administration may be minimal, but the division chosen for an improvement effort must be the one that has the best chance for success. The effort should be visible within the organization, but the risk is minimal. A "back door" approach requires few, if any, conditions for adoption. Strategic opportunities are chosen without administrative support or even acknowledgment, and quality improvement effort is introduced with the knowledge of only its immediate participants.

Summary/Conclusion of Literature Review

Organizational change is taking place today in both the for-profit sector and in organizations in the non-profit sectors such as educational institutions. These changes are often driven by economic pressures to be competitive or to increase the organization's capacity to perform more services with little or no increase in financial support. At times, increased efficiencies may also allow for a reduction in financial resources in one or more areas in order to divert those resources to areas with increased demands. No matter what drives the need for change, there appear to be some common themes for successfully adapting change strategies.

While there is a trend for organizations to be more accepting of change, many of the management systems in place today are out-dated, hierarchical structures that are not flexible or adaptable to new management paradigms. New systems are required to create the atmosphere of a learning organization where ideas from employees are valued and where employees are encouraged to take risks and are not afraid to try new approaches to solving problems. This environment allows for greater staff involvement and thus, is managed in a more participative style. For these change efforts to be most successful, they should also be systematic, cutting across all levels of the organization. Using this approach, change efforts are not isolated in one area or department because successful change efforts usually have a ripple effect that touches multiple levels of an organization.

Efforts to develop and introduce these new systems are taking place in libraries throughout the country as new technologies, new service requirements, and limited financial resources cause institutions to look at how they are organized. Openness and trust must be present in this environment or staff will be reticent to accept change and new management structures. These new structures often include team-based environments with flattened hierarchies and greater staff involvement. In effect, libraries, like other organizations, are finding that the old hierarchical management structures are too bureaucratic for effective management in today's workplace. They must be replaced with a new management paradigm that empowers employees and attempts to balance process, results, and relationships.

Program Evaluation Theory

Stufflebeam's CIPP Model for Program Evaluation (Stufflebeam, 1983) is a decision-oriented evaluation model based on the contention that the most important purpose of program evaluation is not to prove but to improve, that is, to help programs work better for the people they are intended to serve (p. 118). The model consists of four evaluation types – context, input, process, and product – which are used to guide decision-making, (the formative role), and to provide information for accountability, (the summative role). These evaluation components may be used independently, in combination, or in a somewhat linear fashion.

Context evaluation is used to address the overall status of the object under evaluation, whether a program or an institution. This needs analysis would normally be the first phase in a systematic evaluation of an object, defining the institutional context in which some need is present. At this phase the object's strengths and weaknesses are assessed and problems are diagnosed in order to determine the reason for some change, whether that entails the implementation of a new program or the modification of an existing one.

Input evaluation is used to identify and prescribe some program which is intended to satisfy an assessed need. During this phase the environment is scanned to search for alternative solutions as well as barriers and resources that might effect program implementation. Methods used to identify solutions include searching the relevant literature, seeking input from staff, and visiting exemplary programs already in existence in order to assist in the design of the program.

Process evaluation is used to identify and judge procedural activities, to identify defects in the procedural design or its implementation. It is, in effect, an evaluation of the implementation of a plan. Observers and participants are used to judge the quality of the process undertaken in order to assist in carrying out the program.

The purpose of product evaluation is to describe, interpret and judge the outcomes of the program being implemented. It is used "to ascertain the extent to which the program has met the needs of the group it is intended to serve"

(Stufflebeam, 1983, p. 134). As Stufflebeam notes, there is no set prescription for conducting a product evaluation, but might entail any of several methods to interpret a program's worth and merit.

Stufflebeam's evaluation model provided a theoretical framework around which to organize this study. The model served as the conceptual framework for organizing data and provided a methodology to manage and organize the process. It also provided an evaluation tool related to the reorganizational design model which this study assessed.

Procedures for Collection of Data

The consultant introduced the team to a change management model that would guide them through the process of reorganization. This model was called a "Pathway to Action" (Interaction Associates, 1994) and included the following five phases: (1) Process Design, (2) Problem Assessment, (3) Vision, (4) Solution, and (5) Implementation. It was used by the design team during the change effort, and for the purposes of this study is referred to as the action plan. Data were collected in each of the five phases of the change model. The general procedure was to move through the five phases in order. In the Process Design Phase, the overall process and subsequent procedures were established and agreed upon. Next the team moved to create a vision of the new organization in the Vision Phase, and then it began to identify problems inherent in the old organization in the Problem Phase. Then, the team was expected to create solutions to the problems in the Solutions Phase and, finally, when these were agreed upon, the team moved on to implement the proposed solutions in the Implementation Phase. However, the model was considered heuristic in that it could be adapted to each situation as necessary.

The following activities occurred during each phase of the action plan:

1. *Process Design* – During this phase the team developed the ground work for the entire process. It built agreement on the pathway and process for moving through the phases and included the following key agreements:

- Confirm issues to be worked on
- Identify goals of the work effort
- Explore the context surrounding the issue to be worked on
- Do a thorough stakeholder analysis
- Agreement among team members on how decisions will be made as well as the meeting structure and ground rules

2. *Problem Assessment* – This phase determined what the problem was and why it existed and included the following activities:

• Collect, legitimize and understand all perceptions of the problem
• Analyze the problem
• Agreement on problem definition and root causes

3. *Vision* – During this phase a vision of what success should be was developed through the following key activities:

• Solicit a variety of views of the ideal state.
• Create a visual image of success
• Build agreement on the ideal future state

4. *Solution* – The goal of this phase was to identify solution(s) that everyone was willing to support. It included the following activities:

• Identify possible solutions
• Evaluate solutions
• Build agreement on a specific set of solutions to be implemented

5. *Implementation* – During this phase a plan for implementing the decision(s) identified during the solution phase was developed.

• Agree on an action plan – what, who, by when
• Agree on how implementation will be evaluated
• Evaluate impact and team process

The components of Stufflebeam's CIPP model relate to the phases of the "Pathway to Action" introduced by the consultant as identified below.

CIPP	*Pathway to Action*
Context	Problem Phase
Input	Solutions & Vision Phases
Process	Process Design through Implementation
Product	Implementation Phase

The seven members of the PACE Team met regularly to make decisions about strategy, procedures, and analysis. The team also met on an ad hoc basis to address special issues, to interview stakeholders, and to make presentations to the various stakeholders during the process. Stakeholders within the Central University Libraries organization included the Executive Committee (directors of each library unit or functional area), Processing Services staff, Public Services staff of Fondren Library, Hamon Arts Library staff, DeGolyer Library staff, Science Library staff, Collection Development staff, and the Center for Media and Instructional Technology staff. Other stakeholders included faculty, under-graduate students, and graduate students.

Activities during each of these phases were described. The types of data collected during these phases included observations, interviews, and documents. The procedures for data collection during each of the phases were:

Process Design Phase

In this phase, observations included team meetings, any ad hoc meetings that take place, interpersonal and group dynamics among library staff and team members, and any anecdotal data that surfaced during the process. Documents gathered included agendas of team meetings, minutes from meetings, corre-spondence among team members and stakeholders, and notes taken by the researcher during the process.

Problem Assessment Phase

During this phase, observations included team meetings, ad hoc meetings, stakeholder interviews, presentations to stakeholders, interpersonal and group dynamics, and anecdotal data during the process. Documents gathered included agendas of team meetings, minutes from meetings, correspondence among team members and stakeholders, summaries of stakeholder interviews, and notes taken by the researcher. Information from interviews of stakeholders by the team during the Problem Space were collected and analyzed. These interviews consisted of the team interviewing stakeholders in groups of two or more. During the interviews all responses were posted on wall sheets in order for interviewees to verify the accuracy of the documented response. At the conclusion of the inter-views, interviewees were asked if the responses accurately captured their comments. Any needed changes to the comments as recorded were made at that time. By following this method all responses used reflected the mutual under-standing and agreement of both the team members and the interviewees.

Problem Assessment Questions

The following questions were asked of library stakeholders during the problem assessment phase:

(1) What, in your opinion, does your area value most?

(2) What is your worst experience with Processing Services?
(3) What additional demands/requests are your users making that could impact Processing Services?
(4) What problems (long standing, recent, and/or cyclical) have you experienced during interactions with Processing Services?
(5) What additional services would you like Processing Services to provide?
(6) What are the specific needs of your collection?
(7) Who are the key stakeholders in your area and how do you suggest we might interact with them? (Asked of Executive Committee members only.)

A selected group of faculty was also interviewed. They were interviewed by email and were asked the following questions:

(1) Do you request materials to be purchased through Central University Libraries? If yes, how often?
(2) Are you satisfied with the service you receive in purchasing materials? If no or if you have experienced any dissatisfaction with this service, please explain and be as specific as possible.
(3) Do you experience problems in locating materials in the PONI catalog? If yes, please explain.
(4) What services in ordering or locating materials are we not currently providing?

The following questions were asked of students by survey and during group interviews:

(1) How often do you use S.M.U. library materials?
(2) Do the libraries adequately support your studies? If no, please elaborate.
(3) Do you experience problems in locating materials?
(4) Is there enough information in the PONI record to find what you want? If no, please elaborate.
(5) What additional services, especially regarding locating materials, are we not currently providing?
(6) Any additional comments?

Solutions Phase

During this phase I observed team meetings, ad hoc meetings, stakeholder interviews/discussion groups, presentations to stakeholders, interpersonal and group dynamics, and anecdotal data. Documents gathered during this phase included agendas of team meetings, minutes from meetings, correspondence among team members and stakeholders, and notes taken by the researcher during the process. Interviews during the solutions phase were more open ended discussion sessions led by the team. Larger groups of cross-functional staff and members of the administration were brought together in this forum to discuss and offer solutions to the problems and issues brought forward during the problem assessment phase. In general, these were brainstorming sessions with stakeholders, and the ideas/solutions generated were recorded on wall sheets for all to see and verify for accuracy. The available options were narrowed down during additional rounds of discussion sessions with stakeholders until all agreed on proposed solutions. All ideas/solutions generated during this phase were posted on wall sheets during the meetings and summarized in writing to stakeholders in order to confirm agreement. Team members made final recommendations and then solicited agreement from the CUL Executive Committee and library stakeholders.

Vision Phase

This phase was performed primarily by the team. Observations included team meetings and any shared discussions with selected stakeholders as decided on by the team. Documents included correspondence among team members and selected stakeholders as determined by the team, agendas and minutes of team meetings, and notes taken by the researcher.

Implementation Phase

Because implementation of the reorganization plan was an ongoing endeavor, my observations during this phase only included the initial meetings with staff. I observed team meetings, meetings with the staff of Processing Services, presentations to stakeholders, interpersonal and group dynamics, and anecdotal data. I also gathered data from the managers about their assessment of the implementation and their reactions after they concluded the interviews with staff for team assignments.

Concluding Summary Questions

At the conclusion of the process at least one individual from each of the stake-holder groups was interviewed by the researcher to obtain additional information about their perception of the entire process. Members of the PACE Team were interviewed by the researcher at the end of the project to gather their input about the process and the outcomes of the effort. Additional questions were asked of the PACE Team because only the team had knowledge of certain events. These concluding questions, which follow, were open ended.

Stakeholder Questions

(1) How would you judge the overall process of the PACE Project?
(2) How would you judge the interview process during the problem assessment phase?
(3) How would you judge the brainstorming/interview sessions during the solutions phase?
(4) What aspects of the process worked best?
(5) What aspects of the process were most problematic?
(6) How could the process be improved?

PACE Team Questions

(1) How would you judge the overall process?
(2) What aspects of the process were most difficult or problematic?
(3) What aspects of the process were most helpful?
(4) What unexpected issues or problems surfaced during the process?
(5) Were there any modifications to the original process?
(6) Did you feel that the interview process during the problem assessment and solutions phases was beneficial? What was or was not beneficial?
(7) Were there any barriers or problems encountered in coming to agreement on proposed solutions?
(8) Do you think the process was a success? What specifically was successful?
(9) How could the process be improved?

The researcher joined the PACE Team as one of seven team members in September, 1996 when the project began formal operation. However, this study will also include a record of the actions of the three managers during the early development of the process which began in January of 1996. The team completed the design phase of the project in June, 1997, and the implementation phase began immediately thereafter.

Data Analysis

The data were analyzed through a descriptive framework. The entire process from its inception through the conclusion of the design phase was traced and documented. This documentation included personal observations throughout the process as well as involvement in team meetings, correspondence, and interviews with team members. Data collected from stakeholder interviews with the team were coded to identify common themes of both problem perception and solutions. Interviews that the researcher conducted at the conclusion of the change effort with team members and individual stakeholders were compiled and coded to analyze process-related questions about common perceptions of barriers to implementation, functionality, and dysfunctionality. These perceptions, along with the researcher's observations throughout the process, were used to analyze the success of the change effort.

FINDINGS

Time Line of Events

Early in 1996, the three department heads within Processing Services became aware of problems with workflow and related inefficiencies within the department. They approached an organizational development specialist in SMU's Human Resources Department and asked about the possibilities of reorganizing the department, and if that was possible, how they might begin. They continued to meet among themselves and with the organizational development specialist for several months, and, by late spring, they decided to undertake the task of reorganizing the department. The OD specialist recommended that they develop a contract that outlined their roles and the role of the Associate Director for Processing Services. This contract was important because it was a formal acknowledgement of their collective commitment to the project. It noted their expected need for resources and what some of those resources might be including training, documentation, and equipment. Once the contract was completed, the managers continued working with the OD specialist to develop a plan for beginning the project. They presented the proposal to the library director and the Executive Committee of the library and received a commitment to move ahead with the project. The Executive Committee requested that the managers announce the plan to the staff of the Central University Libraries, which they did in mid July 1996.

Upon the recommendation of the Organizational Development specialists, the plan called for a drastic reduction in the amount of work that could be undertaken by the staff of Processing Services during the reorganization. The rationale for such a move was to insure that the reorganization effort be given sufficient time to be successful. Without a reduction in workflow, the project would either not be successful or would take even longer than the nine to twelve months projected. The decision was made to only accept rush requests or those requests for items required within a specified time, usually for direct instructional support. While the decision to allow a reduction in work was agreed upon by the Executive Committee, there was some reluctance to do so. At the presentation to the staff there was both concern and surprise at such a decision, as well as confusion about the impact of such a move. In general, staff did not understand why such a drastic reduction in work going into Processing Services had to take place.

The three department heads had already begun making decisions as a team, but by this time, they were beginning to involve more people from across the university and throughout the libraries. They believed they would need to form focus groups, use assessment tools, analyze current workflow, and obtain advice from other university departments that were undergoing reorganization efforts. They interviewed members of two teams from other departments within the University that were undergoing reorganization and obtained ideas about team structure, size, communication, and commitment. Because of the discussions with and subsequent recommendations from those teams, the department heads formed two subcommittees. One of the recommendations from the university teams related to the importance placed on securing a meeting space for exclusive use by the team. Having this allowed materials to be left out and allowed for impromptu meetings to be called without concern for room availability. A group of staff from Processing Services was then charged with developing a library of change management literature so that the team could have ready access to relevant research.

The managers also began interviewing staff from across the university, the library, and in Processing Services for membership on the reorganization team. Another recommendation from the Organization Development specialist was to have a neutral facilitator work with the team throughout the effort. However, neither of the university OD specialists was available for the required time period, so the managers had to find someone to fill that role. The library director agreed to provide funding to hire a consultant as well as operating expenses for the team. The managers made a recommendation to the library director for team membership, and the recommendation was accepted. The team was formally established in September, 1996 and included the three managers from Processing Services, one staff member from Processing Services, two staff members from other library units (including the author), and the outside consultant, for a total of seven members.

The first meeting of the team took place on September 24, 1996. Upon the recommendation of the two university organizational development specialists this first meeting was a day-long retreat held at a location outside the library. Both OD specialists were present and acted as facilitators for the meeting. The purpose of the meeting was to learn how teams should function for optimum performance and for the team members to get to know each other better. Team members were given a behavioral assessment instrument which identified each members behavioral style, characteristics of each style, and how these styles worked together. Several team building exercises were conducted, and the facilitators showed the team some guidelines and introduced them to communication strategies for effective team work.

Process Design Phase
During the first several meetings, the consultant introduced the process by which the team would operate and the overall plan for the reorganization effort. They were Process Design Space, Vision Space, Problem Space, Solution Space, and Implementation Space. For the purpose of this study they will be referred to as phases.

The first several meetings of the team were devoted to defining team member roles, clarifying ground rules for meetings, drafting a mission statement, deciding on the team's decision making strategy, and understanding the concept of building agreement. The consultant began to introduce and outline the meeting management strategy her company employed, which was a collaborative, consensus building model. The team also decided it should have a name by which to be identified during the process. After some discussion the name chosen was the PACE Team. PACE was an acronym for Processing for Access and Collection Enrichment.

At the third team meeting, the entire team was introduced for the first time to the Executive Committee (E.C.). During that meeting, the team asked the E.C. for its support throughout the project. Even though the team had already begun to function, the consultant believed it important to formally receive agreement from the Executive Committee that the project should proceed. With no objections from the Executive Committee, the team received confirmation to move ahead with the reorganization project.

The next step in the Process Design Phase was to do a stakeholder analysis. The consultant identified stakeholders as those who would be impacted by changes in Processing Services or those who might sabotage the reorganization process. A stakeholder analysis was begun by the team listing any potential group effected by the PACE Project. The key stakeholders identified were students, faculty, the CUL Executive Committee, Processing Services staff, other CUL staff, and the staff of Instructional Technology Services, the university's administrative computing services. These were then grouped by themes including users/patrons, administration, donors, staff, vendors, and indirect users. Along with each stakeholder, the team identified a potential "win" for each stakeholder – something that might help or be good for the stakeholder. After listing a number of these wins, the team decided to pare down the list and include only "key" stakeholders; that is, those that would have a direct impact on the design process or be directly affected by the results. Examples of these "winning situations" for stakeholders included such items as "timely access," "quicker response," "save money," "more efficient use of staff," "increased productivity," "job satisfaction," "reduce duplication," and "increased participation in decision-making and process design."

In order to obtain feedback on the list of stakeholders, the team met with the library director in mid-October to ask for her input and assessment. They clarified the "win" for each stakeholder group and got her input on how to survey the Executive Committee. During the next two weeks the team finalized the stakeholder list and began formulating questions for the next phase which was the problem assessment phase. Team members divided the list among themselves and wrote questions for each stakeholder group. A process map, which is a visual representation of the process with time lines for each phase and a list of activities to be undertaken during each phase, was begun during this time frame. This process map indicated the activities to date and projected general time frames for the remaining phases. The team was asked by the library director to make a presentation at the next open Executive Committee meeting in early November. Because the process map was considered an important component of the presentation, the team spent extra time in its construction.

In early November the team made its presentation to the Executive Committee. For that presentation, the team decided to model the meeting management method it had been using for team meetings while asking the E.C. members for their input on the stakeholder list. The team brought in charts with team member roles, purpose, and the desired outcome for this presentation. E.C. members were told that they would soon be called to set up interviews to begin the problem phase of the project. With this presentation and the final stakeholder analysis, the process design phase was completed.

Vision Phase
While the team was concluding the Process Design Phase, the consultant wanted the team to begin drafting a vision statement which was to be completed before moving into the problem assessment phase. This phase called for creating a vision of what the new organization would look like, written as a short narrative. After several unsuccessful attempts, however, the team decided that they did not have enough information yet to formulate a vision. Instead, the consultant and the team decided to move on to the next phase and create the vision later in the process. Staying with this phase and struggling any longer might have caused the team to lose momentum, which might, in turn, have slowed the process even more.

Problem Phase

The team decided to interview the Executive Committee members first during the problem phase of the project. A letter was sent to each E.C. member which included the PACE Team mission statement, the purpose and desired outcomes for the meeting, the questions they would be asked during the interview, and a request that they identify which of their staff members should be interviewed to represent stakeholders from the other library units that used Processing Services. E.C. members were interviewed in pairs between November 21 and November 25. The library director was interviewed separately in early December. In general, these interviews were very informative and helpful for the team. Most of the E.C. members felt good about being asked for their feedback, and they willingly contributed some very honest comments for the team to include in the problem document which would be the next step in the process. Each E.C. member also gave the team the name of staff members from each of their units to interview.

For these and all subsequent interview sessions during the problem phase, stakeholders were given the same set of questions. E.C. members were asked additional questions concerning what they valued in their units. All comments were recorded on wall chart pads for all to see. Participants were told to clarify their comments if they were not recorded to their satisfaction. At the end of each session stakeholders were asked to give the team feedback on how the meeting went. This was called the Plus/Delta part of the agenda, and it generally took only a few minutes. Plus's were those things viewed positively by the participants, and the Deltas were things participants would change about the meeting. The team used these comments to improve subsequent sessions.

All participants were asked during this phase to focus only on their perceptions of problems related to interactions with Processing Services. They were discouraged from attempting to solve problems. The reason for this approach was a desire to keep from getting distracted by attempting to fix problems along the way. The action plan called for all problems to be compiled first and then later to be presented to all stakeholders so that everyone would see the array of problems/needs compiled in one document. Requiring the stakeholders to only offer problems and needs statements did prove to be somewhat trying, however, especially during the first few interviews. It was always very natural for stakeholders to offer solutions to the problems they identified. But at the beginning of each interview session, the team always clarified that the purpose of the conversation was only to solicit problem statements.

During the latter part of October, it became clear that the staff of Processing Services had a great deal of anxiety and frustration about the PACE Project. They apparently did not understand what the team was doing, saw little in the way of results up to that point, and believed they were not being asked for their input into the process. Little communication had taken place between the staff of Processing Services and the team. Therefore, with the help of the consultant, it was decided to have a series of three meetings with only the staff of Processing Services in order to ease their frustrations and give them a chance to express their concerns. The meetings were facilitated by the consultant, and did not include the rest of the PACE Team. This series of meetings had not been planned, but the team believed it was important to have them in order to relieve any anxiety and concerns before the situation became more serious. While the team had not intended to conduct the problem assessment interviews in this fashion, these meetings were considered the Processing Services staff's time for problem assessment. This was the only group from the libraries that was not interviewed by the PACE Team during this phase. It was also the only group that began to look for solutions prior to the formal beginning of the solutions phase.

In late November, the team was given a debriefing of these three meetings with the Processing Services staff. They learned that five problem themes had been developed. During the solutions stage of these meetings, a recommendation was made by the staff to create an interim team to work on unassigned duties resulting from a backlog of uncataloged materials that had begun to accumulate when a staff member in serials left in February of 1996. The staff believed they could clear the backlog in a relatively short time. In response to this recommendation, the PACE Team decided to formally charter a team to perform this task. This team became known as the Backlog Team, and its purpose was to expedite the processing of serial records that had been left unassigned when the staff person left. The managers from Processing Services did not want to assign staff members to the chartered team, preferring that the staff self-select its membership. This was done, and the PACE Team met with the members of the chartered team in early December. At that time, the team presented a formal charter to the staff, and, after some negotiation, the charter was accepted by all parties.

During this time period, the PACE Team was asked by the library director to make a presentation at the annual all-CUL staff meeting in January. The team wanted to complete the process map for that presentation and spent time periodically during the next several weeks working on the map and the content of the presentation. At the same time, work continued on strategizing about how to interview the remainder of the stakeholders. The decision was made to set up group interviews with each library unit's staff as recommended by the E.C. members. These seven group interviews were completed by January 31.

In order to speed up the interview process and because the team believed that the faculty would have little knowledge about Processing Services activities, it was decided to survey a small, representative group of faculty by e-mail in mid-February. The results of this survey were as expected. The faculty offered little input into the problem phase other than a comment that processing of materials was sometimes slow. Other comments from the faculty concerned connection to the online catalog and a problem in narrowing searches. A group of undergraduate students from an organization that represented a diverse membership was interviewed at a club meeting in mid-February. A print survey of these same questions was also distributed to graduate students who were in the libraries as patrons during the same time period. The comments from both student groups spoke primarily to public service problems and concerns about the collection. Therefore, no significant information was garnered from their comments. Nevertheless, it was important to interview these groups so that all stakeholders would have had input into the process.

The presentation to all CUL staff was held on January 8, 1997. During that presentation, the team gave a history of the project, the reasons for beginning the project, and how the team functioned. The team took questions from the staff and took the opportunity to clarify the time line for completion of the project. The process map which visually represented all activities from the beginning of the project through the projected implementation phase was also presented.

As the team was working through the interviews with various stakeholders, discussions began about the need to document the current workflow. The belief was that a documentation of current activities in Processing Services was necessary in order to effectively compare any proposed new processes with old processes. Because the process of documenting the workflow would likely take quite some time, the team decided to charter a second team charged with that task as soon as possible. The team was asked to create a method for assessing the existing workflow. To accomplish this task they created a workflow survey to determine all the tasks each staff member performed and a Workflow Path Sheet to determine the flow of materials through the department.

By mid-February all interviews with stakeholders had been completed and the team decided to have an all-day meeting to read through all of the approximately four hundred comments received during the problem phase and group them into categories. All the comments had been typed and were presented to the team members at that meeting. Comments were sorted by stakeholder group with accompanying comments. The plan for the day was to read each comment and assign each of them to a theme which would then be recorded on wall charts. These themes, or categories, developed as the comments were read. Because the team did not finish assigning each problem statement to one of the categories during the one-day retreat, several weeks of intense work were spent completing the task. Eleven categories were eventually consolidated into the five major themes of Communication, CUL Management, Processing Services Management, Workflow, and Training.

After categorizing the problem statements into themes, the team began looking for root causes for the problems identified. The root causes represented specific underlying reasons for a related group of problem statements. This task was particularly difficult because the team had to look at problems from the perspectives of both Processing Services and library management. The team continued the process of root cause analysis and met with the library director once more to solicit her perspective on problems and their relationship to root causes.

Root cause analysis was completed in early March, and, on March 18, the team made a presentation to the Executive Committee. A Problem Assessment Document was created prior to that meeting and presented to each member of the Executive Committee. That document included an overview and history of the process to date, the complete list of problem statements that had been gathered from all stakeholders, and the root cause analysis. The goal of this presentation was to obtain agreement from the committee that these were the problems and root causes that needed to be addressed in the solutions phase. The consultant believed it was very important to get a "buy-in" from the E.C. before proceeding to the next phase. Her view was that, without an agreement that these were the root causes and related problems that needed to solved, it would be difficult to obtain acceptance of any proposed solutions. As part of the document for that presentation, the team listed the category, root causes under each category and representative problem statements that supported each root cause. The presentation and the document were well received by the Executive Committee.

It was decided at that meeting with the E.C. that the team should present the Problem Document to Processing Services staff before distributing it to other library units. That meeting took place on April 2 with the library director there to introduce the presentation. The goal of that presentation was obtain from this group an agreement that these were, in fact, the problems that needed to be addressed in the next phase. While the staff seemed to accept the assessment of the problems presented in the document, they were unhappy about not being given enough time to read them in advance. The library director and the team countered by explaining that it was important to view such information in the right context and expressing their concern that the information might have been misunderstood without an appropriate introduction. By the end of the presentation, the staff agreed with the assessment of the PACE Team about the problems and their root causes.

Solutions Phase

The purpose of the Solutions Phase was to generate ideas about how to solve the problems identified in the Problem Phase. The first team meeting in the Solutions Phase took place on April 4. At that time the team decided to work through this phase by conducting three large, cross-departmental brainstorming sessions which included staff at all levels, including E.C. members. The team wanted to have staff from all library units distributed among the sessions to provide an opportunity for a good cross-fertilization of ideas. During these sessions one or two team members facilitated the discussion and another recorded comments on wall sheets. Each attendee was given a copy of the problem assessment document and asked to refer to the root cause analysis page. The procedure used was to go through the list of themes and root causes and ask staff to offer solutions in a brainstorming session. Discussion or criticism of any proposed solution was discouraged in order to allow for the free flow of ideas. In general, these meetings were very successful. Staff seemed to enjoy hearing comments from other units. One unexpected result was that some solutions statements were offered that might be used to solve issues unrelated to the original problem statements.

Once the brainstorming sessions were completed, the PACE Team decided to have their own time for offering solutions, and one meeting was devoted to that process. They also met again with the staff of Processing Services and the library director separately in early May to solicit additional input. This time, the compilation of solutions statements from the brainstorming sessions were given to the staff prior to the meeting.

Vision Phase

While in the middle of the discussions on which solutions to incorporate into a new organization plan, the consultant suggested that the team needed to begin again to formulate a vision statement. Because the team was beginning to have a better sense of how the new organization might be constructed, she felt that this was a more appropriate time to complete this task. The team looked at examples of several mission statements and began to look at the values that were most important for the new organization. They decided to structure the vision around the three issues of process, relationships, and results, and empha-size the concept of the learning organization. By the end of May, the vision statement was completed.

As the team continued to discuss the reorganization based upon feedback from stakeholders and from discussions among themselves, it became clear that the new division would be a merger of the Serials, Cataloging, and Acquisitions Departments. However, it had a great deal of difficulty determining some organizing principle for structuring the flow of work into and through the division. The decision was made to organize the flow of materials by type of material; that is, whether an item was a one-time firm order or a continuation such as a serial or journal. The decision was also made to move to a team-based work environment. Work continued on refining the ideas, and, by early June, the first visual representation of the proposed reorganization with its teams was first developed. Within two weeks, the team had determined the core components of the reorganized division. It included a total of nine teams, eight of which were exclusively within Processing Services. The teams were the Processing Priorities Team, Leadership Team, Priorities Implementation Team, Continuations Team, Requisitions Team, Training Team, Technology Team, Bibliographic Control Team, and the Vendor Relations Team. The reorganization plan called for the division to be managed by a Leadership Team consisting of five staff, three as heads of specific teams regarded as essential for management representation and the two original managers, who desired at-large leadership roles. The three teams with representation on the Leadership Team were the Priorities Implementation Team, the Training Team, and the Technology Team.

In mid-June the team met with the organizational development specialist again to ask for assistance in determining how to assign team member roles and work in a team-based environment. He suggested looking at the current skill set of each employee and determining their motivation and willingness to learn new skills. He also suggested interviewing each staff member and asking them which team or teams they wanted to be on while creating teams with members motivated to work on certain tasks. This would give them the opportunity to make a change in their job responsibilities if they desired. He suggested that he and a colleague offer a team-building workshop to the staff in order to prepare them for the new work environment.

The library director was notified that the team would be prepared to present its plan to the Executive Committee within a few weeks. It was decided to present the proposal to Processing Services Staff first, however, to make sure that the team had their support. On June 16, the first draft proposal was presented to the staff. At that time all proposed teams were presented and the roles of each defined. The team leaders had been solicited in advance and were also announced at that time. The members of the Leadership Team were also announced publicly for the first time. Staff members were told about the interview process for team assignment, and a time line was set for those interviews.

After incorporating some minor suggestions from staff, the team completed its preparation for the final presentation to the Executive Committee. The team wanted to present its plan and, hopefully, receive the approval of the E.C. to move ahead. On June 24, 1997 the team presented the new organization plan to that group. At that presentation, E.C. members were given a revised document that included all solution statements, the team-based structure of the division, leadership of the teams, along with the original problem themes and root causes. The PACE Team presented the team structure with an explanation of each team's function and how the plan addressed the concerns raised during the Problem Phase. E.C. members were asked for their input, and, after some discussion, they were asked if they agreed with the team's recommendations. Approval was given to move ahead with the proposal, thus concluding the Solutions Phase of the project. The Implementation Phase was set to begin.

SUMMARY OF FINDINGS, CONCLUSIONS, AND IMPLICATIONS

This study assessed the results of an organizational change effort in a university library using a qualitative, case study methodology. While there are numerous models in existence to manage a change effort, this particular effort was organized around a model called the *Pathway to Action* brought to the library by the consultant. This model laid the foundation for the change effort and organized the steps taken by the design team to move through the process. The phases of the model called for distinct actions during each phase, providing a linear, yet flexible organizing principle to manage the process. The research questions for this study were driven by the consultant's model and organized by Stufflebeam's CIPP model for program evaluation. As per Stufflebeam, this model is designed, not to prove, but to improve programs so that they work better for those they are intended to help. Stufflebeam's CIPP model overlays the Pathway to Action and provides a theoretical model to evaluate the change effort.

The efficacy of the consultant's model, which became the PACE Project at this university, was tested to determine if its use would result in a successful change effort. The actions called for in this model are derived from the literature on organizational development and managed change. As Kanter, Stein, and Jick (1992) pointed out, the new management paradigm describes "flexible organizations, adaptable to change, with relatively few levels of formal hierarchy and loose boundaries among functions and units, sensitive and responsive to the environment; concerned with stakeholders of all sorts . . . These organizations empower people to take action and be entrepreneurial . . ." (p. 3).

From the perspective of both the process and the end product which resulted from this change effort, the PACE Project fit within this definition. Schneider, Brief, and Guzzo (1996) emphasized the need for change efforts to affect both the climate and culture of an organization. A successful effort should affect multiple levels of an organization. Laabs (1996) stressed the importance of everyone in the organization becoming involved and engaged in the change effort. On mutiple levels, from the Executive Committee to students, the PACE Project provided opportunities for staff and library patrons to offer their input as key stakeholders. The team was given the freedom to find solutions to the previous problems within the division.

As the literature on the learning organization also points out, organizations should attempt to solve problems from a systems perspective. The learning organization speaks to the desire for team learning and a free-flow of ideas because groups are able to come to insights not always possible by individuals. As Senge (1990) states, "Teams, not individuals, are the fundamental learning unit in modern organizations" (p. 10). The PACE Project was a team-based project that operated under a collaborative, consensus-building process. The team made all decisions by consensus and often dialogued extensively before coming to agreement. As stated earlier, the model did call for inclusion of stakeholders from all levels. This approach was designed to provide an awareness of all issues throughout the organization that might effect the final reorganization design. The final plan did, in fact, include a forum for library-wide discussion of issues that effected the division. In terms of the four approaches to change identified by Kovel-Jarboe, this model fit the "managed change" approach in which change is targeted for a specific area. With this approach, the length of time for implementation is relatively long, but there is less likelihood for major losses in productivity.

Summary of Conclusions

As the PACE Team discovered, the volume of work involved in a reorganization effort is enormous. It is difficult to foresee that in advance. Reorganization efforts must be built upon the existing culture of the organization, and the organization's political culture and the general work culture of the staff must be considered. Being aware of the environment and the identity of stakeholders within that environment are also important. While it may be difficult to prescribe an exact formula for success in these efforts, several key elements appear to make success more probable. Support of a formal reorganization effort from the top is critical for success, and it was essential in this environment to have the support of the library director and the Executive Committee. Any team charged with such an effort must also have adequate resources available and must be given a great deal of freedom and autonomy to choose appropriate strategies. To gain that support, such a team must also communicate with and get input from staff at all levels. While it may be impossible to receive support and "buy in" from every staff member or even every manager, everyone in the organization must understand the reason for the reorganization and see the support given it by upper management.

Having an organizing framework to guide a reorganization effort is also an essential component for success. The *Pathway to Action* is one such framework. Such a formal process structure will assist any team to plan its action strategies and provide a framework to guide its steps. Specific meeting strategies such as those implemented in this project are also very helpful to keep a reorganization team focused and on task. The larger organizing framework and the specific meeting management structure combined can provide much needed direction. Such direction allows for reorganization groups to systematically plan a change effort while working with and being sensitive to the unique aspects of the organization in which they work. At the same time, the individual and group will to undertake a change effort for the good of an organization cannot be taken lightly. Ultimately, any change effort must successfully balance processes, results, and the relationships among the individuals that make it all possible.

While time consuming and, at times, difficult, this particular change process was worth the effort. It did result in a "new way of doing things" at this library, and, in general, the staff was able to see the value of the change effort. The greatest challenges during this process were obtaining staff "buy in," especially at the beginning of the project, and maintaining appropriate communication levels. Staff members from all levels of the library were confused about the need for this reorganization, how it would take place, and exactly what involvement they would have in the change effort. Communication did improve over time, but the team struggled for much of the year to catch up from the awkward start. Especially in organizational cultures resistant to change, a reorganization effort should be handled sensitively, its purpose should be clearly stated, and it should provide an opportunity for staff input. The key ingredients that made the change effort at this library successful included top management support, a consideration of the organizational culture, staff input, and an organizing framework around which to manage the change effort. In observing the library culture at this university nearly four years after the reorganization, it appears that, overall, the staff understands that change is sometimes necessary, and that appropriate changes can, indeed, create new efficiencies that benefit both the library and its patrons.

REFERENCES

Argyris, C. (1977). Double Loop Learning in Organizations. *Harvard Business Review* (September–October), 115–125.

Argyris, C., & Schon, D. A. (1978). *Organizational Learning: A Theory of Action Perspective.* Reading, MA: Addison Wesley.

Clack, M. E. (1995). Managing Organizational Change: The Harvard College Library Experience. *Serials Librarian, 25*(3/4), 149–161.

Denton, D. K. (1995). Nine Ways to Create an Atmosphere for Change. *HR Magazine, 41,* 76–81.

Goble, D. S., & Brown K. (1996). What If They Started Talking Talking? New Roles for Staff in Change Management – A Case Study. *The Serials Librarian, 28*(3/4), 197–207.

Kanter, R. M., Stein, B. A., & Jick, T. D. (1992). *The Challenge of Organizational Change.* New York: The Free Press.

Kovel-Jarboe, P. (1996). Quality Improvement: A Strategy for Planned Organizational Change. *Library Trends, 44,* 605–630.

Kramlinger, T. (1991). Training's Role in a Learning Organization. *Training, 29,* 46–51.

Laabs, J. J. (1996). Expert Advice on How to Move Forward with Change. *Personnel Journal, 75,* 54–63.

Lewin, K. (1951). *Field Theory in Social Science.* New York: Harper and Row.

McGill, M. E., Slocum, J. W., & Lei, D. (1992). Management Practices in Learning Organizations. *Organizational Dynamics,* (Summer), 5–17.

Reengineering: Increasing Your Odds of Success (1994). Executive Briefing. Interaction Associates, Inc., Cambridge, MA.

Schneider, B., Brief A. P., & Guzzo, R. A. (1996). Creating a Climate and Culture for Sustainable Organizational Change. *Organizational Dynamics, 24,* 7–19.

Senge, P. (1990). *The Fifth Discipline: The Art and Practice of the Learning Organization.* New York: Doubleday/Currency.

Seymour, D. (Ed.) (1994). *Total Quality Management on Campus: Is It Worth Doing?* New Directions for Higher Education Series, no. 86, Vol. XXII, no. 2.

Seymour, D. (1996). *Once Upon a Campus.* Phoenix: The Oryx Press.

Shaughnessy, T. W. (1995). Lessons From Restructuring the Library. *The Journal of Academic Librarianship,* (July), 251–256.

Stufflebeam, D. L. (1983). The CIPP Model for Program Evaluation. In: G. F. Madders, M. S. Scriven & D. L. Stufflebeam (Eds), *Evaluation Models: Viewpoints on Educational and Human Services Evaluation.* Boston: Kluwer-Nijhoff Publishing.

Stufflebeam, D. L., & William W. (1983). An Analysis of Alternative Approaches to Evaluation. In: G. F. Madders, M. S. Scriven & D. L. Stufflebeam (Eds), *Evaluation Models: Viewpoints on Educational and Human Services Evaluation.* Boston: Kluwer-Nijhoff Publishing.

Tuttle, C. T. (1994). Is Total Quality Worth the Effort? How Do We Know? In: D. Seymour (Ed.), *Total Quality Management on Campus: Is It Worth Doing? New Directions for Higher Education* no. 86, Vol. XXII, no 2.

Worrell, D. (1995). The Learning Organization: Management Theory for the Information Age or New Age Fad? *The Journal of Academic Librarianship,* (September), 351–357.

eBOOK COLLECTION DEVELOPMENT AND MANAGEMENT: THE QUANDARY OF ESTABLISHING POLICIES AND GUIDELINES FOR ACADEMIC LIBRARY COLLECTIONS

Roger Durbin, James Nalen, Diana Chlebek
and Nancy Pitre

eBooks are upon us, or so it would seem. Numerous announcements and articles have appeared that either proclaim the rise of another new company and its impact on the academic market or that bemoan the influence of the newest technology on our intellectual heritage and the habits of our library users. As recently as February 2001, *Library Journal* reported on a survey (albeit undertaken by a publisher) which declared that "electronic texts are making strides in America's colleges" (Rogers, 2001, p. 31). On the other hand, Nicholson Baker has presumably asserted that "librarians have been far too quick to throw out books and newspapers once they have obtained microfilmed or digitized copies" ("Technology and the future," 2001).

Goldie Blumenstyk (2001), writing in *The Chronicle of Higher Education*, summarized the state of things by contrasting the claims of distributors like netLibrary and Questia with the uneasiness of librarians who are contemplating the purchase (or some other form of access) to electronic books for faculty and students. Providers at times act as though they have all the materials necessary for a successful educational experience, whereas librarians are keenly aware of

Advances in Library Administration and Organization, Volume 19, pages 59–84.
ISBN: 0-7623-0868-0

the differences in curricula in the academic community, and thus the need for diversified collections. Claims that electronic books make study "faster" beg comments about the economic necessity of being able to afford the computer or other equipment and software that will allow for appropriate access.

Maybe the time has come to take a few steps back and look at this particular dilemma. Instead of engaging in the debate, or wandering far afield in the anxiety it seemingly causes, librarians need to draw upon the skills they have in collection building for their particular academic institutions in order to assess the role of electronic books and texts in terms of their applicability to their programs. Anyone who recalls the nervousness caused by the introduction of microforms and electronic serials understands that there are ways to work new formats into the essential obligations librarians have to their users, and that most of the worries at the time these formats appeared had nothing to do with librarians and their roles. And anyone who remembers the consternation of librarians when the debate about whether VHS or Beta would win the day will no doubt see the value in understanding the market before leaping into the fray.

If academic librarians approach the quandaries that abound with regard to electronic books through established procedures and policies for sound collection development and management, they will be the better for it. "The unique role, the added value, of academic librarians," as Virginia Tech's collection development policy so clearly puts it, "has always been to bring together an understanding of the publishing world and the resources it makes available with an understanding of the academic enterprise and the local institution." Using this reasoning, librarians seek "then to acquire relevant materials and make them available in a cost-effective manner using the most powerful means available. The new technologies do not change this basic nexus of academic information, but rather help to extend our reach" ("Goals of collection development," 2000).

This study is to serve as a systematic and objective look at the nature and capabilities of eBooks in terms of the market development of these products in order to create a sound basis for collection development policies with regard to them. This examination will show that librarians have in place the means to incorporate many of the possibilities eBooks offer (their impact on distance education being one of them). Librarians also can develop appropriate guidelines and criteria for selection of these resources as they have for other formats. Given these two outcomes, librarians will be able to do something else that they have historically accomplished. They can help to influence the industry by providing rationales for the development of the kinds of products that librarians and their users are interested in, and by outlining the requirements that the products must have if publishers and distributors ever hope to sell them in the academic arena.

WHAT ARE eBOOKS?

One of the first considerations, or challenges, in dealing with this topic, is to describe exactly what we intend when we use the term "eBooks." Janet Balas (2001, p. 56) attempted a definition by separating electronic content, which she calls an "e-book," from electronic hardware devices for reading them (what she refers to as an "e-book reader.") Though helpful, the distinction poses additional questions, for there are formal dimensions and further content considerations that need to be taken into account as a workable definition is developed.

The most readily identifiable type of eBook is simply an electronic version of a print resource. The Gutenberg collection of public domain texts is based on machine-readable forms of existing writings, and, for its part, netLibrary has pretty much defined its business using this same definition (Connaway, 2000). Indeed, those who make the National Book Awards have declared eBooks to be eligible for the annual prize. The announcement, however, discusses eBooks as being effectively an electronic-only version of what is basically a print document, which explains the rule insisting that publishers submit "a hard copy of the work, printed and bound on 8 ½ by 11 inch paper" for consideration. ("eBooks now eligible," 2001)

However, librarians have been confronted with printed materials that have a CD-ROM slipped into a back pocket. At times, the electronic portion is merely an adjunct to the text, that is, it is truly accompanying material. On other occasions, though, the electronic portion is fundamental to the conceptual matter, and, in fact, may be the principal piece of content. It may be computer software, but it is distributed as a component of the printed text, and is thus part of the book material. If this same work is re-published totally in electronic format by an eBook supplier like netLibrary or Questia, then the definition of book is expanded further.

The description widens when we consider what publishers are doing in the creation of textbook materials. In some instances, the primary textbook may be in printed form, with an electronic workbook or supplementary materials available over the Internet. These works seem much like a book with a CD-ROM, as described above. However, when the principal text is electronic, with hyperlinks in the body to glossaries, workbooks, and perhaps computer software that is to be used in conjunction with the chapter content, then we are talking about something else entirely.

These materials may resemble what academic librarians think of as course packs, or "anthologies," created as bundles of related information that supplement a course textbook. For example, companies like Digital Springs publish undergraduate and graduate business texts. Each text comes with "a website, up-to-date resources," and "access to several online business databases" ("Web ancillaries," n.d.). Addison-Wesley offers what it calls *eStudySolutions*. It is, the company says, "the first student portal that features digital textbooks, student solution manuals, study guides, lab books, and more" in downloadable form ("eStudySolutions," n.d.). New York University Press is involved with what some might consider to be true eBooks in that they exist (and can only exist and still make sense) in electronic form. There are variations in design considerations for the presentation of textual material. In a work called *The Buddha Smiled*, by Pratik Kanjilal, we get some notion of what is at stake. As the author himself mentions:

> This work is an exploration of the manner in which hypertext allows a story to be broken up and told in many different ways, of how the mould of traditional storytelling, essentially a linear process, has been broken. The lateral options that hypertext presents . . . are its strength, because they hand over control to the reader. The challenge to the writer is to maintain an overall narrative structure even though he or she has lost control over the plot ("NYU Press Prize," n.d.).

Clearly, as monographic materials ("books" in some people's lexicon) become intrinsically electronic, more interactive, and "packaged" with other types of information, collection development choices become increasingly complicated. Simpler policies of giving consideration to the replacement of lost, damaged, or aged materials by electronic versions lose meaning when the text is principally electronic to begin with. The bundling of related materials around a particular course, or text, for a professor has long been an offshoot of collection growth and management. If publishers get into this arena, and further into areas such as interactive fiction and multimedia theses and dissertations, policies with regard to the selection and purchase of these materials may indeed change in some academic institutions.

THE eBOOK MARKET

Much of the discussion about the future growth in the industry is set within the context of subjective feelings towards the reading of books on computer screens. A wide range of opinions exist on this topic; however, it seems clear that, in the long run, eBooks will have to appeal to a sufficiently large number of consumers in order to sustain the industry. Sandra Morgan (2001) sees great promise in the eBook: "Whether electronic publishing is an industry in its infancy or adolescence, the growth will continue and as market trends develop, it's apparent there will be room for everyone to share in the revenue stream regardless of position in the market place." While the scale of the eBook industry is currently insignificant in comparison to the publishing industry as a whole, research firms like Forrester Research predict that revenue generated by the sale of eBooks will grow to nearly $218 million by 2002 (Rawlinson, 2001).

Librarians have a role to play in the development of this appeal via their collection development policies, which inform publishers and vendors about the needs of library users. Before embarking on a discussion of the role of librarians, it is necessary to ask where the market is headed with regard to eBooks and their content, and how publishers and distributors stand vis-à-vis academic institutions?

According to Ken Brooks, president of Publishing Dimensions, there were historically two types of distribution in publishing; however, with the advent of digital distribution, there are now three: physical distribution of printed books to consumers; the distribution of publishing rights to third parties; and the electronic distribution of content to consumers or third parties. Electronic distribution of content includes the production of eBooks, whether for download or for viewing online, and print-on-demand services (POD). Consumers of the electronic distribution of content include publishers, individuals, schools and libraries. The transition from physical distribution to electronic distribution of content to consumers within the publishing industry will occur over a changing landscape of electronic delivery and access formats (cf. Morgan, 2001).

Meanwhile, it is apparent that the eBooks market is being developed without much input from academic librarians, perhaps because most collection development policies do not make reference to eBooks. Indeed it may be that libraries are being particularly cautious about collecting this new electronic resource, because eBook commerce is being so aggressively promoted as a "push" industry by vendors and publishers who are trying to create a need for the product. In addition, both the nature and the impact of the eBook on scholarly research, pedagogy, library collections and use are still open to much debate and uncertainty in academia. As Thomas Peters, Director of the Center for Library Initiatives, observes when he describes what he designates as the "e-book movement": ". . . The dominant characteristic of this movement – technological, economic, cultural, social, or cognitive – is not yet apparent" (Peters, 2001, p. 201). As David Kirkpatrick reported in the *New York Times*, publishers "say slow sales are caused by clumsy technology, along with high prices for the ephemeral, purely digital editions" (Kirkpatrick, 2001). However, several eBook providers have begun to engage with academic libraries to deliver electronic content to library users.

The nature of this engagement has been largely determined by suppliers, but the result is that relationships between provider and library (and library user) vary considerably. For example, netLibrary fully intends to work with libraries as its primary clientele, and has had some success at the consortium level, with its "academic library" component for OhioLink. Questia is taking another path; it wants to hook up directly with students and other individuals for one-on-one sales, as does yet another company, Versaware (Rogers, 2001, p. 31).

Ebrary, which has an academic history in that it stems from an individual's work at the University of Utah and Stanford University, has in mind a partnership with libraries (among others), using them as middlemen to help sell books to students, for which libraries (and the publishers) will receive a share in the take. ebrary also established recently a partnership with OCLC to have bibliographic records created that will lead users to its bibliographic site for exploration and purchase. The company has added materials related to business, finance, and computers to a few of its vortals (or structured, discipline-related collections of materials) that include journal articles, other resources, along with monographs, as the first of the vertical collections ebrary will make available through OCLC's WorldCat ("Ebrary announces membership," 2001). All these scenarios portray a kind of package deal. That is, one must take all ebrary has to offer, but need only use what is desired; in short, one must "buy the bookstore" to get the one or two titles he or she may really want. The notion of selection and structured literature to support specific programs is totally and glaringly absent, and the idea that libraries will participate in what amounts to commercial ventures as a kind of sales force for these enterprises goes beyond traditional notions of service to library clientele. Indeed, right now, libraries that point to distributors' web sites, where faculty and students can purchase material around the library, are already effectively involved as advertisers for someone else's business.

Textbook and course pack producers, like XanEdu (www.xanedu.com), Ecollege (www.ecollege.com), and netLibrary's Metatext (www.metatext.com), are focusing on college faculty and students in their arrangements. The companies supply to faculty free review copies as temptation to use their versions to support classes. Some compilers (behaving much like academic librarians) are even willing to work with faculty to create customized versions of their courses to accommodate eBooks. Moreover, suppliers heavily promote to professors the unique pedagogical opportunities that eBook technology may provide to teach new critical thinking skills and explorative reading behavior through the use of interactive text modification and "chat rooms."

The market niche, everyone is being assured, will evolve in the textbooks and course pack business, since by renting access to eBooks materials, publishers can prevent the losses they usually incur from recycled books (that is, when students buy used copies). "Publishers can rent entire books or individual chapters by the day, week or semester. A printed book that costs $100 can be rented online for as little as $50, while profit margins are maintained" (Costello, 2001). All that may ·be fine, but this approach avoids access to the range of historical materials and those in other formats, like audiotape and videotape, that can be available for students and their inquiries outside the classroom, and focuses content solely on pre-selected publisher based material.

There is evidence that some publishers and distributors are providing products and services that put them in direct competition with the work of librarians. Barnes and Nobles has announced that it supports MightyWords' vision of what it is calling the Mighty Network, that is, "a network of e-commerce leaders that distribute MightyWords' extensive catalog of professional titles. Partners in the Mighty Network include Barnes & Noble.com, Desaware, Fatbrain and WirelessAdvisor.com." The announcement emphasizes Fatbrain (Barnes and Noble's online arm) as having a "core proposition of offering employees of corporate partners a quick and easy way to order professional and technical books, training and other publicly available materials" ("MightyWords and Fatbrain team to deliver," 2001). One gathers that companies can profile from Fatbrain to customize appropriate literature for their own purposes, and make the resources available through the Fatbrain service. Employees can go to the site to purchase and read pre-selected materials.

In a sense, Barnes and Noble is doing the corporate library's work for them, as still other suppliers, which have hired librarians to work for them, may end up trying to do for academic libraries. As companies package materials, to include electronic texts that appear and behave like traditional monographic materials, they touch upon collection development and management issues for libraries. They also venture into related library services customarily associated with librarians' bibliographic knowledge – that is, the areas of faculty liaison, bibliography preparation and course-support services as well as offsetting the particular, and important, dimensions of instruction in the use of libraries and the teaching of information gathering skills.

ISSUES FOR ACADEMIC LIBRARIANS

The problems for academic librarians are many given all the approaches that publishers and suppliers are taking. First, except for netLibrary, none apparently makes it easy to purchase library copies to be cataloged into individual library catalogs and circulated as is any other book. Indeed, it took over a year of negotiation through OhioLINK to work out the possibility and to arrange for the cataloging records from netLibrary, and these are still not completely available as of this writing. While publishers and vendors want customers to point to their web site and buy or use materials from that location, most libraries do not want to have to point to the company site for eBook materials. Rather, they need them in the catalog where records for all other resources available to support a particular course of study are situated, or as part of bundled electronic information packages for electronic reserves or as library support for distance education, with direct pointers to the desired book.

The University of Akron's experience with the purchase of eBooks has revealed that the only way the materials could be used, that is read by and circulated to faculty and students, was to print them out, bind them, and put them on the shelf. The publishers could conceive of no way to allow that same sort of transaction to occur electronically, but would, Akron's librarians were assured, be happy to sell individual copies to as many prospective buyers as could be identified. Clearly, this is not an acceptable option.

eBook providers seem to assume that academic libraries want all of their materials and will buy them as a package, rather than just selecting those that fit the educational mission of the institutions. Libraries seemingly just have the option of buying them all, or providing access to the site, but then must limit, or try to constrain, what students and faculty can get to. It is something like when libraries bought huge microform sets of materials in order to obtain the few within them that might be needed to support the particular curricular emphasis. At other times, they were forced to purchase the collected works of a composer simply to get the one specific score that was needed. All this is not in the interests of academic institutions, for librarians want to have the necessary ability to tailor their collections to meet specific classroom and research needs to contain costs and make those collections usable. Publishers need to be told as much.

Even netLibrary has only made publisher-based type of library arrangements (for OhioLink solely on the consortial level), and not at the specific institutional level necessary for programmatic help to individual libraries. There are publishers within its collection who would be, and probably have been, written out of many library approval plans because of the nature of the content (like popular treatments) or type of material (like textbooks or study guides) that are simply not wanted in specific institutions despite their purported value in a general collection.

Everyone concerned needs to examine the implications. Any faculty member who enters into an agreement with a publisher, and points to a Web site, may be legally on his or her own or may be binding the institution in ways that make it liable for their behavior. Academic librarians can and must advise faculty away from such arrangements, and work with campus legal offices to make certain that students are being served well.

There are myriad problems surrounding license agreements and other arrangements for the processing and use of eBook materials. One need only think of the situation with regard to books with CD-ROMs in the back pocket. In some libraries, collection developers are given a range of choices. For one thing, at the University of Akron, librarians never honor the caveat that "by breaking the seal," they automatically agree to abide by whatever lies on the other side. Based on printed information, collection builders may decide that they do not really need the CD-ROM and so send the book on to be cataloged while the electronic portion is destroyed. They might also decide that the CD-ROM is important, but not critically so, and therefore send the book on while negotiations over the CD-ROM occur. If an agreement cannot be reached, the electronic portion is destroyed and the printed material stays on the shelf. Collection managers may also decide to wait to resolve the licensing matters. If an agreement is reached, all is cataloged together; if not, the material is returned.

Librarians will probably have to enter into arrangements that are equally time-consuming, labor-intensive, and, therefore, expensive with regard to eBooks for the foreseeable future, or at least until the seeming fear of usage and fear of loss of revenue passes and until the barriers to easy circulation are surmounted. Libraries may even have to create lists of publishers who will not negotiate, and establish "bottom lines" for what the library is willing to do to provide service, as they do for all sorts of materials in other media. Librarians' decisions may have to be the same; some publishers simply will not get the business unless they learn how to collaborate and find ways to market and sell their products to libraries. If publishers want the academic library market for their eBooks, they will need to find ways to make available circulating copies of specific titles, and allow for purchase parameters in a variety of ways – publisher, subject, series, and others – that are meaningful to the academic programs being supported.

At the moment, fear and confusion seem to reign. Many new "players" in the industry are being created while others are disappearing. ITKnowledge folded, and there have been huge layoffs of employees at two of the major companies in this business – Questia and netLibrary – in the past months. Others worry that too much material is being converted away from print without enough thought given to whether the shifts are necessary or wise. "Most librarians say they can't risk buying a needed book solely in e-book form, for fear that it might someday be removed from the online collection by the e-book company or the publisher. So they buy the print book, too. That's a lesson they've learned the hard way in buying" databases of full text articles and "digital journals over the past few years. Companies supplying them with journals have sometimes decided to drop titles from their databases, leaving the libraries without access to journals for which they had no print backups" (Blumenstyk, 2001). With particular note to eBooks, the means to purchase a single title from a single publisher of an eBook – and make it available for use and circulation (and interlibrary loan) through online catalogs within usual cataloging conventions – runs from extremely difficult to impossible. This is a state of affairs that librarians find undesirable, for it goes against the impulse to provide information content and to deliver materials to faculty, students, and other users in cost effective and meaningful ways that reflect the curricula and research interests of the institution.

ISSUES OF ACCESSIBILITY AND USAGE

Collection development policies take for granted that materials selected under general or topical criteria can be made accessible to all library users. This requirement also includes an assumption that librarians will serve those who are physically, visually or hearing-impaired and, in many cases, individuals who are neither students nor faculty of the university or college. These user communities generally also can and need to be able to take advantage of the full functionality of selected materials. For example, print monographs can be made accessible to visually impaired users through the use of adaptive equipment or through campus services designed to record course textbooks for student use. Anonymous unaffiliated library users, or "walk-ins," typically may have some measure of access to the library's print collection but not to the network that supports access to electronic materials.

User accessibility for all comprises a key part of a library's service plan, and the collection of eBooks must be developed with that challenge in mind. The recent development of standards for eBooks under the aegis of the Open eBook Forum (OeBF) signals a significant step in addressing this intent (www.openebook.org). The OeBF standards serve as a guide for publishers and eBook suppliers, providing a common format in which to release data. The standards also are meant to guide the relationship between publishers and eBook users, where the latter are able to purchase or otherwise access an eBook from any authorized supplier and display the work on any type of device. Providers such as netLibrary have announced that they will adopt these standards for their products.

The OeBF standards incorporate elements of the World Wide Web Consortium (W3C) Web Accessibility Initiative (WAI) guidelines (www.w3.org/WAI). These guidelines are designed to make Web content accessible to people with disabilities by specifying technical standards for Web design that make it possible for the visually-impaired to use screen reader technology with Web pages. They also are intended for those who cannot access a personal computer through the use of a mouse because of a physical disability, and for other Web users with disabilities who want access to the highest level of Web content possible. Screen reader technologies, such as JAWS, should be able to read aloud the content of a Website that adheres to the W3C guidelines. netLibrary's eBooks are relatively accessible using JAWS for Windows 3.5. However, this version of JAWS is unable to read figures contained within eBooks that exist only in an image format. To address this problem, text equivalents should be provided for figures and other illustrations to accommodate systems and software that cannot reproduce them in a text format. eBooks that are supplied in Adobe Acrobat's PDF format pose significant problems for screen readers such as JAWS, which are currently incompatible with this format. The caveat to librarians is clear. The decision to purchase eBooks that cannot, for technical reasons, be accessed by library users with disabilities must be carefully weighed against their utility, and accommodations must be made in the context of the service program of the library if the decision is made to go ahead.

Many libraries attempt to draw as wide a circle as is possible and permissible around their community of users. For example, the University of Akron makes many of its resources, both print and electronic, accessible to students, faculty, staff, alumni and the wider community alike, although the level of access may differ among these groups of users. The collection of eBooks poses a challenge to this type of service delivery plan. Access to eBooks provided by netLibrary, for example, requires a valid IP address. Unaffiliated library users may access netLibrary eBooks within the library; however, they will be prevented from accessing these same materials from a home or other remote computer. Affiliated users are able to access eBooks remotely, but others cannot.

Unaffiliated users may borrow from the University of Akron's print collection through a "community borrower card" program, in which this group of users enjoys library privileges that are analogous to those received by affiliated users. The present set-up for netLibrary does not provide this same level of access. Thus, the rules governing essentially the same content has to change, so that the policy on use varies only because of technological quirks.

Libraries may also have formal, contractual service agreements with business and industry companies, or other institutional users of their materials and services. The problems of anonymous users are exacerbated, since the greatest need corporate users may have is for access to the library's materials from remote sites. In short, accommodations need to be made for the subtle, but telling the difference between affiliated and unaffiliated users and authorized and unauthorized ones who may not fall neatly into the usual two categories.

netLibrary eBooks can be accessed through a standard web browser. eBook borrowers can access their currently checked out eBooks from any browser that meets the technical specifications required. However, the added functionality of these works – including annotating and highlighting features – may only be accessible after downloading netLibrary's eBook reader to a personal computer. Since many library users do not have access to a personal computer at home, their use of these materials will have to take place in the library or in other computer labs on campus. One problem is that, in many institutions, firewalls typically prevent the downloading of unauthorized software to networked computers. This restricts the added functionality of eBooks to only those users who are able to access the eBook reader. There have been complaints and warnings in this area from library users who regard this condition as being analogous to the medieval idea of books being chained to the walls. Thus eBook technology and the ways that we might have to provide access to them do not always represent a great leap forward , and in some areas force a regression in library service.[1]

A collection development policy for eBooks, or the incorporation of eBooks into existing topical policies, should specify that these works must meet the OeBF standards, particularly with regards to W3C's set of guidelines. Selected eBooks must also be accessible to all members of the library's community of authorized and anonymous users. This access might be differentiated, perhaps permitting "community borrowers" to access eBooks only on-site. Thus, access should not be solely based on a user's personal information as contained in library records. Unaffiliated users' access to eBooks should be roughly equivalent to their access to print monograph collections. An eBooks provider's business model need not see such access as a monetary threat, since it does not necessarily preclude this group of users from purchasing their own copies at some point in time (Peters, 2001, pp. 56–57).

eBooks should also not require use of specialized reader software or devices provided by the library in order to access content or take advantage of their added functionality (e.g. highlighting and annotating). Ideally, such functionality and content should be accessible through a standard Web browser, or through specialized devices owned by library users. The library should ultimately be able to deliver purchased eBooks content in whatever format the library user requires (Peters, 2001, p. 58).

Though not our concern here, librarians and their professional organizations are addressing policy issues and long-term strategies related to e-book readers. The American Library Association's (ALA) Presidential Task Force, under the auspices of the Office for Information Technology Policy, is working on an ideal eBook model for libraries and library users. "The Bibliofuture group," it says, "has proposed a library standard for e-books ... the purpose of [which] is twofold: to define the minimal features for e-book reader hardware and software (to avoid unwanted and unnecessary features) and to define the minimal rights for the owners and users of e-book reader hardware and software" (Peters, 2001). Here, clearly, is a specialized concern for usability and the role of the format in libraries is apparent.

Generally, collection development policies assume that library users will be able to locate materials in an efficient and effective manner, with access frequently provided through the library's public access catalog. The University of Akron has access to MARC records for netLibrary eBooks through its consortium agreement with OhioLINK. OhioLINK obtains MARC records from OCLC; OhioLINK members can then download these records into their local systems. Alternatively, users may be directed by their library to the OhioLINK central catalog to access eBooks.

However, The University of Akron directs users to electronic serials organized by the University of Pennsylvania on its "On-Line Books Page" in a different fashion. Users can access them only through a link provided to the Web site (http://digital.library.upenn.edu/books/) from The University of Akron's homepage. There is no access to title specific information in the local online catalog, nor is there a title entry under the larger heading "On-Line Books Page." This division of access is somewhat mirrored in the OhioLINK consortium catalog (however, a bibliographic record for the "On-Line Books Page" itself is found in the larger catalog). It seems reasonable, though, that in the future selectors will want to identify monographic titles in the public domain that meet the criteria outlined in topical collection development policies, and that these titles will be made accessible through local catalogs.

Libraries may provide access to their collections of eBooks through their Web site instead of, or in addition to, through local catalogs. For instance, many libraries provide a link to the netLibrary Web site directly from their homepages; researchers can use this link to directly access netLibrary offerings that have been selected by the library, and to netLibrary's collection of "free" or public domain eBooks. However, missing from this type of promotional access is a corresponding explanation of how to access these works, or indeed what eBooks are. While a user might find such a guide at the netLibrary Web site, librarians should be providing such guidance along with their promotion of this resource. North Carolina State University Libraries offers such guidance from its Web site, but this seems to be the exception rather than the rule ("New technologies available," 1999).

Given the costs – in both staff time and money – involved in cataloging electronic materials, it is important to insure that these works will continue to be available before a commitment is made in this area. For print collections, libraries make efforts to shelve these assets efficiently and effectively and also undertake security and preservation measures to make the works available over the long-term. In the electronic world, collection managers should be looking for the same type of long-term availability of materials, so that cataloging will be worth the costs incurred. The same values of security for materials and efficiency and effectiveness in retrieving them must be present in a provider's approach to eBooks. In the parlance of librarianship, hot links from catalogs to discontinued Web sites are the equivalent of maintaining the cataloging of lost books without a notation accounting for their absence from the shelves.

Library users should be able to connect seamlessly from the library's catalog to individual titles without having to spend considerable time locating the desired item. Providers should ensure this level of accessibility by making eBooks technically compliant with changing library operating systems. For example, if a library must adopt a new web browser for its public computers, providers will need to work with the library to ensure that its eBooks are still accessible through this new browser. License agreements should require such adaptability. If these conditions cannot be met through the license agreement, it may not be worth the costs involved to develop traditional cataloging data.

Ultimately, bibliographic data (or metadata) for eBooks should be augmented by the inclusion of their electronic content in local catalogs. Lynn Connaway (2000) suggests that true digital catalogs should not only provide links between eBooks and other library materials, but should also incorporate the ability to search across the electronic content of eBooks. While it may be premature to require such functionality from content providers, future collection development policies should include these criteria as highly desirable in selection guidelines.

TEACHING FACULTY AND COLLECTION MANAGEMENT

As noted above, several providers offer integrated sets of electronic materials along with eBooks for many courses. Once a student has purchased access to a particular work for a class, she or he then has access to these supplementary materials, many of which are available only in electronic form. If a student does not purchase the electronic version of the textbook, but uses a copy that a faculty member has placed on reserve in the library instead, equal access must be arrived at through other means – namely, through the library's collection. In many cases, this is not possible.

For example, Wizeup.com, an eBook provider that works with many academic textbook publishers to deliver content to students, derives supplementary readings from Gale Group's Infotrac College Edition. While the library might provide access to all of the titles contained in Infotrac, this access will not appear as seamless as that provided by Wizeup. At the same time, students may be required to pay for access to full-text journals contained in this packaged version of Infotrac, even if the library already subscribes to a version of this database on behalf of the university community. This represents an unnecessary duplication of resources, much like departmental reading rooms that use scarce resources to unnecessarily duplicate resources. Favored publishers do not mind, because such situations represent increased revenue for them as they sell additional copies of a limited number of titles, but librarians do. It may be possible for librarians to work with such providers of electronic textbook packages in order to minimize this kind of duplication while ameliorating publishers' concerns about their profits.

Librarians have also traditionally been involved in the very same type of linking between resources that is the one of the strengths of true eBooks. Pathfinders, bibliographies, course guides and topical websites all attempt to link together disparate resources on a topic in the interests of a library user. eBooks accomplish this same goal, frequently in a more seamless manner than do traditional library-developed guides. These new models will demand that librarians rethink how resources are presented to students. They will be required to determine how their wide range of resources can be made easier to find, and how they can make it easier to determine which resources are going to be useful for a given topic. They will also need to rethink their services to teaching faculty, and offer them a service similar to Wizeup, that is, one that brings together both print and electronic resources (to include some that are not necessarily part of the library's present collection) in support of a particular course.

The University of Akron already has experience in this area as result of its use of Docutek's electronic reserve system, Eres. Through it, the library is able to gather disparate source materials, to include scanned electronic journals for which the library seeks (and pays for) copyright permission to include materials specified by faculty. Chapters from books can be scanned in as well under the same provisions. Unpublished papers, guides to additional resources, links to books in the library's online catalog, and a host of other information add significant information support to the classroom experience.

Faculty themselves have experience developing their own course packs, using software such as WebCT. However, the eBooks provided by Questia, netLibrary and Wizeup offer expanded functionality not found in "off-the-shelf" software packages, particularly features like annotating and highlighting; it is this sort of functionality that will increasingly appeal to users (Hughes, 2001; Rogers, 2001; Summerfield & Mandel, 1999).

Librarians need to be the integrators, or negotiators, who find ways to bring together all these multiple approaches to providing classroom support for faculty. Since bibliographers have traditionally developed materials that link together various library resources, we should expect to play such a role in the types of linking that occur with regard to eBooks and other electronic resources, along with other appropriate resources, whatever their format may happen to be. The key should be to select, gather, and organize suitable and necessary materials in support of individual courses of study. There needs to be a commitment, or perhaps a recommitment on the part of librarians, to renew and refocus their faculty liaison efforts and work with their teaching colleagues more closely. The process is a well-established one in academic librarianship. The advent of eBooks does not change either the role or the responsibility that goes along with it. Rather, it adds an interesting component that must be worked through. An eBook provider that delivers content in a wholly proprietary manner will limit our ability to engage in this type of activity.

The development of off-the-shelf electronic course packets that include an electronic textbook and supplemental readings presents another challenge to bibliographic instruction and information literacy programs designed to provide students with the skills needed to access curricular support materials. While this type of access might meet the immediate needs of students enrolled in a particular course, it does not help them gain information-seeking skills. This situation is not new for academic librarians, nor for teaching faculty. There has always been the danger of an over-reliance on "anthologies" on reserve in the library, or the overuse of reserve room services. Just as librarians have always steered faculty away from gathering everything students may possibly want during a semester (or indeed more than they might have time to use), they need to move faculty away from this type of thinking with regard to course packs. While students may succeed in an introductory sociology course where an electronic course packet has been made available, they may fall apart in advanced courses in the same discipline when they are required to seek out and use significant amounts of secondary literature on an original topic of inquiry, an event for which they might be ill-prepared because of the absence of basic information literacy skills.

One could argue, if the availability of electronic course packets were sufficiently widespread across the curriculum, including all disciplines and levels therein, that this would not present a problem. However, given that most electronic course packets right now cover only introductory material and are available only in a few disciplines, the curricular experience, at least in terms of learning to gather and evaluate information, will tend to be uneven across the curriculum. Ultimately, it will be unfair to students who will consequently lack the ability to gather information related to their field of study or other interests. Librarians need to assume that faculty will find such a scenario unacceptable, and thereby conceive and implement a better educational experience for students.

In the real world, all needed information is seldom presented in a box for purchase, and that is why academic librarians have been rethinking their instructional programs with a move away from traditional bibliographic instruction (or teaching how to use a particular library) toward programs designed to develop information literacy (whereby students learn the skills necessary to gather, evaluate, organize, and use materials in the appropriate arena). As a result, academic libraries are refocusing instruction programs to include a new instructional role for librarians, where they assist both faculty and students in the "post-retrieval processing of texts" (Peters, 2001, pp. 55, 60). They help users develop the ability to evaluate "information and its sources critically," and then incorporate selected information into one's "knowledge base and value system," so that they learn to effectively use it for coursework, other documentation, or decision-making of some sort (Association of College & Research Libraries, 2000). Academic librarians need to become involved in developing appropriate library-related, or information gathering assignments as part of the faculty member's course syllabi, with the aim of insuring that necessary information skills are part of the learning experience.

eBOOKS AND COLLECTION DEVELOPMENT POLICY

Understandably, most academic libraries have not instituted policies about acquiring, using, and integrating eBooks into the collection, given the state of things. There seem to be only a few libraries that mention eBooks as a format to be reckoned with. Probably the clearest reference comes from Kenyon College, where its collection development policy states: "Collecting books still has a high priority at Kenyon, but we also collect electronic alternatives to print sources for several types of materials, including . . . books." But even here, the reference so far is only to consortial purchases made through OhioLink with pointers to vendor sites ("Collection development policy," 2000).

A look through collection development policies at various web sites reveals that most libraries have established separate policies to deal with electronic resources in general, rather than integrating them as format variations within subject-oriented descriptions. This does not seem appropriate, and, after assessing the impact of eBooks on assumptions relating to the development of appropriate collection policies, The University of Akron University Libraries redrafted its Collection Development Policy to incorporate the inclusion of eBooks into the library's collection. Rather than create an entirely separate policy for eBooks, it was felt that integrating the new format into the existing policy would allow this resource to take its place in the collection as supportive of the library's goals for each specific subject area. The main point of the move is to maintain the notion of content as primary in collection decisions, with matters of format considered as ancillary. Additionally, the acquisition of eBooks emphasizes a major goal of the library's recently developed Strategic Plan for 2000–2004: to "utilize technology to enhance educational quality and access to information." It also supported the university's overall aim to create a campus that would be in the forefront of electronic communication, while supporting the most effective methods available for delivery of needed academic and scholarly information.

The policy consists of a General Section that outlines various categories of collection "Organization and Constraints" for each departmental discipline. These include traditional descriptions such as "Scope and Purpose, Curriculum, Geographical Coverage, Language, Period Coverage and Publication Types". With regard to format of materials, up to this point, the policy only referred to audio-visual materials and computer files, but is being expanded to include this description: "the format of eBook collections for general utilization and circulation from any branch of the campus. The selection of specific texts and collections is based on determination of needs of various subject disciplines. These needs may encompass, but are not limited to, the following:

- monographs exclusively available in electronic form
- electronic duplicate copies of print monographs that are in heavy demand
- monographs that undergo frequent revision and must be kept current
- materials that incorporate multi-media aspects or involve interactive electronic text modification.

To the category of "Collection Levels" is added the statement that "eTextbooks are predominantly collected at the level of Initial Study or below. Electronic coursepacks and bundles (i.e. anthologies of information are coordinated through the Head of Collection Management."

Under the category of "Constraints" certain aspects peculiar to eBooks are noted and described:

(1) *Archiving*: Wherever possible eBooks should be purchased with the right to maintain access in perpetuity.
(2) *Usage*: Accommodation of multiple users and access from remote sites should be a provision of eBooks purchase agreements and licensing.

(3) *Technical Support*: Necessary hardware and technical support should be in
place or acquired simultaneously with the purchase of eBook materials.

In addition, a section of "Caveats" is added concerning conditions of purchase
of eBooks in order to guide collection managers in deciding whether or not to
pursue purchase arrangements. These include the:

- maintenance of stable and ongoing access to single eBook titles from vendor
packages
- availability of eBooks for general circulation and interlibrary loan
- maintenance of high standards in format and publication and adequate, user-
friendly access
- licensing of access from most library sites on campus and remote places

The second section of the revised policy that describes subject-specific collection development emphasizes that collection managers will participate in the
selection of specific eBook titles from collections that are purchased by The
University of Akron University Libraries and from consortium-based arrangements, such as netLibrary. Issues of currency, access, the availability of
e-materials according to subject discipline, and appropriation funds that can be
dedicated, will determine the proportion of eBook resources that will be selected
to support the research and curricular needs of each department. Since different
disciplines innovate at different rates, the assumption here is that various
scientific and technical departments, along with business and education,
(particularly pedagogy), will probably purchase more eBooks than will
disciplines in the humanities and social sciences, simply because currently
published eBook collections in these fields are more numerous.

A section on the unique aspects of eBooks purchasing arrangements is also
described. Vendor partnerships with libraries and departments, as well as course-
derived purchases could be arranged, but these need to be reviewed and
approved by the Collection Management Department head and also negotiated
through the University Legal Office.

Overall, a Collection Development Policy that incorporates eBooks as an
alternate format is created with the intent of maintaining flexibility to change
and adapt to a new information environment. The policy also describes
inclusion of eBooks along with selection guidelines for the bibliographer to
follow in purchasing these materials. And this approach to the policy provides
guidance in understanding and working with publishers and suppliers of
prospective materials. However, the world of technology is volatile, and The
University of Akron is taking a judicious approach in extending its collections
in this area. A balance between print and electronic access is deemed

important, since, like other academic libraries, The University of Akron University Libraries conserve crucial intellectual information and important historical records for an extended period of time. Care must be taken to insure that the library provides the information in the most appropriate, flexible, and useful formats that have been developed to date while insuring that the storehouse of information is not trapped within antiquated (or fly-by-night) technologies that can no longer be afforded. While it is important that we begin to ramp up our investment in etexts in general and eBooks specifically, we cannot afford to discontinue buying information in traditional formats until we have more experience with electronic texts.

CONCLUSION: WHAT ARE ACADEMIC LIBRARIES TO DO?

Some may feel the urge to be in the vanguard and embrace any new technology just because it's new. Others may, in fact, prefer to stagnate in what might be regarded as the glacial pace of collection development in academic libraries in the midst of the seeming hyper-kinetic speed surrounding the development of electronic resources, noting as Michael Looney and Mark Sheehan did in a recent *Educause* article, "Textbooks, course books, and other digital learning materials need to be as easy to find, buy, obtain, and use as books bought at a conventional college bookstore or found in the campus library," (Looney & Sheehan, 2001) and, they aren't yet. Nor is there any guarantee that this will happen, especially as long as the emphasis seems to be on the technology (and security and profit issues) of eBooks rather than on the use of eBook technology to make information freely and easily available. The notion of tethering e-content to a particular piece of technology or machinery makes it inconvenient for our clients to obtain and use. "If the process is slow or complicated, eBooks will not catch fire on campus," Looney and Sheehan went on to say, and we agree. It is also unlikely to excite librarians who are responsible to provide educational and learning materials, it seems, until that happens.

But, at the same time, we feel that academic librarians have the ability to have great influence on the role of eBooks in their academic institutions. For one thing, they can work through associations like the Society for Scholarly Publishing (www.sspnet.org) that track the eBooks industry from the vantage of scientific and technical publishers. The Society's annual meetings also provide an arena where publishers, academics and librarians can square off in debates about many thorny aspects of the eBooks industry and its impact on the communication of scholarly research. It would seem that this is a good avenue to pursue the academic librarian's concerns about the eBooks business and the necessary conditions for the inclusion of materials in this format in the curricula and the library service programs for which we are responsible.

Librarians can also deal individually with publishers and suppliers through the acts of purchase and negotiating licenses (plus whatever consortial influence they may have). The resulting negotiations provide a good mechanism through which librarians can influence the market so that they are able to do their work of service to the academic community better. Within the OhioLink consortium, The University of Akron felt obliged to petition NetLibrary that certain other publishers be added to their list, and wanted concrete information on how to make such requests and have them honored. These requests came out of a noticeable absence of publishers available to support international components of the University's program.

Librarians should feel free to take an informed, but hard line in their business dealings with publishers and suppliers. Anyone who has followed the marked changes in how publishers construct license agreements with reference to electronic serials and accompanying CD-ROMs will recognize the shaping influence of librarians. There are perceptible differences in descriptions that allow for academic institutions, multiple user sites, remote access, circulation and interlibrary lending privileges, and the separation of the subscriber from the user. Librarians have taken responsibility for their role when considering matters of use, fairness, and their clientele, while maintaining a willingness to understand the commercial side of the enterprise. Librarians understand that everyone is served if suppliers make a fair profit and charge a fair price that supports the development of products that meet user needs.

But it is very likely through the development of collection policies, guidelines for selection, and descriptions of ways to evaluate and select publishers and vendors, along with close interaction and cooperation with academic faculty that we will have more immediate means to solve our current problems. Through their liaison activities, librarians can get much feedback from faculty and their students about their experience with eBooks, and use the information gathered as leverage with publishers and suppliers. In the mix of those involved – creators, publishers, suppliers and aggregators, librarians, faculty, students, and the casual user – librarians need to understand they are in the middle of it all. They must position themselves so that they can find reasonable, effective, creative, and relevant solutions to provide appropriate content for clients while disentangling the format problems that emerge.

In a short article in *Educause*, Donald Waters outlined four principles for developing digital libraries, a part of which should include eBooks:

(1) create scholarly value by exploiting the distinctive features of the technology.
(2) create collections of coherence and integrity.
(3) protect and foster an intellectual commons for scholarly and educational uses.
(4) be realistic about costs, especially the costs of distributing content and sustaining ongoing operations.

Librarians have always embodied these principles in their professional work. Academic librarians understand their business, and have a solid record of experience; it remains to be seen whether eBook publishers can match them in intention and performance given the difficulties of the eBook industry. As a result, academic librarians are in good position to push their academic agenda both by performing professional services that help them understand the needs of their users while leading the way in insuring that suppliers understand how information should be organized, presented, and delivered.

NOTE

1. Michael Jenkins (2000) describes the restricted access to eBooks that is imposed by publishers as a form of "retro-glue" that affixes to electronic publishing old models of intellectual property ownership" and thus appears to work against the free exchange of ideas and information afforded by the Internet. On the compatibility of free public access to information in the digital library with the interests of the information market of the publishing industry see also Billington (1996), Lamm (1996), Lang (1996), Lyman (1996) and Borgmann (2000).

REFERENCES

Association of College & Research Libraries (2000). Information literacy competency standards for higher education: Standards, performance indicators, and outcomes. Retrieved June 28, 2001, from Association of College & Research Libraries Web site: http://www.ala.org/acrl/ilstandardlo.html

Balas, J. L. (2001). Think like a patron when you consider buying e-books. Computers in Libraries, 21(5), 56–58.

Billington, J. H. (1996). Libraries, the Library of Congress, and the Information Age. Daedalus, 125(4), 35–54.

Blumenstyk, G. (2001). Libraries offer online reference services to one another. Retrieved May 22, 2001, from Chronicle of Higher Education Web site: http://chronicle.com/free/2001/05/2001052201t.htm

Borgmann, C. L. (2000). Toward a Global Digital Library: Progress and Prospects. In: From Gutenberg to the Global Information Infrastructure (pp. 226–269). Cambridge, Mass.: MIT Press.

Collection development policy (2000). Retrieved June 28, 2001, from Kenyon College Library and Information Services Web site: http://lbis.kenyon.edu/colldev/

Connaway, L. S. (2000). Librarians, producers, and vendors: The netLibrary experience. Retrieved June 28, 2001, from Library of Congress Web site: http://lcweb.loc.gov/catdir/bibcontrol/connaway_paper.html

Costello, M. (2001, May 21). E-textbooks from Rovia. *Publishers Weekly, 248,* 45.

eBooks now eligible for National Book Awards (2001). Retrieved June 28, 2001, from theLibraryPlace.com, Web site: http://www.thelibraryplace.com/daily_zoom.cfm?id=334

Ebrary announces membership in OCLC. (2001). Retrieved June 28, 2001, from ebrary Web site: http://www.ebrary.com/news/010612.jsp

EStudySolutions. (n.d.). Retrieved June 28, 2001, from Addison-Wesley Higher Education Web site: http://www.aw.com/estudysolutions/home.html

Fedunok, S. (1996). Hammurabi and the electronic age: Documenting Electronic Collection Decisions. *RQ, 36,* 86–90.

Goals of collection development (2000). Retrieved June 28, 2001, from Virginia Tech University Libraries Web site: http://www.lib.vt.edu/info/colldev/coll_dev_policies/GOALS.html

Hughes, C. A. (2001). The myth of 'obsolescence': The monograph in the digital library. *Portal: Libraries and the Academy, 1*(2), 113–119.

Jenkins, M. (2000). e-books and retro glue protect the vested interest of publishing. *The Chronicle of Higher Education,* June 23, 2000.

Kirkpatrick, D. (2001). Forecasts of an e-book era were, it seems, premature. *New York Times,* August 28, 2001, p. 1.

Lamm, D. S. (1996). Libraries and Publishers: A Partnership at Risk. *Daedalus, 125*(4), 127–146.

Lang, B. (1996). Brick and Bytes: Libraries in Flux. *Daedalus, 125*(4), 221–234.

Looney, M. A., & Sheehan, M. (2001). Eigitizing education: a primer on eBooks. *Educause, 36*(4), 38–46.

Lyman, P. (1996). What is a Digital Library? Technology, Intellectual Property and the Public Interest. *Daedalus, 125*(4), 1–33.

MightyWords and Fatbrain team to deliver digital content (2001). Retrieved June 28, 2001, from fatbrain Web site: http://www1.fatbrain.com/pressreleases/mighty.asp

Morgan, S. (2001). Electronic publishing: Turmoil or growth? *Electronic Publishing Magazine.* Retrieved June 25, 2001, from http://ep.penwellnet.com

New technologies available at the NCSU Libraries: Electronic books (1999). Retrieved June 28, 2001, from North Carolina State University Libraries Web site: http://www.lib.ncsu.edu/colmgmt/ebooks/

NYU Press Prize for Hyperfiction (n.d.). Retrieved June 28, 2001, from NYU Press Web site: http://www.nyupress.nyu.edu/hypertext/

Peters, T. A. (2001). Gutterdämmerung (twilight of the gutter margins): e-Books and libraries. *Library Hi Tech, 19*(1), 50–62.

Peters, T. A. (2001). A Year of Growing Pains for the Electronic Publishing Movement. In: D. Bogart (Ed.), *Library and Book Trade Almanac* (pp. 201–217). New York: R. R. Bowker.

Rawlinson, N. (2001, June). e-Books: Changing the Business of Trade Publishing. Presentation at the annual meeting of the American Library Association, San Francisco, California.

Rogers, M. (2001). Survey reveals college students' growing preference for e-texts. *Library Journal, 126*(2), 31.

Summerfield, M., & Mandel, C. A. (1999). On-line books at Columbia: Early findings on use, satisfaction, and effect. In: R. Ekman & R. E. Quandt (Eds), *Technology and Scholarly Communication* (pp. 282–308). Berkeley: University of California Press.

Technology and the future of academic libraries: a live discussion with Nicholson Baker (2001). Retrieved May 15, 2001, from Chronicle of Higher Education Web site: http://chronicle.com/

Waters, D. Developing digital libraries: four principles for higher education. *Educause*, 37(1), 59.
Web ancillaries (n.d.). Retrieved June 28, 2001, from Coursepaq Web site: http://www.coursepaq.com/
    transition/module_3/3_2modcos.htm

APPENDIX

The University of Akron University Libraries

Collection Development Policy: eBooks and eBook Collections

A. Introduction
In order to meet their primary mission of supporting the teaching and research needs of students and faculty through their collections and services, The University of Akron University Libraries are committed to utilizing technology to enhance educational quality and access to information. The following guidelines address issues that are unique to the Libraries' acquisition of the format of eBooks and eBook collections, since electronic publications are often treated differently from printed publications by publishers and vendors. Because technology and information access change so rapidly it is expected that these guidelines will be under continuing review by the Libraries' Collection Management Department.

B. Definition and Scope
In the context of these guidelines, an eBook is defined as a digital monograph that is searchable, able to be enhanced with cross-references, and linked to other sources and multimedia.
    The criteria set forth below will cover eBook acquisition:

• both within and outside consortial agreements;
• as single-item acquisitions and as bulk collections.

C. General Collection-Related Criteria

(i) Subject-Related Criteria
ebooks and eBook collections considered for acquisition by selectors should:

(1) follow current collection parameters already in place as represented by the currently approved "University of Akron University Libraries Collection Development Policy," particularly as these relate to each departmental discipline, covering categories of "Scope and Purpose, Geographical Coverage, Language, Period Coverage and Publication Types;"

(2) represent materials for utilization and circulation from any branch of the campus and that are broadly accessible under the strictures of current copyright and licensing laws;

(3) enhance and enrich current collections and academic needs of various disciplines. Such needs encompass, but are not limited to, the following:

- monographs exclusively available in electronic form
- electronic duplicates of print monographs in heavy demand
- monographs that undergo frequent revision and must be kept current
- materials that incorporate multi-media aspects or involve interactive text modification

eTextbooks should be predominantly collected at the level of "Initial Study" or below, with few exceptions. Electronic course packs and "course bundles" that are predominantly anthologies of information are excluded from purchase.

(ii) Technology – Related Criteria
Selectors are referred to the technology criteria for collection of electronic resources that are outlined in "Part 1: Checklist for a Collection Policy Statement" made by the ALA RUSA CODES Collection Policy Committee (Fedunok, 1996, pp. 86–87)

D. Constraints

(1) Archiving – Whenever possible, eBooks and eBook collections should be purchased with the right to maintain access in perpetuity.
(2) Access and Usage – Accommodation of multiple users and access from remote sites should be a provision of eBooks purchase agreements and licensing.
(3) Technical Support – Necessary hardware and technical support should be in place or acquired simultaneously with the purchase of eBook materials.

E. Caveats
In considering acquisition of eBooks and eBook collections selectors are advised to check agreements for the following provisions:

(1) Option to select single eBook titles from vendor packages.
(2) Availability of eBooks for general circulation and interlibrary loan.
(3) Provision of high standards in format and publication and adequate, user-friendly access, *including adherence to OeBF (Open eBook Forum Standards)*.
(4) Licensing of access from most library sites on campus.

F. Other Considerations

(1) Subject selectors will participate in the selection of specific eBook titles from general collections that are purchased by the Library and from consortium-based arrangements, e.g. netLibrary, that are purchased with OhioLINK.
(2) Issues of currency, access and availability of eBook materials will, as a rule, determine the proportion of eBook resources that will be selected to support the research and curricular needs of each university department.
(3) Subject selectors may arrange library partnerships with vendors and university departments for course-derived eBook purchases, but these need to be reviewed and approved by the Head of Collection Management and negotiated through the University Legal Office.

INTERNET RESEARCH ETHICS AND INSTITUTIONAL REVIEW BOARD POLICY: NEW CHALLENGES, NEW OPPORTUNITIES

Elizabeth A. Buchanan

INTRODUCTION: NEW CHALLENGES, NEW OPPORTUNITIES FOR RESEARCHERS

The Internet continues to evolve along at least two lines of development: it has since its inception been and continues to be a tremendous resource for researchers seeking and sharing information; and, it is quickly becoming the object or medium of research itself. Challenges face researchers on both of these fronts, from assuring the integrity and validity of data in the first scenario to the actual protection of individuals' privacy and autonomy in the second.

This paper focuses on this second scenario: examining the use of the Internet itself as a medium for conducting research. Online research (or virtual research) is quickly emerging as a unique research methodology, complete with its own methodological specificity, its own guidelines on *how* to conduct research online, and its own codes of researcher conduct. Nowhere is the challenge surrounding online research greater than in the offices of the institutional review boards which find themselves struggling with new

Advances in Library Administration and Organization, Volume 19, pages 85–99.
ISBN: 0-7623-0868-0

protocol language, new means of data selection and collection, and new and increasingly difficult challenges to the ethical treatment and protection of human subjects.

Many, including notably the United States Office for Protection from Research Risks, has seen the tremendous growth in the use of the Internet or the World Wide Web as a medium and a locale for conducting serious research. The Office's first formal workshop on this issue took place in 1999, in light of many inquires surrounding virtual research and ethical conduct. Frankel and Siang (1999) describe the circumstances leading to the workshop "Ethical and Legal Aspects of Human Subjects Research on the Internet:"

> The Office for Protection from Research Risks (OPRR) ... has received inquiries from researchers and Institutional Review Boards (IRB's) members seeking guidance regarding research in this area. Many IRB's recognize their unfamiliarity with the protocols. To both protect human subjects and promote innovative and scientifically sound research, it is important to consider the ethical, legal, and technical issues associated with this burgeoning area of research (p. 2).

The goal of this paper is to provide organizations dealing with the rapid influx of this new research design a base from which to make appropriate decisions regarding the protection of human subjects in the realm of the virtual. Such issues as public versus private domains, privacy, confidentiality, and data integrity are among the pertinent issues discussed.

RESEARCH ETHICS IN GENERAL

Research ethics itself is a solidified field, in general, and distinct methodologies, such as naturalistic inquiry or experimental research, each embody their own ethical codes and protocols. Overriding the specificity of each type of research methodology are three major areas of research ethics: autonomy, or respect for persons, justice, and beneficence. Resulting from trials and experiments conducted during World War II, these principles have developed out of early violations of ethical conduct in research. For example, horrendous violations of research ethics are named in the Nuremberg Trials, Milgram and Tuskegee studies, among others. In the United States, institutional bodies were created to respond and to produce formal frameworks for the protection of human subjects. This is reflected in the *National Commission for the Protection of Human Subjects of Biomedical and Behavioral Research* (1975–1979) and the *President's Commission for the Study of Ethical Problems in Medicine and Biomedical and Behavioral Research* (1979–1982). The National Commission created the regulatory framework of biomedical and behavioral research. This is encoded in the *Belmont Report* and especially, in Title 45, Code of Federal Regulations, Part 46 (45 CFR 46) (May, 2000).

The principles of human subject protection, originating from biomedical research, have been appropriated by the social sciences as well. It should be evident that all types of research that impact human beings must be guided by strict forms of protection. The National Commission wrote in 1979 that:

> The expression 'basic ethical principles' refers to those general judgments that serve as a basic justification for the many particular ethical prescriptions and evaluations of human actions. Three basic principles, among those generally accepted in our cultural tradition, are particularly relevant to the ethics of research involving human subjects: the principles of respect of persons, beneficence and justice (np).

The aspect of respect for persons, or autonomy, demands that researchers acknowledge subjects as autonomous agents, and those individuals with diminished capacities must receive special protection. "An autonomous person is an individual capable of deliberation about personal goals and of acting under the direction of such deliberation. To respect autonomy is to give weight to autonomous persons' considered opinions and choices while refraining from obstructing their actions unless they are clearly detrimental to others" (National Commission, 1979, np).

The main vehicle of protection of respect for persons is through "informed consent." Participants must give their informed consent, indicating understanding and full awareness of the risks and benefits of the research in which they are involved. The National Commission wrote of this principle:

> The voluntary consent of the human subject is absolutely essential. This means that the person involved should have legal capacity to give consent; should be so situated as to be able to exercise free power of choice without the intervention of any element of force, fraud, deceit, duress, over-reaching, or other ulterior form of constraint or coercion; and should have sufficient knowledge and comprehension of the elements of the subject matter involved as to enable him to make an understanding and enlightened decision. This latter element requires that before the acceptance of an affirmative decision by the experimental subject there should be made known to him the nature, duration and purpose of the experiment; the method and means by which it is to be conducted; all inconveniences and hazards reasonably to be expected; and the effects upon his health or person which may possibly come from his participation in the experiment.

Further, the *Institutional Review Board Guidebook* clearly describes the importance of informed consent in chapter 3, "Basic IRB Review:" "It is too often forgotten that informed consent is an ongoing process, not a piece of paper or a discrete moment in time. Informed consent assures that prospective human subjects will understand the nature of the research and can knowledgeably and

voluntarily decide whether or not to participate" (np). Notably, the principle of informed consent takes on new challenges in the realm of the virtual, due to the spatial and temporal dislocation of researcher and subjects. Researchers operating in the virtual, as I will describe, need additional means to assure participant consent.

Furthermore, beneficence, meaning simply being kind or good, takes on an extended meaning in the realm of research ethics. The Office of Human Research Protection (n.d.) defines beneficence as "an ethical principle discussed in *The Belmont Report* that entails an obligation to protect persons from harm. "The principle of beneficence can be expressed in two general rules: (1) do not harm; and (2) protect from harm by maximizing possible benefits and minimizing possible risks of harm." Researchers must maximize benefits and goods while minimizing harm and risk that may result from research. Harm in social science research may be psychological harm as opposed to physical distress as in the cases of clinical trials or experimental studies. Researchers conducting focus groups or interviews, typically associated with qualitative research, must ensure that participants are not going to be hurt in any way by the types of questions being asked, the ways in which they are asked, or the ways in which the data will be used. Researchers must also protect any associations between the data and participants. IRB's will assess risk and benefits along a number of points. These include:

(1) identify the risks associated with the research, as distinguished from the risks of therapies the subjects would receive even if not participating in research;
(2) determine that the risks will be minimized to the extent possible . . .;
(3) identify the probable benefits to be derived from the research;
(4) determine that the risks are reasonable in relation to be benefits to subjects, if any, and the importance of the knowledge to be gained;
(5) assure that potential subjects will be provided with an accurate and fair description of the risks or discomforts and the anticipated benefits . . . and
(6) determine intervals of periodic review, and, where appropriate, determine that adequate provisions are in place for monitoring the data collected. (Office of Human Research Protection, n.d.)

Of particular interest to researchers conducting online research are risks and benefits surrounding privacy, confidentiality, and anonymity. While physical dislocation and lack of face-to-face contact may, in one regard, provide an additional level of protection, the integrity of online communications may be questionable and therefore, researcher protection of participants may be compromised, despite the researcher's beneficent intentions. As Frankel and Siang (1999) assert, ". . . there is a need to reexamine how the principle of beneficence and current guidelines and requirements translate into the virtual domain, and whether they provide an adequate foundation for protecting human subjects" (p. 3).

The third principle of research ethics is justice, which "seeks a fair distribution of the burdens and benefits associate with research, so that certain individuals do not bear disproportionate risks while others reap the benefits" (Frankel & Siang, 1999, p. 3). Philosophers have long debated the principle of justice, examining such questions as "what is justice?" "what is equality and inequality?" "what are rights and privileges?" and many other deep and debatable questions surrounding justice. In the biomedical realm, the principle of justice has been examined in light of social practices. *The Belmont Report* (1979) states that

> . . . during the 19th and early 20th centuries the burdens of serving as research subjects fell largely upon poor ward patients, while the benefits of improved medical care flowed primarily to private patients. Subsequently, the exploitation of unwilling prisoners as research subjects in Nazi concentration camps was condemned as a particularly flagrant injustice. In this country, in the 1940s, the Tuskegee syphilis study used disadvantaged, rural black men to study the untreated course of a disease that is by no means confined to that population. These subjects were deprived of demonstrably effective treatment in order not to interrupt the project, long after such treatment became generally available (http://ohrp.osophs.dhhs.gov/humansubjects/guidance/belmont.htm#xjust).

Thus, justice pertains to the fair and equitable identification of subjects and the integrity of data collection. Online research certainly presents challenges to these, as the Internet itself is still devoid of racial, gender, ethnic, and economic diversity and individuals may choose to misrepresent themselves online, causing possible inaccuracies to researcher data.

These foundational principles of research ethics – autonomy, beneficence, and justice – must remain in the forefront of all researchers, while those conducting research in the realm of the virtual face additional challenges. They must understand this new terrain as it impacts their research and the ways in which they work with and protect their participants. Moreover, institutional review boards must equip themselves with a new language of research protocols in order to appropriately respond to the new dimensions of virtual research.

EMERGING ISSUES IN THE ETHICS OF VIRTUAL RESEARCH

As technology itself evolves from the social sciences to medical fields, researchers are looking at the potential of the Internet and World Wide Web as a rich terrain for data collection, observation, and study. The "field" of the virtual is rich with communities and life forms that may exist only online, while some communities have a counterpart in the "real" world. All forms of research can be conducted in the realm of the virtual, including survey research, questionnaire, focus group, ethnography, and observation. Each form of research will embody its own ethical challenges particular to its own research specificity, but all share in similarities surrounding the ethics of virtual research. It is expected that the issues presented herein will evolve as technology itself, as well as researcher and IRB understandings of the challenges of online research mature.

The basic foundations of online research are predicated on trust, honesty, and consent. A relationship must be developed between the researcher and the researched that is built on these basic principles, in addition to the afore-mentioned principles of research ethics themselves. This calls for an understanding and adoption of a basic social contract between the two parties that is, unfortunately, not always easy to adopt and maintain. Trust, honesty, and consent are confounded by one significant problem: There is *no* completely secure interaction online – no system is 100% hack-proof, nor is data ever completely safe from intrusion. Thus, participants must be alerted to this reality before they consent to participate. Typically, online participants know this – they know their emails can be intercepted, they know that the channels of delivery online are neither direct nor "pure," and, thus, intrusion can occur at many points.

However, while individuals are prepared to accept this risk for the benefits of online participation, the *use* of their communications for research may still be unacceptable. Researchers must tell participants for what purpose their messages, communications, et cetera, will be used, *and* participants must be completely aware that interception is possible so that they can give full and free, informed consent. Frankel and Siang (1999) discuss the elevated risks research may pose because of lack of understanding by both researchers and subjects of the

> technical and storage capabilities of Internet technologies . . .. The risk of exposure can surface at different stages of research, from data gathering, to data processing, to data storage, and dissemination . . .. The possibility also exists that an e-mail may be sent to the wrong address, leading to potential embarrassment, or worse, for the participant. Furthermore, as data are accumulated and stored over the years, outdated or poorly designed security measures may create more opportunity for risky exposure (pp. 13–14).

Moreover, Mann and Stewart (2000) suggest that the researcher must disclose the public nature of online communications to participants prior to consent. This public nature of online communication may have very negative effects on, or risks to, participants, that must be described. Online abuse – in one case a virtual rape – is prevalent, and researchers should disclose it as a potential risk. Online communications can be viewed by countless individuals, and online etiquette is not always observed. Researchers must prepare a set of guidelines for their research space, if they are setting up their own forums or sites, to protect participants. The Ten Commandments of Computer Ethics may be a starting point (http://www.cpsr.org/program/ethics/cei.html). Additional suggestions for appropriate participation in online environments comes from Shea's *Netiqette* and her "Core Rules for Netiquettte:"

Rule 1: Remember the Human
Rule 2: Adhere to the same standards of behavior online that you follow in real life
Rule 3: Know where you are in cyberspace
Rule 4: Respect other people's time and bandwidth
Rule 5: Make yourself look good online
Rule 6: Share expert knowledge
Rule 7: Help keep flame wars under control
Rule 8: Respect other people's privacy
Rule 9: Don't abuse your power
Rule 10: Be forgiving of other people's mistakes (http://www.albion.com/ netiquette/corerules.html).

The potential for intrusion in online environments must be considered by IRB's who must assess the risks and benefits of the research in light of these conditions. If the risks are too great, where participant's safety or security is jeopardized, the protocol should be rejected or modified. Protocols must reveal that the researcher has made every attempt to protect the communications through firewalls, password protected areas, encryption, or other security devices. Regardless of these attempts, participants must still receive notification that any online study cannot be 100% safe 100% of the time. IRB's should include a model statement in their sample consent forms and protocols for researchers to include. For instance, informed consent letters should contain a simple statement that acknowledges the security risks involved: "I understand that online communications may be at risk for hacking, intrusion, or other violation. Despite this possibility, I consent to participate."

Moreover, it is worthwhile for IRB's to determine a policy concerning required signatures for consent forms for online research. Some European legislation requires written consent and researchers who fail to obtain this are subject to civil action (Mann & Stewart, 2000). Some researchers accept the use of a "Yes/No" statement that participants click to indicate their consent, while others require participants to respond with a code word or message that only he/she and the researcher know to "guarantee" authenticity. The IRB should be consistent in this procedure.

Once consent has been attained and the vulnerability of online communications has been recognized by the researcher and the researched, the next step is for the researcher to determine whether a particular forum, listserve, chat room, bulletin board, or other online locale is considered *by its members* to be a public space or a private space. Defining the boundaries of a site before researching it and its members is paramount for safeguarding autonomy, beneficence, and justice. If the members consider it private, the researcher must go through appropriate channels to obtain consent, permission, and guidelines for his/her participation and observation of the space. Many online communities consider their locale a safe harbor – a site where they can be free to speak out without fear. The analogy to an Alcoholics Anonymous meeting has been used. Within these communities, there is an agreement not to violate each other's trust and to respect each other with utmost dignity. The researcher, as an outsider, must learn and adopt these foundational rules and remember that he or she is a visitor and that the participants can request his or her removal or cessation of research activities at any point.

Researchers may find the information about a site's policies and expectations from the moderator or owner of a particular site. It is worthwhile for a researcher to begin communications with the moderator or owner before any research is implemented and before the researcher proposes the protocol to the IRB; this will ultimately save the researcher time, as planning a research study around an online community that will not consent to be studied is useless.

Defining public and private space online poses challenges and difficulties. Many have come to consider the Internet and Web purely public space for anyone's use. And, different platforms on the Web have different statuses. Some researchers (for instance, the ProjectH Research Group) suggest that USENET is public and may, therefore, be exempt from IRB full review (see Mann & Stewart for discussion, 2000). In their view, USENET would be considered public space and, therefore, open to observation, much like a public park or beach. Participants' consent is assumed to a great degree. Nevertheless, it is important to remember the *IRB Guidebook* and its methodological considerations: "If people are to be observed in places or circumstances in which they have a reasonable expectation of privacy [which many online sites are presumed to have], the research must be reviewed by an IRB" (Chapter 4, Observation). Many mailing lists and bulletin boards require a subscription and define the parameters of the group's membership – in some cases, researchers must convince the owner or moderator that they should be able to subscribe with the understanding that they will not disrupt the normalcy of the community and that the community has given consent to the presence of the researcher. Frankel and Siang (1999) suggest that "evaluation criteria for the level of sensitivity that members of a particular online community may expect be proportional to the community's level of accessibility" (p. 8).

The IRB as well as the researcher must understand the parameters of an online site or community. Frankel and Siang (p. 7) assert that "users of . . . forums form expectations about what and where they are communicating . . . even though the information is public, communicants may perceive a degree of privacy in their communications." Researchers should err on the side of caution and assume higher levels of privacy than lesser.

A serious problem involves a forum or community where some participants consent while others do not. The researcher cannot ignore the non-consenting participant's contributions, though he/she cannot use that information in the analysis and reporting. The researcher should communicate with the list/site owner/moderator about this issue to determine appropriate courses of action. The analogy to an observational study in a classroom where not every student has consented is appropriate. The researcher must understand the dimensions of the classroom, which include the non-consenting students, while collecting and using data on only those who have consented. In an online environment, this may be extremely difficult, as threads or chat logs may depend on the non-consenting individual's messages for coherence. Regardless, it is the researcher's obligation to ignore those messages and work only with the consenting participants. In a qualitative or ethnographic study in particular, the researcher should also describe to the entire community – especially those not consenting – that his or her representation will be biased by the entire community's experiences though direct quoting or description will depend on only those who have consented to participate. By taking this precaution, the researcher will protect him or herself from complaints and conflict in the reporting and release of the research study.

For those who have consented to participate in an online study, researchers should ask participants how they should be identified in written reports – do they want their screen name kept intact or do they want a pseudonym for the screen name? A pseudonym would promote greater confidentiality, but many, including Sherry Turkle in her seminal work studying online communities *Life on the Screen* (1995), suggest that the participants make this decision. Pseudonyms for forums, listservs, and all online communities should be discussed with the owner or moderator, as well as with the participants of the site prior to the inception of the research and again prior to the reporting of the study. It is particularly important to establish the research conventions for the data write-up in consult with the participants. This is a form of member checking, where participants review the research for inaccuracies and misrepresentations. This is most significant in qualitative research and a large deal of research methods literature surrounds this topic.

Finally, researchers must provide a forum where participants can ask questions online before they give their consent to any research projects. This forum should be set up by the researcher before the inception of any research activities and subjects should be alerted to the forum where a full description of the research, the methodologies, the consent conditions, and any other pertinent information about the participants' activities and roles will be contained. The forum must be easy to use and accessible according to the World Wide Web Consortium's guidelines for accessibility. The goal is to empower research participants to understand the research and ask informed questions in order to best make informed decisions.

Turning to the actual use of data from an online environment, the researcher must get permission to use archived data from a list or site. Bakardjieva and Feenberg (2000) suggest that participants must know what their comments and communications might be used for "up front," at the time of communication – not after the fact. Researchers must get participants' permission to observe and analyze archived data and must have a consensus of the group members before such data is tapped. Bakardjieva and Feenberg refer to this as the "non-alienation principle:"

> ... alienation, not privacy, is the actual core of the ethical problem of most virtual community research. While practically everybody is allowed and often welcome to join online communities ... participants seem generally to take it for granted that members are not authorized to use or 'harvest' ... or sell the product of the group participation. To do that, they would be expected to ask for permission preferably before the content has been produced, thus granting participants' right to control their own product. This 'non-alienation principle' should be the basis of emergent social conventions in cyberspace. It would apply to researchers as to anyone else (p. 8).

Furthermore, researchers must get distinct permission to quote online communications – not simply observe interactions. The researcher then must pay close attention to messages that have been forwarded, reposted, or otherwise manipulated, and should seek the original owner of a message before it is quoted in research. Moreover, as Bakardjieva and Feenberg suggest, all online communications reported in research must be discussed with the group under investigation. In online communities that deal with extremely sensitive issues, for instance, sexual abuse, disease, or other extremely difficult areas, researchers must exercise even greater care to secure permission. King, as well as Finn and

Lavitt (quoted in Frankel & Siang, 1999) both relay accounts of violations of subjects when their comments were quoted – the "safe environments" of the online forum were ruined. The researcher violated the "support group" mentality, breaking the bonds of trust that are requisite for online research in particular.

In the virtual, it is certainly easy for researchers to present themselves as one of the group – one who too has been sexually molested or abused as a child or one of a particular ethnic group. The participants, one assumes, would be none the wiser to the truth. Researchers who use deceit or deception online face tremendous difficulties, as peer debriefing, which is required with the use of deception, often becomes impossible in any online environment. Mann and Stewart (2000) discourage the use of deception as online participants are harder to track down after a period of time. In addition, a virtual debriefing may be less efficacious, given the potential for misunderstandings in textual communications, which frequently occur. Studies which require deception must be stringently analyzed by IRB's for the risks and benefits, as the risk factor for harm appears extremely high at this point. If researchers can integrate a true face-to-face meeting for debriefing, the protocol has a better chance of approval.

The principle of justice, recall, demands that subject sampling be fair and equitable. This principle is challenged online as communities on the Internet are often self-formed, based on likeness of interests or other variables. Researchers are drawn to this. As such, self-formed communities comprise a rich and "pure" set of participants from which to draw data. For instance, a researcher interested in studying women who have miscarried may seek permission to observe and study any of the multiple lists, forums, or web sites where such women communicate. Presumably, the women of these groups feel safe discussing the grief, sadness, and pain surrounding miscarriage in a safe environment. The researcher does not have to sample the participants of these communities as one would in typical environment to determine who has miscarried, how many times, and so on. Online, women share this information freely in the spirit of supporting each other.

However, researchers who are sampling open lists and sites may face a skewed population as a direct result of the non-proportional race and gender populations currently online (For more information, see the NTIA's report *Falling Through the Net*, 2000). Researchers should be cognizant of these potential problems in research design, and IRB's should look carefully to ensure researchers are making an effort to ensure representative sampling where appropriate.

Great complexity surrounds online research of minors. Because researchers have an additional responsibility to protect those with diminished capacities, including children who may not have the maturity or understanding to give full and free consent to their participation in research, more rigid standards are in place with consent and research activities. No protocol involving minors is automatically exempt and researchers are required to obtain parental or guardian permission. Mann and Stewart (2000) suggest that researchers must decide if they identify children for participation directly through parents or schools. Because of the ease with which children can click on a "yes, I give consent for my child to participate in this study," IRB recommendations should always stipulate requiring paper consents for online research with minors. Researchers must obtain mailing addresses, and this could prove impossible. Researchers are encouraged to dovetail their online research with minors with schools, libraries, or community centers in order to have a "real" place with which to work with children and their parents or guardians. Protecting children online is and has been, as many are aware, a priority, whether through U.S. legislation or other measures. Researchers must also be cognizant of the dangers they may pose in the virtual realm with minors.

In addition to these research procedures, a number of more technical areas require attention when conducting research online.

TECHNICAL ISSUES IN ONLINE RESEARCH

I have reviewed a number of research protocols where researchers claim that they will only use an email address as an identifier and that there is no way to connect an email with the research subject or any personal information about that email address. Unfortunately, in most cases, this is simply wrong and dangerous ignorance. While getting information about an email address and its owner from an Internet service provider, university, business, or other entity may be time-consuming and somewhat challenging, it can be done. If one wants to find out who eliz1679@uwm.edu is, he/she can "finger" the address on the University of Wisconsin-Milwaukee server, and see that it is a person named Elizabeth Buchanan, when she last logged in and from where; of course, with the "in real life" name, one can search Elizabeth Buchanan on the server, find her office, phone, and other available information. Further, while it may seem overly paranoid, remember that research subjects' protection is paramount: If one is intent on getting the identity of a user at Hotmail or Yahoo, for instance, a few calls to the ISP can typically result in name, address, connection type, and other access information of a user. Network administrators often state that ISP's are notoriously weak in protecting their users if it means a potential lawsuit against them. To avoid potential problems in the legal realm, researchers should be familiar with local data protection laws; they obviously must respect legal and ethical frameworks, and, thus, it is recommended that researchers disclose the jurisdiction under which they are working to participants, who may well be in disparate locales. Data protection laws vary greatly from one country to another, and researchers must appreciate the legal structures in place when they are conducting online research. IRB's are encouraged to be proactive in this regard to assist researchers who may have little or no understanding of information policy.

Another issue surrounding email communications is ensuring that only the participant has access to a particular account. Many households have one shared account and it is the researcher's responsibility to ensure that communications are received only by the intended participant. Suggestions for this include a disclaimer in the subject line that "the following message is for the use of *** only and should not be viewed by anyone else." This is a technique that university advisors and professors are now using when corresponding with distance students to protect confidential communications such as grades, advising information, and the like. This simple action shows a great deal of respect for researcher subjects.

Furthermore, many researchers attempt to circumvent the problem of email identification by providing an email specific to the research study. This is an advisable practice. If researchers are providing participants with accounts, they must allow participants to change passwords at regular intervals. Researchers should provide guidelines for selecting difficult to crack passwords (for instance, use at least one number, one capital letter, one symbol). And relatedly, if researchers use encryption, which is recommended for all online communications, it is his or her responsibility to provide thorough instructions on using it, as some packages are difficult to use. PGP is a well regarded encryption program.

Finally, in traditional research, researchers are required to protect their data and keep it in safe, locked places with restrictions on who has access to it. Typically, paper surveys, field notes, clinical reports, and other data would be protected by the researcher for a specified time frame, after which all records would be destroyed. With data emerging from all digital communications and procedures, researchers have an added burden to protect the data in all forms if the researcher also prints as well as maintains the data electronically. Firstly, data and its identifiers and researcher analysis should be kept on different servers; secondly, the servers should be unique to the research study, not a general purpose or open access server in the case of a university. And thirdly, the researcher must work closely with the network administrator on security measures. The participants should be briefed about these security measures in their consent forms.

As previously noted, changes and advances in technology will dictate changes in the data integrity and protection measures. Researchers must remain aware and informed of developments in technology as they pursue research in online environments.

CONCLUSIONS

The challenges facing researchers in the virtual environment are indeed great. But, the vast diversity of research ground available online matches these challenges and presents a fertile setting for researchers working in fields ranging from the social sciences to the medical fields and sciences to the humanities. Research in the virtual assumes a new set of ethical dilemmas and obligations to which all researchers and IRB's must actively and aggressively respond. Researchers must exercise greater self-regulation and responsibility because of the seeming openness and anonymity of online life. All organizational IRB's should implement awareness and training sessions for researchers interested in this type of research to alert them to these and emerging issues and concerns. Frankel and Siang's (1999) workshop report offers a solid set of guidelines in its "Action Agenda," many of which have been discussed throughout this paper.

Consider a goal of research itself: to extend human knowledge and gain greater understandings of the world around us. Our world has been fundamentally changed by the omnipresence of the Internet and World Wide Web. This is unquestionable. As communities grow and thrive in virtual realities, we must study them to further our knowledge and expand our horizons of understanding of the virtual and the communities that inhabit it. All research conduct must be tempered by an appreciation and adoption of the foundational principles of research ethics. While the atrocities of research abuse seen in past medical experiments seems far removed from our world today and from the world of the virtual, research participants deserve the utmost respect and beneficent and just treatment. Researchers and IRB's alike assume an obligation to respect virtual research and the many challenges it presents. This paper has provided a starting point for developing a standard of ethical research conduct in the realm of the virtual.

REFERENCES

Bakardjieva, M., & Feenberg, A. (2000). Involving the Virtual Subject. Unpublished paper. *Journal of Ethics and Information Technology* (forthcoming).
Frankel, M., & Siang, S. (1999). Ethical and legal aspects of human subjects research on the Internet. A report of a workshop. Washington: American Association for the Advancement

of Science. Available: http://www.aaas.org/spp/dspp/sfrl/projects/intres/main.html. Accessed 1 April 2001.

Mann, C., & Stewart, F. (2000). *Internet Communication and Qualitative Research: A Handbook for Researching Online*. Thousand Oaks: Sage.

May, T. (2000). Research Ethics. Unpublished lecture. Milwaukee: Center for the Study of Bioethics.

National Commission for the Protection of Human Subjects of Biomedical and Behavioral Research (1979). The Belmont Report. Available http://ohrp.osophs.dhhs.gov/humansubjects/guidance/belmont.htm. Accessed 3 May 2001.

National Telecommunications and Information Administration (2000). Falling Through the Net: Toward Digital Inclusion. Available: http://www.ntia.doc.gov/ntiahome/fttn00/contents00.html. Accessed 5 May 2001.

Office of Human Research Protection (No Date). Institutional Review Board Guidebook. Available: http://ohrp.osophs.dhhs.gov/irb/irb_guidebook.htm. Accessed 23 March 2001.

Turkle, S. (1995). *Life on the Screen: Identity in the Age of the Internet*. New York: Simon and Shuster.

ACADEMIC LIBRARY MANAGERS AT WORK: RELATIONSHIPS, CONTACTS AND FOCI OF ATTENTION

Diana Kingston

Relationships management was identified as one of four major themes in an academic library manager's job by a research project in which the jobs of five academic library managers were studied (Kingston, 1999). The other three major themes identified were: Information management, Physical infrastructure and materials management and Structure of work management.

This article in part uses a 'Relationships management' perspective to present some results from the study. Another article considers the usefulness of a generic description of managers' jobs based on the four major 'Themes' (and various sub-themes) which emerged in the study (Kingston, 2001). Appendix A provides some background information on the study and on the five sites which comprised the study sample. In view of the range of differences between the five jobs and the five managers, the various commonalities found to exist in their work were considered important findings. In so far as the commonalities occurred at all five levels of management, they probably indicated generic aspects of management that could be called 'manageal', that is not restricted to senior, 'managerial', levels of management.

The jobs are referred to by their library location or site:

(1)   Site A, where the CEO/head librarian at the largest library site managed 141.1 personnel.
(2)   Site B, where the CEO/head librarian managed 70.9 personnel.
(3)   Site C, where the branch librarian managed 27.3 personnel.

Advances in Library Administration and Organization, Volume 19, pages 101–136.
Copyright © 2002 by Elsevier Science Ltd.
All rights of reproduction in any form reserved.
ISBN: 0-7623-0868-0

(4)   Site D, where the branch librarian managed 11 personnel.
(5)   Site E, where the branch librarian at this smallest site supervised just
           0.2 personnel.

The definition of 'management' used in the study was very general. All levels of management were of interest, including, but not limited to, senior 'managerial' work. The study's quantitative results were reported in terms of '**Work segments**'. Appendix B provides an outline of the concepts and terms used in the study. This article presents a description of the way time was spent by the library managers studied. It reports on the parties associated with the managers' activities, the types of work segments undertaken, their contact activities and the general areas which were the foci of their attention. Normally two sets of tables are presented for each section of the article. These represent different levels of aggregation of the data at the analysis stage of the study. The more aggregated tables are designed to provide overviews. At the more detailed level of description, data category codes (numbers) tend to be used in the tables where the natural language category descriptors are too long.

Consciously or unconsciously, managers continually and to some extent continuously manage various human and institutional or corporate relationships in the course of their work. Relationships may be discussed in various ways which emphasise, for example, such aspects as the parties involved, the purposes of the relationships, their properties or characteristics, the activities undertaken (or otherwise) in the creation, maintenance and demise of relationships, the forms of communication and information used and the resource areas managed through the relationships. For various reasons, some of these aspects were the focus of the present study and others were not.

One strand of management literature which informed the research project was the marketing, particularly, the 'relationships marketing' literature. For example, the work of Berry (1983), Christopher, Payne and Ballantyne (1991), Kotler and Andreasen (1987), McKenna (1991) and Zineldin, Johannisson and Dandridge (1997) provided insights.

THE PARTIES INVOLVED

Those involved in relationships may be described in various ways. Some authors, for example, are interested in social dynamics and may approach a discussion of these dynamics in terms of the individual, the group, the network and/or the organization. Other writers classify the parties involved in relationships in terms of 'markets' which must be managed. For example, Christopher et al. (1991, pp. 21–31) identify and discuss six types of relationship markets:

customer, referral, supplier, employee (recruitment), influence and internal markets. In the present study, one variable was designed particularly to provide information on the types of individuals, groups and organizations with whom the library managers had direct or indirect associations of various kinds. In general terms, the field data were analyzed within a broad marketing philosophy or framework. However, in the literature, no classification scheme for market groups was found to be entirely suitable for this study. A special scheme was therefore devised during the data analysis stage of the study.

Eight major groups of parties associated with managers' work segments were identified by the study. This classification scheme was preferred because it expressed affiliation or otherwise to the home institution (the library and the university). The eight groups identified were:

(1) Library clients/potential clients.
(2) Subordinates of the library manager.
(3) Other colleagues in the same library system (home university).
(4) Other colleagues in the home university, excluding superordinates and others specifically coded elsewhere.
(5) Other libraries and librarians external to the home university's organizational structure.
(6) Other organizations.
(7) Superordinates of the library manager.
(8) Others.

The types of associations taken into account were direct or indirect contacts with the library manager. Also included were parties on behalf of whom the library manager performed tasks. Direct contact was given priority for mention over any indirect contact in a given work segment.

As a group the library managers had dealings with a wide variety of parties, both internal and external to their library organization. In terms of time spent, subordinates other than secretarial assistants top scored at the three (and almost the four) largest sites. At the two smaller sites, library clients top scored. At the largest site, a significant proportion of time was spent in dealings with senior university administration (superordinates). At the second largest site, a significant proportion of time was expended in dealings with the other libraries and librarians (peers in the wider library and information industry). Overall, the results suggested that from a marketing point of view, academic library managers should be skilled in both internal and external relationship marketing and be prepared to deal to varying degrees with a wide variety of parties. Table 1 shows that most time was expended by all five library managers on work segments which had an association with another party.

Table 1.   Party Associated (% of time).

	SITE A	SITE B	SITE C	SITE D	SITE E
Clients	15.6	4.8	9.9	33.5	57.4
Subordinates	40.0	38.5	26.4	27.2	3.5
Home library other	1.6	–	26.8	7.3	9.5
Home Univ. other	3.7	10.5	2.6	1.4	1.3
Other library	8.1	22.0	0.2	1.4	0.1
Other organ'ns	1.8	8.6	5.0	2.9	10.6
Superordinates	17.2	0.5	13.4	12.0	5.0
Others	1.6	7.7	4.2	5.1	2.6
Probable contact	0.8	1.4	3.1	0.7	0.7
None	1.3	1.4	1.5	0.8	3.0
With researcher	8.2	4.4	6.8	4.7	6.2
Total	100	100	100	100	100

Note: Some work segments when library managers flipped through a batch of papers very rapidly (so that the researcher was unable to record whether or not the papers were mail), were coded as 'probable contact'.

The small proportion of time devoted to work segments with no associated party was in the range of 3.0% of time at Site E to 0.8% of time at Site D.

Of the eight groups, library managers at the two largest sites (A and B) spent most time in work segments which had some association with subordinates of various kinds (40.0% and 38.5% respectively). At Site C, the group with which most of the manager's time (26.8%) was associated was colleagues belonging to the home library (other than subordinates or supervisors). At Site C, this was closely followed (at 26.4%) by the same group that ranked first at the two larger sites (subordinates of various kinds). At the two smaller sites (D and E) most time was spent in work segments associated with library users (clients). In addition, it is noted that the managers at Sites C and D spent about the same proportion of time on work segments associated with subordinates (26.4% and 27.2% respectively).

In general, as would be expected, the results for top scoring parties tended to reflect the position of each library manager in the hierarchy of the whole library organization to which they belonged (that is, not merely that part of the whole library which they managed). The two CEO's at Sites A and B were at the top tending to focus down within their library organization (towards subordinates). At the library which was mid-ranking in terms of personnel establishment size (Site C), the manager was tending to focus 'sideways' and upwards to peers and other colleagues elsewhere in the whole library system and also downwards within his branch library (towards subordinates). The library manager at the next step down in size of the branch libraries (D), tended to focus down on subordinates but also outwards towards library clients. At the smallest site (E) the library clients top scored as the focus of the library manager's attention.

Some differences to be noted are the following. There were relatively smaller proportions of time associated with superordinates at Sites B (0.5%) and E (5.0%). In the other libraries, the manager at Site A expended 17.2% of time on work segments associated with superordinates and Sites C and D had similar results (13.4% and 12.0% respectively). The work of the library manager at Site B had a greater association with other libraries and librarians (22.0%). This result would have been influenced by his role as chair of an industry peer group at the time of the field work phase of the study. At Site B, the library manager had greater associations than the other library managers with university administrative staff other than superordinates. The data indicated that this manager tended to interact with the university administrative staff other than superordinates.

Table 2 (which was derived from the detailed level of analysis), shows that library managers at all sites except E spent most time in work segments associated with their own subordinates (category code 32). These were specifically subordinates other than those providing wordprocessing/typing and other secretarial assistance. At Site E, the category with which time most time was associated was clients from academic departments in the home university.

Table 2. Party Associated (categories with most % time).

	SITE A	SITE B	SITE C	SITE D	SITE E
Rank 1	33.0	33.0	23.5	26.0	18.3
	Code 32	Code 32	Code 32	Code 32	Code 6
Rank 2	7.5	18.9	16.3	11.1	15.6
	Code 88	Code 61	Code 41	Code 85	Code 27
Rank 3	6.5	10.5	9.5	9.4	12.5
	Code 61	Code 51	Code 87	Code 6	Code 21

Explanation of codes

6   Home university academic (including faculty).
21   General client focus (information service).
27   General client focus (access service).
32   Subordinate (other than secretary or other code).
41   Other home university library colleague.
51   Home university personnel other than library and academic.
61   Libraries and librarians (not from home university).
85   Superordinate within home library system.
87   Superordinate within home library and other library colleagues and/or subordinates.
88   Superordinate external to home library in company with academic staff and students.

The article returns to consideration of these parties later on. Before that, a description of the general types of work segments in which the library managers engaged is presented.

THE TYPES OF WORK SEGMENTS UNDERTAKEN

Through analysis, four major types of work segment were identified:

(1) Real-time contact

Contact that involved active contact with other parties (person-to-person in real-time, including via telephone).

(2) Contact materials handling

Handling of incoming and outgoing mail and other active documents having a relatively immediate contact function. Mail came in diverse physical formats, including parcels and electronic mail.

(3) Working tools and files handling

Handling of materials such as working tools and files, including organizational documentation, catalogues and pending or holding files.

(4) Other

These segments included non-contact work segments that could not be classified to the above. This included processing of library materials in various ways apart from the actual mailing or despatching of them. The latter was included in work segment type 2 above.

Table 3 and Table 4 show the results for the general types of work segments to which the five library managers devoted the most time. At all sites, the group of activities to which the library manager devoted most time was that labelled 'real-time contact'. Real-time contact included face-to-face and also telephone contact. However, the range in the proportion of time involved was rather large, being 66.6% of time at Site C down to 32.6% at Site E (approximately half). Contact activity including real-time contact will be discussed in more detail below. It would be interesting to repeat the study within the context of the intensive electronic mail regime of the early 21st century. One would expect that the balance of real-time to mail contact would have shifted towards the latter over the intervening time.

The group of activities at Sites A, B and D which consumed the next most time was that labelled 'contact materials handling'. That group included regular mail, voicemail, electronic mail and the shipping of library materials to other parties. The shipping of library materials was a minimal component (0.2% of

Table 3. Work Segment Type (% of time).

	SITE A	SITE B	SITE C	SITE D	SITE E
Real-time contact	53.2	47.4	66.6	59.1	32.6
Contact materials handling	32.2	33.8	7.6	19.1	20.5
Working tools/files	4.1	12.1	16.5	9.7	16.6
Other	2.3	2.2	2.5	7.6	24.1
With researcher	8.2	4.4	6.8	4.7	6.2
Total	100	100	100	100	100

time and less) at each site except Site E where this constituted about a quarter of mail handling time (4.9% of time). At the two larger (and again at the two smaller sites) the managers spent similar proportions of their time on mail. The managers at Sites A and B spent 32.2% and 33.8% of time respectively on that material. On the other hand, those at Sites D and E spent respectively 19.1% and 20.5% of their time on mail.

At Site C the second largest consumption of time involved the handling files or working tools (16.5%) which was approximately the same proportion of time spent on that activity at Site E (16.6%). At Site E, other types of work, which included library materials processing, ranked second in amount of time expended (24.1%) followed by mail (20.5%) which ranked third. In the latter case, as noted above, the statistics included 4.9% of time spent on the receipt or despatch of library materials for various reasons such as interlibrary and other loan traffic, the arrival of new books and the shipping of material to and from the binder.

The managers at the three largest sites spent about the same proportion of time on 'Other', which included the handling of library materials and equipment. Some differences between the sites shown in Table 3 include the following. There was a smaller proportion of time expended on mail by the manager at Site C relative to the other sites. There was a relatively smaller proportion of time spent on working tools and files at Site A. At Site E the relatively greater proportion of time spent on 'Other' such as library materials handling is obvious.

The results from uncollapsed data are presented next. The top scoring individual types of work segment are set out in Table 4.

At all sites, most time was expended on real-time contact where the manager and the contact party were both in the same location (that is, work segments coded with value 10 in the original data). However, in actual percentage terms, noticeably less time was expended on face-to-face contact at Site E (19.3%) in comparison with a range of 51.9% (C) to 36.8% (B) at the four largest sites.

Table 4. Work Segment Type (categories with most % of time).

	SITE A	SITE B	SITE C	SITE D	SITE E
Rank 1	49.9	36.8	51.9	41.9	19.3
	Code 10	Code 10	Code 10	Code 10	Code 10
Rank 2	32.0	33.6	13.1	18.7	15.7
	Code 39	Code 39	Code 50	Code 39	Code 76
Rank 3	3.3	10.6	12.8	15.1	15.5
	Code 29	Code 29	Code 29	Code 29	Code 39

Explanation of codes:

10   Contact (in person, same location).
29   Contact (via telephone, excluding voicemail).
39   Contact (mail).
50   Materials (organisational working tools and files).
76   Materials (information/collection resources in any media).

Later Table 6 will show that the library manager at Site E had more real-time contact time with library clients than with other parties.

At Sites A, B and D, the group of work segments labelled 'mail' received the next most time. At Site C organizational working tools and files received next most time. At Site E, library materials from the collections received the next most time. The third ranking activity at the four largest sites was telephone usage. At Site E it was mail handling.

CONTACT ACTIVITIES

As mentioned above, the study revealed that, overall, each of the library managers' jobs involved a very significant amount of contact activities in the broad sense. This section provides, through an alternative analysis of the data, some additional detail in terms of work segment type.

Table 5 shows that contact activities involved 74.7% or more of the library managers' time, except in the case of Site E. Nevertheless, even at Site E (which was noticeably different in that the number of subordinates with whom the manager might interact with there only totalled approximately an 0.2 EFT of a casual), more than half of the time was dedicated to contact activities.

The greatest proportion of time spent on contact activity occurred at the largest Site (A) and the least at the smallest Site (E). Site D showed slightly more contact than Site C. Thus the total proportion of the library managers' time spent in all types of contact activities (including face-to face/in person, via the telephone and via mail) ranged from 86.4% (Site A) to 54.5% (Site E).

Table 5. Contact Activity (% of time).

	SITE A	SITE B	SITE C	SITE D	SITE E
Same location	49.9	36.8	51.9	41.9	19.3
On hold*	–	–	1.9	2.0	3.9
On hold (telephone)*	–	–	–	–	0.4
Voice mail	–	–	0.1	0.1	0.2
Telephone	3.3	10.6	12.8	15.1	9.1
Dispatch (vols)	0.2	0.2	0.0	0.2	4.9
Mail	32.0	33.6	7.6	18.7	15.5
Delivery checks	0.7	–	–	0.2	0.5
Telephone attempts	0.3	0.7	0.4	2.6	0.7
Subtotal	86.4	81.9	74.7	80.8	54.5
Not contact	5.4	13.7	18.5	14.5	39.3
With researcher	8.2	4.4	6.8	4.7	6.2
Total	100	100	100	100	100

* 'On hold' was used to indicate that a party ('someone' such as a client or a colleague) was actively waiting for the library manager to respond to an inquiry generated by them.

Stated in another way, at Sites B, C, and D the proportion of time which was not spent is contact activity was found to be in the range of 18.5% of time (C) to 13.7% of time (B). At Site A the proportion of time not spent in contact activity was much smaller (remarkably only 5.4% of time). At Site E the proportion of non-contact time was higher than the average at 39.3% of time.

From Table 4 and Table 5 we see that there was quite a variation between sites in some of the percentage values for some categories of contact. Each library manager spent the largest proportion of their time interacting with others in the same location "face-to-face" (work segments which were coded with value 10). The range was 51.9% (Site C) to 19.3% (Site E). Real-time interaction with others (face-to-face and via the telephone) ranged from 64.7% (Site C) to 28.4% (Site E).

Mail took up between 33.6% (Site B) and 7.6% (Site C) of the managers' time, which was a large variation. At the two largest sites (A and B), the managers spent similar proportions of time on mail, that is, about one third of their time was devoted to mail (32.0% of time at Site A and 33.6% of time at Site B).

THE PARTIES AND REAL-TIME CONTACT

The amount of time devoted to real-time contact was analyzed according to the aggregated data for parties associated with work segments. The results of the crosstabulation are presented in Table 6.

Table 6. Party Associated (% of real-time contact time).

	SITE A	SITE B	SITE C	SITE D	SITE E
Clients	15.4	6.6	9.2	37.3	64.9
Subordinates	54.2	57.2	34.7	43.8	10.8
Home library other	2.9	–	30.6	6.3	15.9
Home Univ. other	1.2	11.8	3.0	1.5	2.5
Other library	2.4	13.2	0.2	2.1	–
Other organ'ns	–	8.3	3.2	1.2	1.5
Superordinates	24.0	0.4	17.0	7.5	3.7
Others	–	2.5	2.1	0.2	0.7

At the four largest sites, most real-time contact time was spent with Subordinates. At the two largest sites this was more than half of real-time contact time. The range for the four largest sites was 57.2% of real-time contact time at Site B to 34.7% at Site C. By contrast, at the smallest site (E) most real-time contact time (64.9%) was spent with Clients, far more than with any other group at Site E. With only 0.2 EFT subordinates, the library manager at Site E spent 10.8% of time dealing with them.

There was variation across the sites as to the second and third ranking parties in real-time contact with the library managers. At Site A the manager spent the next ranking proportions of time with his Superordinates (24.0%) and library Clients (15.4%). These contacts would have occurred mostly at scheduled meetings.

At Site B the next rankings were Other libraries and librarians (13.2%) and Home university other (11.8%). The library manager at Site B was chairperson of a national university librarians' committee. It should be noted here perhaps that a substantial proportion of the interaction with other libraries, librarians and his peer group was related to committee business, discussion of national issues affecting university libraries and strategic planning in relation to those issues. Of the five library managers, B devoted the largest proportion of time to the 'Home university other' group of parties and the least to 'Superordinates'. He appeared to be dealing with persons in the university administration other than superordinates on day-to-day financial and other matters.

At Site C the second and third rankings for real-time contact were Home library other (30.6%) and Superordinates (17.0%). Thus this library manager spent from almost one third to almost one half of his time in real-time contact with peers and others located elsewhere in the library structure, for example at the central library. A substantial proportion of this time would have been related to his role in the circulation working party. At Site D the second and third ranking groups in terms of time spent were Clients (37.3%) and Superordinates (7.5%). At Site E the second and third rankings were Home library other (15.9%) and Subordinates (10.8%).

THE PARTIES AND MAIL ACTIVITIES

The results for the mail do not take account of whether the mail was incoming or outgoing to the library manager. The situation was quite complex. In the case of subordinates, for example, some documents moved back and forth between the library manager and subordinates during a consultative process. In some cases, they were draft documents being worked up to a final form. In other cases, an issue was under discussion and a relevant document gathered added pages of comment during its travels between parties within the home site. Some documents were the subject of live discussion between the manager and another party such as a subordinate. This occurred, for example, when one of the parties took a document with them to discuss its contents and perhaps other issues involved in the other's office. Some documents generated telephone conversations, with the latter possibly also spilling over onto topics other than those represented in the document (either by intention or on the spur of the moment).

The degree of attention given to each piece or batch of mail was not given a focus in the present study. The researcher would say from observation that there was an enormous range of attention spans involved, either due to the nature of the material or to the effect of priorities. Some batches of incoming mail were handled quite speedily. Some items representing particular types of material were discarded to the waste bin with notable speed, for example, advertisements. Some documents were put aside for a better opportunity to study them, either at the office or at home. The latter appeared to be particularly the case at the two larger sites. Some incoming items were quickly referred on to another party to deal with, such as a subordinate. In the latter case, the manager would sometimes write a short note to attach to the item being forwarded on. The attached note might have been, for example, a question or an instruction from the library manager. Some mail sessions tended to be intrinsically sorting and/or prioritizing sessions. Such activity might be interspersed with other types of mail activity (for example, writing and editing) during the same session.

The mail came in various physical and informational forms. There was a variety of types including hard copy and email, letters, reports, advertisements and appeals. Further, the data analysis had to produce coding for the whole range of types of materials handled across the five library types involved in the study. Overall, the range of topics handled at each site via the mails was large.

Some indication of this is given in a list of matters from the field log which is provided in Appendix 10 of the original research report (Kingston, 1999).

Table 7 shows that there was variation across the sites as to the top ranking group (party) associated with time spent on contact materials handling. At Site A, most of the contact materials handling time went on mail which the library manager sent to or received from Subordinates (33.0%). At Site B the library manager spent most of the time which he devoted to mail on that received from or sent by him to the group of parties labelled Other libraries and librarians (39.1% of contact materials handling time). This was more than that devoted to his subordinates and reflects his position of chairperson of the national peer group for university librarians.

At Sites C and E the top ranking group was Other organizations (29.3% and 46.4% respectively). At Site D, the top ranking group was Superordinates (33.7% of contact materials handling time).

At Site A the second and third ranking groups of senders or receivers of mail to and/or from the library manager took about the same proportion of his time (19.7% and 19.0% respectively). These were the groups labelled 'Other libraries and librarians' (probably mostly 'peers') and library 'Clients'. At Site C the next ranking group of parties in terms of the library manager's mail time was 'Home library other', that is colleagues and peers within the total home library structure (17.1%). There was a three-way tie for third rank at Site C, with 14.3% of contact materials time being expended on each of the following three groups: Clients, Subordinates and Superordinates. At Site D the library manager spent second most mail time on Clients (16.0%) and third most mail time on the groups labelled 'Home library other' and 'Other libraries and librarians' (both on 14.6%). At Site E the second and third ranking group of parties in terms of time devoted to various forms of contact materials were 'Home library other' (18.5%) and Clients (18.0%).

Table 7. Party Associated (% of contact materials time).

	SITE A	SITE B	SITE C	SITE D	SITE E
Clients	19.0	4.0	14.3	16.0	18.0
Subordinates	33.0	26.5	14.3	3.8	–
Home library other	–	–	17.1	14.6	18.5
Home Univ. other	8.6	7.0	2.1	1.4	1.1
Other library	19.7	39.1	0.7	14.6	0.5
Other organ'ns	5.7	11.2	29.3	9.1	46.4
Superordinates	9.7	1.0	14.3	33.7	6.4
Others	4.3	11.1	7.9	6.2	8.8

INITIATOR AND DIRECTION OF CONTACT ACTIVITY

The field data recorded in general terms the obvious initiator of contact (for example the obvious sender of mail) and the direction of contact (for example whether telephone calls were incoming or outgoing). However, it became clear to the researcher during the data collection stage of the study that there were different levels of initiation of contact activity, especially if ongoing contact about a particular topic occurred over time. The recording of changes in the direction of contact activity was a quite complex matter and not always immediately obvious in the field, particularly in various types of meetings. A decision was taken during the field work that this aspect of work warranted more attention than was possible in the race to record the field data for the major variables.

It is interesting to recount here a comment by Thomas and Ward (1974) which they made in describing one of the two areas of difficulty which the librarians had in completing diary cards for their study. They remarked "even though we specifically asked the immediate source or instigator of an action, many wanted to go right back in time to when the topic first occurred" (p. 56). Team effort and consultative processes appear to be factors revealed by this phenomenon. There were occasions in the present study, for example, when 'several minds' contributed to the compilation of a document which ultimately became in effect a library-wide working document or de facto an official statement by the library in a particular area. At Site A, preparation of a draft strategic plan and also of a national music cataloguing project plan were examples of these processes unfolding.

NUMBER OF PERSONS INVOLVED REAL-TIME

This section provides information on the number of persons, including the library manager, who were involved real-time in the immediate work segment being analysed and coded. Thus, those involved in immediate contact with the library manager, either in person in the same location or via a 'real-time' medium such as the telephone, were included in the count of persons involved in a work segment. In other words, the results represent the actual number of persons in contact, including the manager.

At all sites, more than half of the library manager's time was spent working alone or with one other person. However, within that result there was considerable variation (see Table 8). At Sites A, B and E, most time was spent working alone. This ranged from 62.3% of time at Site E (where the personnel totalled only 1.2 EFT), to 38.5% at Site A. At Sites C and D, however, the manager spent most time with one other person (39.2% and 40.3% respectively).

Table 8. Number of Persons (% of time).

	SITE A	SITE B	SITE C	SITE D	SITE E
Alone	38.5	48.3	26.7	36.9	62.3
2	18.3	25.3	39.2	40.3	27.7
3	11.8	8.9	11.6	3.3	0.1
4	3.8	9.5	0.1	1.0	–
5	0.6	–	1.2	0.4	0.6
6	0.0	–	5.7	2.7	1.7
7	–	1.2	7.1	0.7	0.8
8	–	2.4	0.8	1.8	0.6
9 or more	18.7	–	0.8	8.2	–
With researcher	8.2	4.4	6.8	4.7	6.2
Total	100	100	100	100	100

Site A recorded a much greater proportion of time where the manager was in the company of larger numbers of persons. In 18.7% of time there were 9 or more persons in contact, including the library manager at Site A. The large scheduled meetings held at Site A explain that result.

RESOURCES AREAS MANAGED

For each work segment, one variable provided a summary of the focus of the library manager's attention in terms of the service or administrative area associated with any resources under consideration. This resource area might have been either within the library's internal or external environment, or might have spanned both those environments. The study revealed that all five managers were found to have been presented with continuity and discontinuity in their work and often dealt with rapid changes of focus and scenarios.

The detailed data for this variable were aggregated twice. In the first instance, the aim was to summarize the focus of the manager's attention as being primarily directed towards one of three general areas:

(1) User services.
(2) Bibliographic and information resources management.
(3) Administrative services.

The results are presented in Table 9. At the four larger sites, most time was devoted to administration, between 81.4% (B) and 46.4% (D). At the smallest site most time was devoted to user services work (46.2%).

Table 9. Resource Area: Summary (% of time).

	SITE A	SITE B	SITE C	SITE D	SITE E
User services	11.5	4.4	31.4	24.7	46.2
Info. resources	16.0	5.6	10.4	18.4	26.8
Administration	63.3	81.4	50.1	46.4	19.2
Other	1.0	4.2	1.3	5.8	1.6
With researcher	8.2	4.4	6.8	4.7	6.2
Total	100	100	100	100	100

There was slightly more variation in the second ranking at each site. At Sites A, B and E this time was allocated to information resources management. The range of time was 26.8% (E) to 5.6% (B). At Sites C and D user services received the next most attention in terms of time (31.4% and 24.7% respectively).

The managers at Sites A and B devoted noticeably less time proportionately to the user services area, particularly library manager B with only 4.4%. Also, this manager was less involved in information resources management than the others. In a comparison across the five sites on the information resources management area, this area received more of the library manager's time at Site E (26.8%). Incidentally, Table 10 below shows this to be mainly collection maintenance work. There was a large range across the five sites in the proportion of time which administration took up (81.4% at Site B down to only 19.2% at the smallest site, E). At Library B, a much greater proportion of time was expended on 'administration' than at the other libraries, probably because of the added administration resulting from his position as chairperson of the national university librarians' peer group committee.

In the second aggregation of data, the three above-mentioned major areas of work were broken down into subgroupings as shown in Table 10.

At Sites A (19.1%), B (29.1%) and D (31.5%) most time was devoted to human resources administration work. At Sites C (25.1%) and E (34.3%) most time was devoted to lending services and document supply. At Site C the focus was more on 'backroom' activity such as problem solving and the design of procedures. On the other hand at Site E service aspects (such as the issue and discharge of loans) predominated. It is noted that at Site C, human resources administration had almost as much time (24.7%) devoted to it as was devoted to lending services and document supply (25.1%) by the same library manager C.

Some differences found were as follows. In contrast to the library managers at the three largest sites, those at the two smaller sites did not spend much or

Table 10.   Resource Area (% of time).

	SITE A	SITE B	SITE C	SITE D	SITE E
Inform'n services	1.2	0.2	4.7	16.8	11.8
Lending services	9.7	2.9	25.1	7.6	34.3
Bibliog. services	4.0	–	1.2	0.5	2.1
Coll'n maint'ce	0.6	0.0	1.2	3.7	22.7
Info. res. dev.	11.3	5.5	8.1	14.3	1.9
Human resources	19.1	29.1	24.7	31.5	10.6
Finance resources	14.2	18.4	10.2	0.2	–
Physical resources	1.6	9.2	3.1	3.0	2.5
Admin. info.	10.7	16.7	4.9	6.0	5.4
Other	19.4	13.3	10.0	11.9	2.3
With researcher	8.2	4.5	6.8	4.7	6.2
Total	100	100	100	100	100

any time on financial management. The percentages of time were 0.2% (D) and 0.0% (E). At Site E 22.7% of time was devoted to collection maintenance work, whereas it received no or little time at the other sites (the range was 3.7% at D down to 0.0% at B). On the other hand, the library manager at Site E spent little time on information resources development work (1.9%). This probably reflects the centralization of information resources management and processing at the library organization to which Site E belonged. Overall there were traces of various types of client service, human resources management and collection management work in the jobs of all five library managers. Finally, the detailed output tables reveal that most time at the various libraries was spent on the individually coded categories shown in Table 11. This shows that there was quite a deal of variation between sites.

SUMMARY

In summary, in terms of time spent, the top ranking features of the library managers' work involved:

(1) contact activities of various kinds;
(2) another party in various ways;
(3) subordinates or clients in particular;
(4) human resources or lending services as the focus of attention.

The article now returns to a general discussion of the Relationships management theme.

Table 11. Resource Area (categories with most % of time).

	SITE A	SITE B	SITE C	SITE D	SITE E
Rank 1	17.7	8.6	12.5	14.0	19.1
	Code 98	Code 69	Code 23	Code 18	Code 57
Rank 2	8.5	8.0	8.5	9.1	8.9
	Code 82	Code 98	Code 83	Code 52	Code 39
Rank 3	5.1	7.8	7.2	6.8	8.0
	Code 29	Code 81	Code 98	Code 68	Code 15

Explanation of codes

15	Reference/reader advisor service.
18	Group reader education.
23	Circulation records management.
29	Reciprocal borrowing and other reciprocal services.
39	Shelving/reshelving/respacing/shelf tidying.
52	Information resources – initial stages of establishment of access by any means (acquisition, licence agreement).
57	Binding, conservation, preservation, repair, restoration.
68	Chat (any medium).
69	Organising people aspects of meetings, groups, travel.
81	Budget in general.
82	Income/balance in credit.
83	Accounting/financial record management.
98	Administration in several areas.

RELATIONSHIPS MANAGEMENT

Based on the results of the present study and a knowledge of the disparate literature which deals with various disciplines including the social, human resources, marketing, communication and psychosocial aspects of management, the researcher formed the view that a Relationships Management (RM) core theme exists. It should be stressed that the term 'Relationships Management' is used here in a 'neutral' sense, so as to cover both positive and negative aspects of the theme. Again, the phrase 'Relationships Management' is intended to cover a comprehensive range of types of relationships, for example, from one-to-one interpersonal relationships through collective relationships to formalised inter-organizational relationships. In the LIS literature, elements of the 'Relationships Management' theme already exist in various manifestations and to varying degrees. In particular, issues touched on by authors within different branches of traditional library user services are relevant to the RM theme. For example, this occurs within such areas as circulation, interlibrary loans, reference work, reader education (including information literacy and bibliographic instruction) and electronic literature services.

Some examples pertinent to the Relationships Management theme in LIS literature follow. There has been some interest in the communication patterns of academic librarians (for example, Xu, 1996). The role of interpersonal communication in the reference interview has received some attention (for example, Grogan, 1992). The importance of library staff relating to user needs in readers' advisory work has been stressed by Prytherch and Barthel (1988). Again, Kong (1996) listed "communication skills, public relations savvy, and the ability to effectively relate to a diverse clientele" (p. 21) among core competencies for academic reference librarians. Owen (1996) also stressed communication at the library enquiry desk and presented strategies for understanding users' questions.

A relevant literature on quality client-focussed service has been gradually developing. For example, Whitlatch (1995) discussed the concept of TQM (total quality management) as relevant to the library customer and reference services. Hernon (1996) stressed the importance of customer service quality, and Hernon and Altman (1996) promoted customer service quality as the key indicator of academic library performance. Bundy (1997) discussed the higher education environment and emergent issues relevant to client-focussed services in academic libraries. Heery and Morgan (1996) also identified key issues in the environment and suggested strategies that modern academic libraries undertake or adopt to meet future challenges. Some of these have 'Relationships Management' aspects, such as the need for librarians to develop "interpersonal and communication skills", "credibility with academic staff" and "teaching and training". They also note that important management responsibilities include the need to adopt "participative decision-making models", "greater emphasis on teamwork" and the "gradual breakdown of hierarchical staffing structures" (pp. 133, 142).

McGregor (1997) stressed the importance of all aspects of human resources management to quality assessment in an academic library. Baldwin (1996) has written about the management of human resources in academic libraries. Giesecke (1997) has edited another edition of a volume published by the American Library Association to provide practical help for new supervisors. Cherrett (1997) discussed the concept of partnerships (with suppliers, other libraries and client groups) developed in the interest of client service. The building of partnerships between computing and library professionals has also been discussed (for example, Lipow & Creth, 1995).

The LIS literature also contains well established strands of material devoted to other types of relationships such as inter-library cooperation and library networks, including interlibrary loan and document supply networks. Communications protocols and standards are used to facilitate relationships in this area. At a more general level, Powell (1979) asserted that librarians form a "human connection between people and the information or knowledge" (p. ix) that they need. She stressed the importance of librarians' considering the affective dimensions of working with library colleagues and library users. Fisher (1996) concluded anecdotally that, within a library, successful managers are "the ones who can develop a positive relationship with a work group as a whole, as well as positive relationships with the individual members of the work group" (p. 55).

In the present study, the Relationships Management core theme was found to be relevant in various ways to library user services, also intra- and inter-organizational parties as the focus of the library manager's attention, and human resources management. At all sites, few work segments were coded as having no party associated with them. Overall, managers as a group were part of a complex network with different types of contact parties. A study of each of the eight groups of parties might be considered as sub-themes. Clients (library users) and their service emerge as a one possible sub-theme, Subordinates and their management as another.

In the present study, in all cases, most time was spent in some form of contact, direct or indirect. In particular, most time was spent in real-time contact (including telephone calls). Broken down, most time was spent specifically in face-to-face contact. As a group, the managers were required to be competent in various modes of contact, both direct (face-to face, via the telephone, in meetings, in classes and in reference interviews) and less direct (mail in various physical forms: paper documents, electronic documents and parcels). The inevitable conclusion is that librarians must have a wide range of communication and interpersonal skills. In the public user/client services area this includes sets of skills required for effective reference interviewing, preparation and presentation of reader education classes, borrower management and the client interface in general. In dealing with parties of influence internal and external to the home university, communication skills which are relevant relate to the effective presentation of information, review and argument, promotion and persuasion. Further, the raft of communication and interpersonal skills required for the management of subordinates is clearly required. Heery and Morgan (1996) note the importance of staff or human resources management as academic librarians meet the challenges presented by the forces of change.

It has been asserted that "Only customers justify the existence of a library" (Hernon & Altman 1996, p. 3). This statement, of course, begs various questions including 'Which customer type and when?' Nevertheless, it is an important point of view. The study recorded service to diverse sub-groups of clients, from external non-primary library users, through undergraduate students to academic researchers at the home institution. Skill in dealing with a wide range of client needs is called for. Further, there was evidence in the present study that library staff, both relatively higher and lower in the same organizational hierarchy, were called on to provide various client services which are normally considered quite skilled. For example, the reader's advisor at Site D and the manager at Site E both performed electronic literature searches for researchers in their clientele. Thus the range of library personnel requiring electronic information skills and client interviewing skills is extensive.

There was also evidence that supervision functions were undertaken by individuals from relatively low ranked grades of staff upwards. It is clearly not only so-called 'middle' and 'top' ranks of staff who need to be included in the relationships management training programmes of academic LIS organizations.

The management literature deals with intra- and inter-organizational relationships under various topics or discipline areas. One such area is 'organizational behavior'. It is possible to include a historical and comparative approach to this area as many authors do (for example, Guillen, 1995). Another large area is so-called 'human resources management' (see for example, Anthony, Perrewe & Kacmar, 1996; Beardwell & Holden, 1997). This includes human resources planning, recruitment, job design, organizational structure, distribution of personnel, ethical treatment and development of staff, evaluation and supervision. Human resources management purports to provide a strategic focus compared to traditional personnel management (for example see Beardwell & Holden, 1997, p. 21). As mentioned earlier, marketing is another general area containing elements of relevance to RM (such as the concepts of internal and external market target groups).

Examples of other specific topics of discussion in the literature which include elements of RM are teamwork (for example, Katzenbach, 1993), leadership (for example Sayles, 1979), group dynamics, power and politics (for example Pfeffer, 1981) and organizational climate and culture (Denison, 1996). There also are bodies of literature dealing with alliances (for example, Osborn and Hagedoorn, 1997) and networks (for example, Carroll & Teo, 1996; Jones, Hesterly & Borgatti, 1997; Brass, Butterfield & Skaggs, 1998). Moorman, Blakely and Niehoff (1998) have discussed procedural justice and organizational citizenship behavior. Becker (1998) has discussed integrity in human resource management.

Watson (1994) argues that from years of research studies of what managers actually do at work that the image that has taken shape in the literature of "management as essentially and inherently a social and moral activity" (p. 223).

Linstead (1996) argues that since management is a social process, ideas and methods drawn from social anthropology offer insights into significant areas of management such as an understanding of the cultural processes at work in organizations, appraisal of management practices and the nature of organizational change and its management. Townley (1994) discusses the underlying importance of 'emotional labor' and the underlying psychosocial elements of work. She also outlines a Foucauldian analysis of ubiquitous phenomenon of power in relationships and its appropriate or ethical use which she holds emerges from that analysis.

A Relationships Management (RM) framework would seem to provide a useful mechanism for integrating the study of disparate areas such as those mentioned above, and for studying the contrasts and connections between various paradigms (Schultz & Hatch, 1996).

SOME IMPLICATIONS OF THE RELATIONSHIPS MANAGEMENT FRAMEWORK

The Relationship Management (RM) concept appears to offer a potentially very useful, integrating framework in three areas of the LIS sector: research, education and library operations. It has relevance for library and information organization management studies at both the macro and the micro levels. It is also relevant for use both within and across organizations and institutions. The establishment of a project dedicated to the development of this theme as a tool to integrate and advance 'manageal' knowledge and its application would be a worthwhile goal for the LIS profession. Work by interested individuals and organizations would be needed for the articulation and mapping of content for agenda, programs or curricula based on the RM framework. This would be achievable through cooperation between educators, practitioners and researchers.

Staff development implications are important. There were indications in the reported study of the need for 'manageal' learning opportunities in the workplace for less experienced or less 'senior' staff. In other words, staff development implications are important in the light of the finding that 'manageal' strands of work appear to be required of incumbents who are located relatively low in organizational hierarchies right through to CEO's. It may be that staff development has in the past been rather too compartmentalized both 'vertically' (as suggested above) and 'horizontally'. For example, the issue of the sets of communication and other skills required for library and information workers across a range of activities should be explored and documented in a coherent, comprehensive way. Further, as noted earlier in the article, clients are just one of eight potential groups (parties) of varying degrees of importance to the successful operation of a library and information organization. Again, there needs to be a coherent and comprehensive view taken of the range of parties with and for whom librarians work. This coherent view may then be built into educational and training programs for librarians.

The results also suggest that the four major themes mentioned at the commencement of this article provide a framework which may be useful for the analysis, design, description and comparison of jobs within and across organizations. At the least, the study provides a platform for further research, educational and institutional initiatives to develop the Relationships Management (RM) theme framework. Further, it would be worthwhile for educational and library institutions to undertake extensive, comprehensive audits using the four themes framework to articulate the knowledge, skills and attitudes required by library staff related to:

(1) Relationships management.
(2) Information management.
(3) Physical resources and infrastructure management.
(4) Structure of work management.

REFERENCES

Anthony, W. P., Perrewe, P. L., & Kacmar, K. M. (1996). *Strategic Human Resource Management*. Fort Worth: Dryden Press.

Baldwin, D. A. (1996). *The academic librarian's human resources handbook: Employer rights and responsibilities*. Englewood Cliffs, CO: Libraries Unlimited.

Beardwell, I., & Holden, L. (Eds) (1997). *Human resources management: A contemporary perspective* (2nd ed.). London: Pitman.

Becker, T. E. (1998). Integrity in organizations: beyond honesty and conscientiousness. *Academy of Management Review, 23*(1), 154–161.

Berry, L. L. (1983). Relationship marketing. In: L. L. Berry, G. L. Shostack & G. D. Upa (Eds), *Emerging Perspectives On Services Marketing* (pp. 25–28). Chicago: American Marketing Association.

Brass, D. J., Butterfield, K. D., & Skaggs, B. C. (1998). Relationships and unethical behavior: A social network perspective. *Academy of Management Review, 23*(1), 14–31.

Bundy, A. (1997). Investing for a future: Client-focussed Australian academic libraries in the 1990s. *Australian Library Journal, 46*(4), 354–369.

Carroll, G. R., & Teo, A. C. (1996). On the social networks of managers. *Academy of Management Journal, 39*(2), 421–440.

Cherrett, C. (1997). Bringing the services together: How partnerships add value for the client. *Australian Library Journal, 46*(4), 370–375.

Christopher, M., Payne, A., & Ballantyne, D. (1991). *Relationship marketing: Bringing quality, customer service and marketing together*. Oxford: Butterworth-Heinemann.

Denison, D. R. (1996). What is the difference between organizational culture and organizational climate? A native's point of view on a decade of paradigm wars. *Academy of Management Review, 21*(3), 619–654.

Fisher, W. (1996). Library management: The latest fad, a dismal science or just plain work. *Library Acquisition: Practice and Theory, 20*(1), 49–56.

Giesecke, J. (Ed.) (1997). *Practical help for new supervisors* (3rd ed.). Chicago, IL: American Library Association.

Grogan, D. J. (1992). *Practical Reference Work* (2nd ed.). London: Library Association Publishing.

Guillen, M. F. (1994). *Models of management: Work, authority, and organization in a comparative perspective.* Chicago: University of Chicago Press.

Heery, M., & Morgan, S. (1996). *Practical strategies for the modern academic library.* London: Aslib.

Hernon, P. (1996). Service quality in libraries and treating users as customers and non-users as lost or never-gained customers: Editorial. *Journal of Academic Librarianship, 22*(3), 171–172.

Hernon, P., & Altman, E. (1996). *Service quality in academic libraries.* Norwood, NJ: Ablex Publishing Corporation.

Jones, C., Hesterly, W. S., & Borgatti, S. P. (1997). A general theory of network governance: Exchange conditions and social mechanisms. *Academy of Management Review, 22*(October), 911–945.

Katzenbach, J. R., & Smith, D. K. (1993). *The wisdom of teams: Creating the high-performance organization.* Boston: Harvard Business School Press.

Kim, J. T. (1998). Management, Contingency In: J. M. Shafritz (Ed.), *International Encyclopedia of Public Policy and Administration* (pp. 1344–1348). Boulder: Westview.

Kingston, D. E. (1999). Academic library managers at work: An analysis of five cases. Unpublished doctoral dissertation, University of New South Wales, Kensington.

Kingston, D. E. (2001). Themes and sub-themes in managers' work. *Australian Academic and Research Libraries, 32*(4), 308–320.

Kong, L. M. (1996). Academic reference librarians: Under the microscope. *Reference Librarian, 54*, 21–27.

Kotler, P., & Andreasen, A. R. (1987). *Strategic marketing for nonprofit organizations* (3rd ed.). Englewood Cliffs, N.J.: Prentice Hall.

Linstead, S. (1996). Understanding management: Culture, critique and change. In: S. Linstead, R. G. Small & P. Jeffcutt (Eds), *Understanding Management* (pp.11–33). London: Sage.

Lipow, A. G., & Creth, S. D. (Eds) (1995). Building partnerships: Computing and library professionals: The proceedings of Library Solutions Institute Number 3, Chicago, Illinois, May 12–14, 1994. Berkeley, CA: Library Solutions Press.

McGregor, F. (1997). Quality assessment: Combating complacency. *Australian Library Journal, 46*(1), 82–92.

McKenna, R. (1991). *Relationship marketing: Successful strategies for the age of the customer.* Reading, MA: Addison-Wesley.

Mintzberg, H. (1973). *The nature of managerial work.* New York: Harper and Row.

Moorman, R. H., Blakely, G. L., & Niehoff, B. P. (1998). Does perceived organizational support mediate the relationship between procedural justice and organizational citizenship behavior? *Academy of Management Journal, 41*(3), 351–357.

Osborn, R. N., & Hagedoorn, J. (1997). The institutionalization and evolutionary dynamics of interorganizational alliances and networks. *Academy of Management Journal, 40*(2), 261–278.

Owen, T. (1996). *Success at the enquiry desk*. London: Library Association Publishing.

Pfeffer, J. (1981). *Power in organizations*. Boston: Pitman.

Powell, J. (1979). *Peoplework: Communication dynamics for librarians*. Chicago: American Library Association.

Prytherch, R., & Barthel, J. (1988). *The basics of readers' advisory work*. London: Clive Bingley.

Sayles, L. R. (1979). *Leadership: What effective managers really do . . . and how they do it*. New York: McGraw-Hill.

Schultz, M., & Hatch, M. J. (1996). Living with multiple paradigms: The case of paradigm interplay in organizational culture studies. *Academy of Management Review, 21*(2), 529–557.

Stewart, R. (1989). Studies of managerial jobs and behavior: The ways forward. *Journal of Management Studies, 26*(1), 1–10.

Thomas, P. A., & Ward, V. A. (1974). Management activities of librarians in the UK. In: EURIM: A European Conference on Research into the Management of Information Services and Libraries 20–22 November, 1973 (pp. 55–65). London: Aslib.

Townley, B. (1994). *Reframing human resource management: Power, ethics and the subject at work*. London: Sage.

Watson, T. J. (1994). *In search of management: Culture, chaos and control in managerial work*. London: Routledge.

Whitlatch, J. B. (1995). Customer service: Implications for reference practice. *Reference Librarian, 49/50*, 5–24.

Xu, H. (1996). Type and level of position in academic libraries related to communication behavior. *Journal of Academic Librarianship, 22*(4), 257–266.

Yin, R. K. (1994). *Case study research: Design and methods* (2nd ed.). Thousand Oaks, CA: Sage Publications.

Zineldin, M., Johannisson, B., & Dandridge, T. C. (1997). *Strategic relationship management: A multi-dimensional perspective: Towards a new co-opetive framework on managing, marketing and organizing*. Stockholm: Almqvist & Wiksell International.

APPENDIX A:
BACKGROUND INFORMATION ABOUT THE STUDY

This article is derived from a diagonal multi-case study of five academic library managers' jobs (Kingston, 1999). The study design, including definition of the variables studied, and full results are reported elsewhere together with a review of the literature (Kingston, 1999). The study used a multiple-case cross comparison technique based on a diagonal cross-section of cases (Yin, 1994, pp. 44–51, p. 135). The study was concerned with generic 'manageal' work which may be found at all levels of management. The results were expressed statistically (quantitatively) and complemented by qualitative information.

In terms of research focus, the author acknowledged distinctions between the study of: (a) an organization in which a manager works, (b) its external environments, (c) related job(s), (d) related groups, (e) a particular job, and (f) an individual incumbent (see also Stewart, 1989, p. 5). While these distinctions relate to research focus, in reality each of the six research areas deals with an aspect of work which is inextricably intertwined with the others in various ways. The field observations made by the researcher could be said to have focused on the area between the 'incumbent' (or 'person') and the 'job' in the above list. On balance, the research study was concerned with the job of the manager rather than the person doing the job and with what the job brought to the manager, rather than what the manager brought to the job. Nevertheless, it was accepted that these two factors were and are not necessarily independent of each other.

Table 12. Library Sites – Internal Environment.

	PERSONS MANAGED	MONOG. VOLUMES	SERIAL VOLUMES	SERIAL TITLES
SITE A	141.1	860299	570493	13061
SITE B	70.9	310833	133213	7119
SITE C	27.3	158875	11644	1407
SITE D	11	*	*	*
SITE E	0.2	*	*	*

Notes:
* The organisation at Sites D and E was unable to supply statistics on the collections in these branch libraries.
– Library C also held a sizeable audio-visual collection.

Table 13. Library Sites – External Environment.

	*FAC. N	ACADEMIC FTE	STUDENT EFTSU	CITY POPULATION
SITE A	11	1759	11239	1071100
SITE B	8	881	9035	249500
SITE C	4	1363	11931	454800
SITE D	1	2771	8671	297900
SITE E	1**	2771	8671	297900

Notes:
Academic FTE and Student EFTSU statistics refer to the whole university not just to the faculty mainly served by the library.

* N = Number of Faculties mainly served by the Site.
** Site E served a Research School, rather than a Faculty.

The study aimed within its scope and limitations to identify commonalities (and, inevitably, disparities) between the work of five managers whose jobs were overtly different in various ways, as summarised for example in Table 12 and Table 13. Table 12 compares the personnel and holdings of the five libraries and Table 13 provides some demographic data.

The research problem investigated by the study was the extent to which certain aspects of work were universal or common in a diagonal cross-section of jobs. The five library managers whose jobs were studied were at different stages in their career, undertook different types of professional activities outside their own institutions and were located at different positions within their organizational hierarchy. The library organizations ranged from large to small as indicated by Table 12.

Currently, the terminology of management studies has a paucity of qualifiers or adjectives to substitute for the general nouns 'management' and 'manager'. This paucity of terminology has to some extent hindered discussion. For example, the term 'managerial' has overtones of most relevance to the CEO's of, and also senior managers in, large or otherwise substantial organizations. This raises such questions as: How might the research terminology be enhanced to advance discussion on the commonalities and the differences between the work of various cohorts of managers? Are there common themes running through the work of all levels of management, that is from the work performed by managers in 'lower status' positions, CEO's of smaller organizations, managers located in the middle of organizational hierarchies, through to CEO's of, and senior managers in, large organizations? In the study, the researcher was trying in effect to distinguish between concepts of work that might be termed (to coin an adjective) 'manageal' (that is, relevant to all management levels and types) and 'managerial' (that is, most relevant to senior management levels).

The library managers were in charge of geographically distinct main or branch libraries in four Australian universities. Thus, each manager had the type of autonomy afforded by a separate location on campus and was in a sense in a boundary-spanning position between the library and the university community served by the library. The jobs of these five managers represented a diagonal cross-section of jobs in various respects: for example, the size of unit managed, level in university organizational hierarchy, potential for influence in various industrial sectors and indeed their actual and potential impact in human and financial terms.

At the two larger sites (A and B) the library managers were CEO's of the whole library organization within their respective universities. At Sites A and B, traditional 'managerial' or 'executive' level decision making, planning and human and financial resources management functions were included in the library manager's role. Clearly, however, the functional roles of the three branch library managers (Sites C, D and E) in relation to their respective whole library organizations (that is, where someone else was the CEO), were different from that point of view from those of the library managers at Sites A and B. In other words, the inclusion of the smaller sites was not intended to suggest that the roles and activities of their library managers were 'managerial' in the more traditional sense. Nor was the researcher suggesting that library technical or processing operations were 'managerial' in the traditional sense.

At the heart of the study was the recognition of the usefulness of contingency theory (Kim, 1998). It is used to explain the great diversity in management, in that specific contexts, situations and environments influence management and vice versa. As mentioned, each of the five libraries in the present study was very different from the others in terms of the size of its personnel establishment and other features. Therefore the assumption was that findings of commonalities between the jobs of the five library managers would be of potential significance. The researcher essentially observed the five managers' actions and analyzed these along eleven variables, some of which were derived from Mintzberg's classic study (Mintzberg, 1973). The researcher's perspective could not be identical to that of the individuals in the jobs, nor was a 'whole organization' perspective adopted.

The concept of a 'Work segment' was employed to structure both the field observation and the analysis phases of the study. The original report analyzed both the amount of time spent in various kinds of work segments and also the number of work segments involved in particular types of activity.

Of particular interest in the study were the following characteristics of work segments: (1) the parties associated with work segments; (2) the general type of work segments undertaken; (3) the modes of contact involved; (4) types of communication and information resources used; (5) the resource areas which were the foci of the managers' attention; (6) the links between various work segments which indicated continuity (or otherwise) in the managers' work; and (7) the physical resources managed. Further, as indicated in Appendix C, additional analysis of the data provided some limited information for comparison with Mintzberg's classic study on managerial work (Mintzberg, 1973).

APPENDIX B:
OUTLINE OF CONCEPTS USED IN THE STUDY

Activity. A descriptive summary of what the library manager was doing in a work segment. One variable was devoted to the analysis of such summaries. This variable provided one of the six structural parameters which defined a 'Work segment'. The data analysis phase of the study identified several major types or groups of activity.

Chief executive officer. The person in the library with overall responsibility for its operation. For convenience, the abbreviation 'CEO' was sometimes used. The more generic term 'Manager' was sometimes used instead of this term.

Contact. A process by which the manager was in touch with another party. In this study, 'contact' was interpreted in the broadest sense of the term. The contact might be direct or indirect. It included contact via mail. The process was described as 'live' or 'real-time' contact if the manager was in the company of another party or was talking to them in real-time mode for example, by telephone.

Contingency variable. A variable which may be considered part of the context, situation or environment in which a manager works. Contingency variables are said to influence what a manager does and the nature of the manager's job and vice versa. Examples of contingency variables are: the size of a library, the hierarchical position of the manager and the mission of the library's parent organization.

Data, Structured. In this study, data recorded in the field logbooks according to seven predetermined groups. In fact, study data were recorded into seven columns in the field notebooks. The first six columns were reserved for: Start hour, Start minute, Situation, Location/Place, Information/Mail form, Party/Contact/Direction. In these six columns mnemonic codes were used wherever possible to facilitate recording. The column for the seventh predetermined group of data was reserved for any work description required by the circumstances under observation at any particular time. *See also* Data, Unstructured.

Data, Unstructured. Field data recorded in the field notebooks in the column labelled for recording of 'Focus/Topic/Process/Other details. These data included descriptions of events as they unfolded, verbatim details of conversations, briefings from the library manager and any other relevant details not recorded under other categories of data.

Desk work. This term referred to one type of work 'Medium' described by Mintzberg (1973, pp. 235, 240) as: Time the manager spends at his desk, processing mail, scheduling activities, writing letters, and communicating with his secretary; or, Periods when managers work alone, or with their secretaries, in the confines of their offices. Note that 'Location' or 'Place' (specifically, the manager's own office or desk) was a major parameter of the 'Desk work' Medium.

Duration of work segment. The amount of time devoted to an individual work segment by a manager. Specifically, the period of time between the start of one work segment and the start of the following work segment. An interruption was deemed to terminate a work segment. Work segments of less than one minute were recorded as zero minutes in duration and were included in the analysis.

Environment. A milieu which a manager or another party operated in, dealt with or paid attention to. An environment may be an industry, an institution, a particular organization or a profession. It may also refer to geographical areas. Note, however, that in this study the physical location or place where an activity occurred was coded as a 'Location' as defined below. *See also* Location of work segment.

Focus. Anything to which a manager attended. This included management of resources such as equipment, finance, place, personnel and time.

Focus theme or topic – resource area. A summary of the focus of the library manager's attention in terms of the service or administrative area associated with any resources under consideration. This resource area might have been either within the library's internal or external environment, or might have spanned both those environments.

In transit. A non-contact work segment when the manager was in transit on business within the library or elsewhere on campus during work.

Interruption. An interruption was deemed to have terminated a work segment. It might have been an unexpected interruption, for example by the appearance of a colleague or a library user. On occasion, library managers interrupted themselves on a particular task. See Work segment links.

Job. The totality of the manager's operations and their contexts, including functions, activities and roles in relation to the library and parent organization. It also included the various situations with which the manager was confronted in the course of the working day. In common parlance and in this study, the word 'job' is very general in meaning and is useful because of its generality.

Library. A functionally or geographically distinct library service. This definition includes a branch library service.

Location of work segment. A place on campus where the library manager was at work. This was usually a functional area in a library, university administrative office or faculty domain. Location included areas on campus such as footways and other traffic ways. The physical place where a work segment occurred, such as a particular office or part of a library.

Manage. This term was used in the very broadest sense of the term. No meaning represented in regular English dictionaries was excluded. All functions normally associated in common parlance with the word 'manage' were considered relevant, including the allocation, control and direction of staff and other resources.

Manager. The person in charge of a whole library or a geographically distinct branch library. The function of a manager is to control and direct an organization, its staff and other resources by a wide variety of means, as indicated above in the comments on usage of the term 'manage'.

Materials. Any objects, equipment or information resources, unless qualified further by context as in the next entry in the Glossary. In this study information materials used in a work segment were described in two separate ways. Firstly they were described in terms of their physical form. Secondly, they were described in terms of their informational or literary genre.

Materials handled – informational or literary form. The content of information resources used by the library manager, expressed in terms of genre or form. The conceptual structure of library, bibliographic and mail items as distinct from their physical format. Use of materials included direct touching, physical movement or remote activation, such as the use of remote electronic media via a computer network connection. Used to describe 'information material' or 'library material'.

Materials handled – physical form. Objects used by the library manager in a work segment. These materials included informational media and office and other equipment. Use of materials included direct touching, physical movement and remote activation, such as the use of remote electronic media via a computer network connection.

Medium. This was a term used by Henry Mintzberg to describe five scenarios wherein a manager operates (Mintzberg, 1973, pp. 242–243). In the present study, it was used to facilitate comparison with Mintzberg's results. There were five types of 'Medium': Desk work, Scheduled meeting, Telephone call, Tour and Unscheduled meeting.

Meeting, Scheduled. One type of scenario or 'Medium' in the Mintzberg scheme. Specifically, a pre-arranged meeting, normally initiated by the date and the clock.

Meeting, Unscheduled. One type of scenario or 'Medium' in the Mintzberg scheme. Specifically, a meeting in the manager's office, arranged hastily, as when someone just dropped in (Mintzberg, 1973, p. 235). All contact that the manager had with his secretary were excluded (Mintzberg, 1973, p. 271). Contacts with the researcher in the manager's office were excluded. In the context of the 'Medium', this term did not refer to an unscheduled meeting which took place outside the manager's office. Mintzberg referred to the latter as a 'Tour'.

Mintzberg's Chronology Record Scheme. A scheme which summarized work performed by managers in terms of five types of work scenarios: Desk work, Scheduled meetings, Telephone calls, Tours and Unscheduled meetings (Mintzberg, 1973, p. 271). Mintzberg sometimes referred to these five types of work sessions as five types of 'media' and at other times as five types of 'activity'.

Number of persons involved real-time in work segment. The number of persons, including the library manager, who were involved real-time in the immediate work segment being analysed and coded. Thus those involved in immediate contact with the library manager either in person in the same location or via a 'real-time' medium such as the telephone were included in the count of persons involved in a work segment.

Participant. This was a person engaged simultaneously in an activity with and including the library manager. That is, the manager was always counted as one participant. Telephone callers were included. Persons not in real-time or live contact with the manager were excluded, such as senders of mail. *See* Number of persons involved real-time in work segment.

Party. A description of a person, officer, group, institution or organization, including the manager. The description summarised the official work relationship or otherwise between the manager and the other party.

Party associated with work segment. A person, group or organization with whom the library manager was directly or indirectly associated in a work segment. Such association included direct or indirect contact with the library manager. Also included were parties on behalf of whom the library manager performed tasks. 'Party' was one of the six structural parameters which defined a 'Work segment'.

Personal time. This time was recorded in the field, but excluded from the results of the study. It included, for example, lunch breaks (even though contact with colleagues may have occurred) and the occasional personal telephone call. Personal time was considered to be 'time out' from the study.

Resource. Any means or wherewithal inside or outside the library by which the librarian manager ensured its operation and development. Resources included energy, equipment, finances, information, people, place, space and time.

Session. One occurrence of a Mintzberg work scenario. A 'Work session' might or might not correspond in time with a 'Work segment'.

Situation. A field logbook column heading. In this column changes in the type of 'Work segment' (and as appropriate 'Medium' in the Mintzberg scheme) were recorded.

Size of library. Library size is a complex concept. Here one particular size variable was of special interest: the number of library personnel. Unless otherwise stated, in this study 'size' referred to the number of library personnel reporting to the library manager. This concept played a role in the selection of subjects for the present research study.

Telephone call. This term was used to describe one type of work scenario or 'Medium' in the Mintzberg scheme. Telephone calls screened or made by the secretary were excluded (Mintzberg, 1973, p. 242).

Time. The phenomenon measured by a clock or watch. Recorded time was crucial as an indicator of the commencement of each work segment in the field data. It was also fundamental to the basic accounting for time process which was one of the first steps in the data analysis process in the study. See also Duration of a work segment.

Tour. This was one type of work scenario or 'Medium' described by Mintzberg as a chance meeting in the hall, or a promenade taken by the manager to observe activity and to deliver information (Mintzberg, 1973, p. 235).

Work segment. This was a basic concept for data collection and analysis in the study. It referred to a period of work in which there was no change in six work parameters: the 'Activity' performed by the manager, the 'Location', the 'Materials handled (physical form), 'Materials handled (informational/ literary form)', 'Work segment type' and the 'Parties associated with work segment'.

Work segment links. An expression of association between separate work segments. This association included progress in dealing with a particular matter or theme throughout a particular day over more than one work segment.

Work segment type. The general and immediate character of a work segment, particularly in relation to the type of contacts between the library manager and others. Data analysis identified four main types of work segment. Some work segments involved active contact with another party and others did not.

APPENDIX C:
MINTZBERG'S CHRONOLOGY RECORD SCHEME

There is historical interest in the framework used by Henry Mintzberg (1973) to describe the work of managers (for example, through his Chronology Record scheme).

The Mintzberg Chronology Record scheme summarized work performed by managers in terms of five types of work session: Desk work, Scheduled meetings, Telephone calls, Tours and Unscheduled meetings (Mintzberg, 1973, p. 271). Mintzberg sometimes referred to these five types of work session as five types of 'media' and at other times as five types of 'activity'.

Because the data in the present study were structured on the concept of a 'work segment', rather than primarily based on 'location' as in Mintzberg, the types of comparisons possible were somewhat limited. However, through additional analysis, work segments were each coded as one of five major types of work as described by Mintzberg's Chronology Record scheme.

(1) Desk work

This term referred to a work 'Medium' described by Mintzberg (1973, pp. 235, 240) as either: Time the manager spends at his desk, processing mail, scheduling activities, writing letters, and communicating with his secretary: or, Periods when managers work alone, or with their secretaries, in the confines of their offices. Note that 'Location' (specifically, the manager's own office or desk) is a parameter of the 'Desk work' session.

(2) Scheduled meeting

A prearranged meeting, normally initiated by the date and the clock.

(3) Telephone call

All use of the telephone by the library manager in the library manager's own office.

(4) Tour

According to Mintzberg (1973, p. 43), the tour provided the manager with the opportunity to observe activity without prearrangement. But it could

include a chance meeting in the hall or a promenade taken by the manager
to deliver information (Mintzberg, 1973, p. 235).

(5) Unscheduled meeting

A meeting in the manager's office, arranged hastily, as when someone just
dropped in (Mintzberg, 1973, p. 235). All contacts that the manager had
with his secretary were excluded (Mintzberg, 1973, p. 271).

In various ways, Mintzberg's five activity descriptors had to be adapted to cover
the wide spectrum of the library managers' work covered in this study. For
example, the descriptor 'Tour' was the closest available to cover service point
and other activity away from the manager's own office. In the present study,
as Table 14 shows, there was variation between the sites overall. The results
presented in Table 14 will be discussed below, followed by a mention of
Mintzberg's results.

In the present study, the highest proportions of time were spent as follows:
Scheduled Meetings at Site A, Desk work at Sites B and E, and the 'Tour' (not
in own office) at Sites C and D. At the two larger sites (A and B), the categories of activity which ranked second in the proportion of time devoted to
them were: Desk work (at Site A 38.2% of time) and Scheduled meetings (at
Site B 17.8% of time). At Site A the the difference between the top and second
ranking scenarios was only 1.2% of time. That is, manager A spent approximately the same proportion of time on Scheduled meetings (39.4% of time) as
on Desk work (38.2% of time). Scheduled meetings accounted for only 5.5%
of work segments at Site A. Therefore, this manager's time was to a certain
extent relatively more prestructured by a rather fewer than greater number of
lengthy scheduled meetings.

Table 14. Analysis by Mintzberg Scheme (% of time).

	SITE A	SITE B	SITE C	SITE D	SITE E
Desk work	38.2	43.4	23.2	27.6	36.9
Scheduled meeting	39.4	17.8	22.2	8.9	3.4
Telephone call *	3.6	10.4	11.8	17.3	10.0
Tour **	7.7	17.5	29.1	33.1	34.0
Unscheduled meeting	2.8	6.5	6.9	8.4	9.5
With researcher	8.2	4.4	6.8	4.7	6.2
Total	100	100	100	100	100

Notes:
* Excludes telephone calls not made from the manager's own office.
** Includes telephone calls and unscheduled meetings away from the manager's own office.

Conforming to this picture of the relatively more (but by no means entirely) 'pre-structured day' at Site A was the finding that only 2.8% of library manager A's time was spent in Unscheduled meetings in his own office. This was a smaller proportion of time spent in such Unscheduled meetings than at the other sites (where the range of time was 9.5% at the smallest site dropping successively to 6.5% at Site B). Some Unscheduled meetings would have been grouped under the 'Tour' category (that is, if they had occurred outside the library manager's own office). Manager A also spent less time than the other managers on Telephone calls (i.e. those made from his own office). This may have been because some were screened by his secretary, including those that occurred when he was out of contact or otherwise occupied, such as during Scheduled meetings. So, Library manager A spent a smaller proportion of time in Telephone calls, Tours and Unscheduled meetings than the other managers. In other words, his time was concentrated into fewer types of scenarios (namely, Scheduled meetings and Desk work).

The managers at the three smallest sites tended to be more 'mobile' than those at the larger sites. At Sites (C and D) the top ranking scenario was the 'Tour', that is away from the manager's own office. The second ranked scenario in terms of time was Desk work (own desk). At Site C the three top ranked scenarios took up almost similar proportion of time 29.1% (Tour), 23.2% (Desk work) and 22.2% (Scheduled meeting). At Site E the second ranking scenario was the 'Tour' (not in own office). Like Site A, the proportion of time spent in the top ranked and second ranked scenario was similar (36.9% of time on Desk work and 34.0% of time on Tour). However, unlike Site A, at Site E the library manager's office also functioned as a service point. From that point of view the statistics for the 'Desk work' scenario give a false impression in the case of Site E. At Site E, the proportion of time expended in Scheduled meetings was very small. It has already been noted that the researcher learned that the library manager had declined to attend a meeting (which had been scheduled the same day as a data collection date) because researcher observation status had been declined by the chair. Off campus meetings were not included in the study.

A comparison of the relevant results that is, Table 10 of Mintzberg's study (Mintzberg, 1973, pp. 242–243) and Table 14 of the present study, reveals the following.

The library managers in the present study tended to spend more time in the desk work scenario (including mail handling) than Mintzberg's 'composite manager' who spent 22% of time on desk work. However two individual library managers (A with 38.3% and C with 23.2% of time) spent about the same proportion of time in this scenario as two of Mintzberg's individual managers A (38% of time) and B (23% of time).

As to Scheduled meetings, except for one case (library Site A), the library managers tended to spend significantly less time than the Mintzberg managers in that scenario. This is the case for both the Mintzberg 'composite' manager (59% of time in scheduled meetings) and the individual Mintzberg managers who spent between 75% and 38% of their time in scheduled meetings. At the largest library site (A), 39.4% of time was spent in scheduled meetings (similar to Mintzberg manager A).

As to telephone calls made from the library manager's office, except for library manager D who spent 17.3% of time on the telephone or attempting to make calls, the range of the proportion of time expended on 'phone calls was roughly similar to the Mintzberg finding which was 9% of time down to 4% of time, with 6% of time for the composite manager. The library managers other than D spent between 11.8% and 3.6% of time on telephone usage.

Regarding the 'Tour' scenario (not in own office, except for scheduled meetings) the result was as follows. Generally speaking, the library managers were significantly more mobile than the Mintzberg managers. There were notable exceptions in both studies, namely the library manager at the largest site A, who was recorded as out of his office 7.7% of time (excluding scheduled meetings) and the Mintzberg manager A (10% of time). The Mintzberg result for the 'Tour' scenario was 3% of time for the 'composite' manager and a range of 10% to 0% of time for the individual managers. The range of time for the library managers was 43.0% (Site E) to 7.7% (Site A). Some of this time was spent assisting library Clients away from the manager's own office.

As to Unscheduled meetings in the manager's own office, the library managers on the whole recorded a little less time in unscheduled meetings than the Mintzberg managers. However, some unscheduled meetings in the present study were recorded under the 'Tour' scenario because they occurred outside the library manager's office. In the Mintzberg study the range of time spent in unscheduled meetings was from 18% to 3% of time, with 10% for the 'composite' manager. The Mintzberg manager with the 18% result was a noticeably higher scorer on unscheduled meetings than the other four cases in that study. In the present study the range was 9.5% of time at Site E (where the office was also a service point) to 2.8% of time at Site A.

CURRENT ISSUES IN HIGHER EDUCATION QUALITY ASSURANCE: AN INTRODUCTION FOR ACADEMIC LIBRARY ADMINISTRATORS

Jean Mulhern

Today's academic library leader needs a dual perspective to provide high quality library resources and services. The challenge is to align the traditional (horizontal) definition of library with a re-envisioned library needed to support new local (vertical) learning environments. As they emerge, these learning environments will require unique definitions of *library*, specific to the missions and purposes of parent institutions. For the library, there will be increased emphasis on demonstrating "worthwhileness" to local constituents and less concern with horizontal peer library comparisons.

More and more, the quality of the academic library will be directly linked to the parent institution's vision of a high quality operation. As experienced change agents, librarians should and can participate actively in institutional (not just library) strategic and assessment planning. Understanding institutional quality assurance, therefore, becomes paramount to librarians.

General quality assurance issues in higher education can be divided into two categories, internal institutional concerns and external oversight pressures. Both categories require detailed internal definitional framing since the term *quality* is subjective and must be negotiated within institutions of higher education that are dynamically complex internally and in a multi-dimensional global environment. In this paper I conclude that in the future the thriving institution will employ

Advances in Library Administration and Organization, Volume 19, pages 137–164.
Copyright © 2002 by Elsevier Science Ltd.
All rights of reproduction in any form reserved.
ISBN: 0-7623-0868-0

coordinated quality assurance strategies to control its customized response to inevitable change. Further, I conclude that external pressure for quality assurance will continue with the addition of a push for international standards.

Regarding quality assurance, academic library leaders must, as noted above, maintain a dual focus, a bifocal lens, if you will. Through one lens, for the short distance, they must see the way to provide high quality library resources and services as defined by professional consensus (the horizontal perspective), using library-specific quality assurance strategies. Focusing through the second lens, for the longer distance, they need to assert "library" into the emerging local teaching/learning environments (the vertical integration perspective).

These "re-envisioned" environments will likely feature definitions of "library" specific to the mission and purposes of the individual institution. Strong influences shaping these environments will be changes driven by technology, newer instruction strategies, and *new* students. The issues central to quality assurance at the institutional level are outlined in this essay which is organized to include a discussion of the challenges of defining *quality* and *quality assurance*; the theories, constraints, and trends related to quality assurance; and, finally, some predictions related to quality assurance. This essay focuses on general institutional concerns with quality assurance since those concerns in turn signal likely changes that are on the horizon for librarians.

The nation's largest regional accrediting body, the North Central Association, Higher Learning Commission (NCA) assumes this holistic concept in its challenge: "Higher education library staff need to evaluate their overall efforts, to collect evidence that something worthwhile is happening to students because the library exists. How, where, and in what form to collect this information are up to each institution, and the effective use of the information to improve its learning resources depends on an institution's traditions, structure, orientation, and particular situation" (1997, p. 48). Academic librarians are already sensing that much more weight is placed on vertical mission achievement and less emphasis on the library as a separate entity in regional accreditation evaluators' reports in the past few years [Author's observation based on peer contacts in the NCA and Southern Association of Colleges and Schools (SACS) areas]. More and more, quality of "library" will be directly linked to the parent institution's vision of institutional quality. The broad assumption is that a strong, high quality academic library is by definition one that is fully integrated into and essential to the success of its institution's mission and purposes. Such a unit cannot be measured in isolation and is more closely allied with its home institution than with libraries in other institutions. To contribute to institutional goals, the library may look and operate very differently from libraries in other institutions. Library services developed for students of the University of Phoenix (an online distance education provider) would certainly be different from those that would best serve the students of Oglala Lakota College in South Dakota or Vanderbilt University in Nashville. Assessing library quality from the institutional perspective becomes concomitant with assessing the quality of the parent institution.

A college or university (in fact any institution of higher education) is a complex organization operating in an overlapping set of dynamic environments. These ever-changing environments – the civic, social, economic, academic, and technological – interact like multi-colored jewels tumbling in a kaleidoscope. Providers of higher education also tumble about in the kaleidoscope, jostling with other providers for different positions as the scope is passed from student to faculty member to donor to government grant evaluator to legislator. Each viewer experiences the display differently; and each stakeholder sees the institution differently, using different criteria. Quality may seem to be in the eye of the beholder but the institution must take control of its own measures of quality and develop a process to maintain its direction and purpose. No institution can be all things to all stakeholders, and none should try.

DEFINITIONS

Defining Quality

Quality assurance initiatives in higher education, however earnest, must stop before they can start, at the point of defining "quality." Who assesses? What is being assessed, one program, one college, or a group of institutions? By what criteria? By what standards? By what values? Under what assumptions? Over what time frame? For what purposes? Formal or informal? Internal or comparative? Who decides who assesses? Who assesses the assessor? It all depends; answers are contextual, not absolute. Regardless of which "answers" are selected by any given institution, asking and answering the questions ride on the institutions' core values and priorities.

Stephen D. Spangehl, director of the North Central Association's Academic Quality Improvement Project (AQIP), offers his definition of the word *quality*:

> Most of us use *quality* loosely, with many different meanings .... Generally, individual students seek higher education to satisfy multiple purposes. And most institutions serve disparate groups with dissimilar goals. Thus an institution's educators must work hard to understand their stakeholders' diverse purposes, to decide which ones are essential and which are merely desirable, and to evaluate carefully how to best fulfill each need. Typically an institution will be perceived as high quality for satisfying one purpose, low for another. Ranking one institution as having higher overall quality than another is what makes

cumulative rankings, like those in *U.S. News and World Reports*, so offensive. Global, abstract talk about quality is neither logical nor useful. If thinking about quality is to lead to improvement, it's critical we remember for whom and for what purpose we do what we do (2001, On-Line).

Quality Assurance – Dialogue on Definition

Since there can be no one "right way" to define quality in higher education, activities relating to that topic must start with detailed operational definitions and assumptions. Even within the smallest college, academic leaders face the daunting task of coordinating and facilitating multiple internal and external criteria defining quality with multiple processes of quality assessment. To make sense of it all and to communicate effectively with the many stakeholders, the leadership usually seeks to develop a strategic plan. Strategic planning, fully realized, is a process for identifying, organizing, prioritizing, and implementing the campus effort to achieve local goals within the context of the organization's mission. Since strategic planning is the institution's process of deciding to "launch an expedition to climb a selected mountain," then quality assurance is what must happen to ensure the success of the expedition. Quality assurance assures that the supplying of base camps, two-way communications, equipment repairs, health checks, and progress reporting, all essential to sustaining the mountain climbing expedition, take place appropriately and in a timely fashion. Quality assurance in higher education is the way that each institution nourishes, monitors, refines, asserts, and sustains its efforts to achieve its educational vision. Ironically, while institutions recognize strategic planning as an internal operation, quality assurance (Were the plans fulfilled in the manner and at the levels specified?) can become confused with other external processes such as accreditation reviews and can be lost in the shuffle of daily responsibilities.

The term *quality assurance* in higher education draws meaning from the diverse fields of manufacturing technology, business, organizational management, and administrative leadership. The Institute of Telecommunication Sciences of the United States Department of Commerce (Institute, 2001) offers an example of a technical definition for quality assurance:

> Quality assurance (QA): (1). All actions taken to ensure that standards and procedures are adhered to and that delivered products or services meet performance requirements. (2). The planned systematic activities necessary to ensure that a component, module, or system conforms to established technical requirements. (3). The policy, procedures, and systematic actions established in an enterprise for the purpose of providing and maintaining a specified degree of confidence in data integrity and accuracy throughout the lifecycle of the data, which includes input, update, manipulation, and output (On-line).

Although far too empirical for most teaching/learning purposes, this technical definition of quality assurance provides ample justification for a college to implement an array of quality assurance strategies to monitor its variety of systems and processes. Regardless of how quality assurance is defined, its key component is the looping of data/information gathering, analysis, and decision-making for goal achievement. Looping gives rolling feedback to realign efforts toward progress.

The application of *quality assurance* to education is most advanced in the United Kingdom and in Europe and centers on the work of the International Network for Quality Assurance Agencies in Higher Education (INQAAHE) that publishes a journal called *Quality in Higher Education*. A second journal titled *Quality Assurance in Education* is also published in the U.K.

For the purposes of this paper, the term *quality assurance* combines the technical meaning with concepts inherent in such common American phrases as *strategic planning, measuring institutional effectiveness, quality control, quality improvement, institutional assessment*, and the current catch phrase, *student learning assessment*. Not inherent in the term is any prescription of specific research methods or techniques, which are chosen at the discretion of the institution in line with its interpretation of its information needs. Standardized tests, for example, are not mandated by quality assurance.

Beyond this general definition, quality assurance in higher education can be understood in terms of scope. In the narrowest sense, in every faculty lounge in the country *distance education* is THE topic of conversation and quality assurance is the chief concern. Skeptics wonder whether a degree earned through distance education is equivalent to one earned in a campus classroom. Will faculty have the same autonomy and control of learning? Will students experience true intellectual growth and development? How can students possibly receive personalized library service? Others ask whether the traditional campus classroom (or library) is all that effective for teaching and learning and where is the evidence one way or the other? Distance education debates expose both concerns for consistent program excellence and insecurities with quality assurance – fear of change and/or loss of control.

At the institutional level, quality assurance might be a carefully designed process motivated and led from within. For example, presidents of such diverse institutions as Kent State University (OH), Edison State Community College (OH), Concordia University (IL), and Maranatha Baptist Bible College (WI) are leading their institutions in an alternative NCA regional accreditation process called Academic Quality Improvement Project (AQIP), which had 27 participating institutions as of October 2001 (North Central, AQIP, 2001). Continuous quality improvement strategies of many types are at the heart of AQIP, which engages volunteer institutions in annual reporting cycles and frequent peer dialogue on quality improvement. AQIP institutions are exempt from comprehensive self-studies and campus evaluations every five to 10 years since they are involved in continuous self-monitoring and improvement processes.

Quality assurance can also be a limited institutional response to an external pressure or an internal crisis. An example would be a college faculty working with the financial aid officer to define *satisfactory progress* and to implement policies and procedures to comply with federal financial aid administration guidelines (U.S. Department of Education, 2001).

Finally, expectations for quality assurance can emerge from the public sector or from an external perspective. At this level, accrediting agencies evaluate members, legislators look for value for public investment, donors select worthy recipients, and students compare institutions (for admission or transfer).

As an effective institutional leadership practice, quality assurance in higher education has both its proponents and its detractors. By showcasing thriving institutions, some studies argue for common acceptance of a particular quality assurance strategy. On the other hand, there are doubters who question whether a special focus on quality assurance is necessary. For such doubters, the concept of quality assurance is redundant, even a drain on institution energy and resources. They assert that higher education has evolved its traditional practices (admissions standards, tenure, shared governance, IRBs) for just that purpose, to sustain high quality. They see high quality as a synonym for higher education; any administrative problems in an institution are rooted in failure to sustain tradition. This essay next offers a review of the issues swirling around this controversial topic.

BACKGROUND ISSUES

Quality Assurance and Organizational Theory

Defining quality assurance in higher education includes understanding it in the context of organizational theory. McDonald and Micikas (1994) cite theorist Kim S. Cameron (p. 21) as the first author writing on the measurement of institutional effectiveness to discard the notion of a single ideal measure in favor of "multivariate and dimensionalized ones" (p. 22). Cameron, as a positivist, "argues for testing a comprehensive set of effectiveness criteria rather than an exhaustive set which, presumably, could never be known" (p. 22). Further, "the multiple perspectives (models) must always be considered in relationship to one another" (p. 22). Cameron's work continues to inform current research on organizational effectiveness. Lysons, Hatherly and Mitchell (1998) studied four types of academic institutions in Great Britain and concurred with Cameron concerning the importance of using multiple assessment strategies to account for the complex competing values in play. Today, many regional and disciplinary accreditation bodies require institutions to use multiple measures when assessing effectiveness of student learning for self-studies. The concept of measures can be interpreted broadly to include both quantitative and qualitative data/information gathering and analysis.

McDonald and Micikas (1994) summarize Cameron's (1986) list of themes common to most studies of organizational effectiveness (quality). These themes include the following:

(1) Because no conceptualization of an organization is comprehensive, no conceptualization of an effective organization can be comprehensive. As the metaphor describing an organization changes, so does the definition or appropriate model of organizational effectiveness.
(2) Consensus regarding the best, or [at least, a] sufficient, set of indicators of effectiveness is impossible to obtain. Criteria are based on the values and preferences of individuals, and no specifiable construct boundaries exist.
(3) Different models of effectiveness are useful for research in different circumstances. Their usefulness depends on the purposes and constraints placed on the organizational effectiveness investigation.
(4) Organizational effectiveness is mainly a problem-driven construct rather than a theory-driven construct (pp. 29–30).

Looking specifically at organizations in higher education, the application of various quality assurance strategies has met with resistance. This resistance has come particularly from faculty. Resistance (reluctance, serious doubt, skepticism) is justified based on some or all of the following arguments:

• Higher education has evolved its governance systems, policies, and practices for the purpose of quality control. Traditional practices are tailored to the needs of higher education.
• Higher education is too different from business or government entities to use the quality assurance templates developed for those venues.
• Translation of existing quality assurance templates is too difficult and requires too much effort to use for unknown benefits.
• The products of higher education (learning, research, and service) are not easily measurable and may not demonstrate their full impact for decades after delivery.
• The profile of students is too variable and their goals too diverse to make a quality standard of learning achievable.

- In some institutions, their various activities (learning, research, and service) compete internally for resources and also may be supported intentionally at different levels of "quality."

An example of this debate, which focuses on TQM (Total Quality Management principles), has emerged in the *Journal of Quality Management*. Business management professors Robert Orwig and Lawrence Jauch (1997) argued against TQM as a bad fit for higher education. They cited problems with continuous improvement, customer focus, and hierarchical management systems. Two faculty members from Central Missouri State University, Ralph Mullin and George Wilson (1998) challenged Jauch and Orwig. The Missouri duo countered that TQM principles were misrepresented and too narrowly interpreted. They argued that, properly applied, TQM would enable academe to make quantum leaps in quality improvement and that "customer focus" and "catering to customers' whims" were not identical concepts. More importantly, they urged that faculty resistance to various *controls* (monitoring or measuring strategies) not be confused with an institution *in control* of its processes.

Mullin and Wilson concluded that the first step toward quality assurance in an institution should be an examination of the underlying assumptions shoring up current governance structures, policies, procedures, and practices. Higher education institutions, implied Mullin and Wilson, have taken on the appearance of dysfunctional extended families subsisting within ramshackle mazes consisting of a couple of original rooms copied from Harvard College and numerous add-ons and lean-tos. To remedy this situation, they contend that it is time to put all assumptions and traditions back on the drawing board. In terms of purposes and constituents, they suggest that institutional leaders ask: "Can this college or that university afford to continue to operate as it has?" Or, "could the University of Phoenix, with its distance education strategy and its for-profit and entrepreneurial stance, really be a better idea?"

To continue the dialogue, Jauch and Orwig (2000) chided Mullin and Wilson for calling for outright revolution and radical reorganization in academe. Jauch and Orwig called instead for keeping the debate on quality in higher education within the realm of reality. Although taking opposite sides in this debate, both sets of authors acknowledged that one distinctive characteristic of academe has been shared governance, the tradition in which faculty play a strong role in program design and decision making "through peer processes and collegial bodies. Nevertheless, dominance of academics in decision making about quality is now being directly challenged by the quality movement's emphasis on customers" (Lindsay, 1994, as cited by Izadi, Kashef & Stadt, 1996). Not surprisingly, shifts (or fear of shifts) in the power structure are at the heart of the struggle.

Quality assurance in higher education, obviously, is a hot debate. Those seeking to maintain current institutional processes and structures are labeled old guard, knee-jerk resisters, modernists, pragmatists, or realists. Those looking toward examining underlying assumptions and amenable to restructuring and change are impractical idealists, revolutionaries, post-modernists, or common-sense change advocates.

History of Quality Assurance in American Higher Education

For more than 300 years, colleges and universities have been subjected to published quality assessments rating general prestige or the reputation of specific programs or services (Mulhern, 2001). Reputation, determined in the courts of professional and public opinion, builds on perceptions of how well the institution fulfills its various purposes or how impressive are its resources. Institutions themselves also have benchmarked their operations on course-credit-completion information (the numbers) (Mullin & Wilson, 1998) and on the amounts of donations, research sponsorship, and endowment (the dollars). Institutions active in quality assurance today may be driving purposefully to control (and to publicize) those factors that in their estimation seem to matter most to reputation or prestige. The terms *reputation* and *prestige*, then, have the same subjective interpretation problems as the elusive definition of quality (Goldman, Gates & Brewer, 2001).

Academe, by its nature, is conservative, building onto or reacting to an existing knowledge base. In this same conservative mode, then, where past experience has value, higher education institutions in the United States have developed through continuous benchmarking on the practices of just a few prestigious institutions, beginning with Harvard and Yale. In their recent RAND report, Goldman et al. (2001) described a research study on perceptions of reputation and prestige in higher education. Reputation has short-term qualities and attaches itself to specific programs or aspects of an institution in comparison to other institutions. The authors defined prestige as a perceived general status chosen for pursuit or defense by an institution that uses its resources to increase "the quality of incoming students, the amount of federal research funding, and the success of athletics programs" (p. B13). The RAND study found that institutions can and do choose *not* to pursue prestige because of its high costs and necessary diversion of resources and attention from other more valued goals. A study by West Point researcher Bruce Keith (2001) reported a disconnect between changes in institutional outcomes and prestige; regardless of the changes, prestige rankings remained stable over time. "Yet, ironically, the institutions that have shunned that strategy [pursuit of prestige] are the ones transforming the nature of higher education at the beginning of the 21st century" (Goldman et al., B15). To continue to benchmark against other institutions, particularly if they are selected based on prestige, may be a hollow exercise.

Mullin and Wilson (1998) critiqued the traditional criteria for defining quality in academe. They point out that both the reputation/resources and course-credit-completion criteria showcase the "business," or output functions, of the academy. They noted that some detractors of quality assurance praise traditional academe and decry the current quality assurance movement in those same terms. As alternatives, they cite Astin (1992) and Hutchings and Marchese (1990) who called for student-focused outcomes or value-added learning (p. 295).

Aiming to shake up the academic establishment and to break the cycle of reinforcing business-as-usual in traditional higher education, Patrick M. Callan (2000), head of the Pew Trusts-funded National Center for Public Policy and Higher Education, led a recent study of public higher education. Callan's findings are summarized in *Measuring Up 2000*, the first report card that grades the 50 states on their performance in higher education. Unfortunately, when states get graded publicly, the public institutions involved will undoubtedly feel political pressure to change and improve the grades. Callan's report looked at higher education in terms of "who gets to college in each state, how well prepared they are, who gets through, and what those years of study produce" (Connell, 2001). The grades Callan assigned were not high (National Center for Public Policy, 2000). He plans additional research to include the testing of college students in order to develop conclusions about the quality of teaching and learning in higher education. Note that there already are focused licensure tests (with institution-specific passage rates available) for such fields as law, nursing, and most recently in some states, teacher preparation.

In a presentation about his report, Callan focused on the key issue of quality assurance in higher education – definition. He asserted through analogy that academe, even though it is looking for its keys under the lamppost where the light is better, has really lost them in the shadows (Connell, 2001). If the keys are ways to monitor and increase quality, institutions are most interested in employing those strategies that track the goals most successfully met or easily achieved. They leave in the shadows quality assurance for institutional topics likely to make a poor showing or to be difficult to assess. Depending on how quality is defined and assured, an institution can coast on prestige and past practices or can target institutional practices or programs for upgrade or change. Depending on how authentically strategic planning and quality assurance are embraced, an institution can design and deliver a high-performing educational experience that meets the identified needs of its specific clientele.

Quality Assurance: Impetus for the Current Interest

In the 1970s many manufacturing firms in Japan credited much of their success to the application of the philosophy and strategies of Total Quality Management (TQM) promoted by W. Edwards Deming (1982), and corporations in the United States noted that success, developed their own TQM programs. TQM also was adapted for use by other types of organizations, including government agencies and non-profit entities throughout the world. Academe has been a relative latecomer to this kind of strategic management practice. Nevertheless, spurred by financial downturns and consumer activism, public pressure has increased on all organizations, particularly those financed with public funds, to demonstrate value and productivity. Reflecting that concern, legislators have aimed to control escalating costs in higher education and to increase public confidence with academe. Through legislation and a variety of agency rules and regulations, government has begun to demand accountability using criteria based on test-results and economic efficiency. Following the introduction of achievement and high-stakes student testing in K-12 schools, the realization of national standardized testing of college students may be very near. Peter Ewell, a critic of *Measuring Up 2000* and a proponent of other ways to assess learning, has predicted "if all goes well, a new National Assessment of Adult Literacy will be administered in 2002. A proposal is now on the table to administer the survey to samples of college sophomores and seniors in addition to the general population, and the tasks used to assess these students will reflect authentic college-level abilities" (Ewell, 2000).

States authorize the operation of institutions of higher education and exercise extensive control over public institutions (especially concerning quality assurance). The federal government extended its reach into higher education through its financial support of the Land Grant institutions beginning in 1862 (Brubacher & Rudy, 1997). In fact, it was based on dissatisfaction with the type and quality of education offered by the existing liberal arts colleges that led to the increasing demand for more pragmatic education. Today, tied to federal support for higher education programs are federal regulations applied to research, financial aid, and grants. Other federal laws regulate the quality of practices related to admissions, employment, facilities design, and liability.

The federal government circuitously linked itself to voluntary higher education accreditation in 1952 when it tied student federal financial aid for Korean Conflict veterans to attendance at accredited institutions. (Brubacher & Rudy, 1997). Immediately accreditation became, not voluntary, but essential for financial survival for many colleges. The most interesting recent development has been the move of the federal government to accredit the accrediting agencies.

The Secretary of Education is charged with certifying the accrediting agencies and works with a membership organization called the Council on Higher Education Accreditation (CHEA, 2001, On-Line). CHEA coordinates accreditation activities and promotes institutional self-regulation through sixty accrediting agencies. Failure to promote and monitor institutional "quality," especially through the use of effective penalties, could remove an agency from the federally approved list maintained by the Department of Education. Institutions accredited through an unlisted agency would lose federal funds.

The specter of increased direct federal and state regulation of academe also is an issue with accrediting agencies. The Pew Center for Higher Education Policy Analysis has been tracking state trends toward restructuring publicly funded institutions and toward standardized testing of their students (Pew Trusts, 2001). In response, to preserve the concept of self-regulation for their member institutions, accrediting agencies strengthened their accrediting processes and are working to dispel public perceptions of soft standards. For instance, among others, NCA now requires a process documenting value-added student learning as one of its required proofs of institution viability. In 2001, the Southern Association of Colleges and Schools placed two colleges on probation and officially warned seven other institutions. (McMurtrie, 2001). Such actions have been rare in the past and not publicized, but they are becoming more frequent.

Regulated professions provide an additional set of requirements with the list expanding from medicine to social work and teaching. Even sports leagues (like the NCAA or NAIA) assert quality assurance expectations on individual institution members through minimum standards for participation and concern for graduation rates (Suggs, 2001). Foundations, backed with financial clout, exert pressure. For example, the Knight Foundation's Commission on Intercollegiate Athletics recently issued a report advising college presidents to take charge of college sports, citing low student retention and graduation rates and escalating costs (Suggs, 2001).

A second impetus toward quality assurance is the growing list of competitive alternatives available for advanced and professional education, research, and service, all purposes of traditional academe. Nothing spurs change faster than competition. Students are pursuing knowledge and skills through workplace opportunities, distance education provided by employers or for-profits, online education, and certificate training and testing. Geographical barriers have disappeared; international education is now possible online. Research is pursued worldwide and can be government subsidized or privately funded. Through electronic communication, options for researchers to collaborate are international and no longer tied to one site. In turn, sources of information and service to society have expanded to include K-12, corporations, government agencies, and philanthropy. To compete with these alternatives, academe has to authenticate its continuing value.

In the past year, 2000–2001, institutions of higher education in Ohio (and nationwide) have been constrained as they competed for a diminished pool of financial resources with the K-12 educational community and other state responsibilities, including prison operation. In late 2001, downturns in the economy and national crises increased the competition for decreasing pools of public and private funds. Such competition requires academic institutions to demonstrate the quality and value of their contributions to an increasingly skeptical society (Hebel, 2001).

The picture is clear. Higher education is becoming increasingly marginalized with increasing restrictions and competitive alternatives for all its mission-driven purposes. To address this situation, institutions must assure the quality of their endeavors and show results in terms appreciated by their constituencies. At issue is whether an essentially reactive, defensive posture to questions of quality assurance in higher education is too little, too late. Can traditional higher education as currently structured withstand such broad, high-pressure scrutiny based on quality criteria externally defined? Should it stand on tradition or should it re-engineer itself? A distance education entrepreneur, nodding toward the Harvards, Yales, and Stanfords, has indicated "we will eat their lunch" (Stahl, 2001). Institutions must decide whether this is likely.

ISSUES CONSTRAINING IMPLEMENTATION

Informed by Cameron's findings, as summarized by McDonald and Micikas (1994), and sensitized to the *quality* debate in academe, it is necessary to visit the quality assurance movement in higher education. There are several constraining issues complicating the translation of general quality assurance principles to the needs of higher education in general or to those of a specific college or university. These issues all relate to identifying the primary driver (definition) of institutional quality.

First, the extreme complexity of the academic organization invites a misleading reduction in attempts to attach a quality rating to a particular program (like a library) or to an entire institution. As Mullin and Wilson (1998) suggested, institutional complexity has accumulated incrementally in the historical development of higher education in America. The pattern has been one of increasing the number of purposes, broadening the student profile, increasing the size, broadening governance, sharing decision-making, and diversifying sources of funding. Business corporations may address quality assurance through similar diversification, but they also have systems for detailed monitoring of outcomes and for determining the overall impact of changes on the viability of the organization. Corporations such as Procter & Gamble are well known for diversifying product lines while, at the same time, trimming incompatible products. In just the past year, that company has experimented with Culinary Sol, a cooking school, and has sold off its popular, yet incompatible, Crisco and Jif product lines (Proctor & Gamble, 2001). Similarly, the atypical and non-traditional DeVry, Inc. technical institutes model businesses in launching and testing new academic programs and in deciding when to discontinue others (Borrego, 2001).

In its background role of sustaining the common foundations of a diverse society, academe can make a reasoned case for conservation of its lengthy menu of purposes and programs. Without access to deep pockets and with its monopoly loosening, however, priority should be to direct resources toward programs and services that can best meet public expectations of high quality. Limited resources and competition elevate the need for response and change. For example, just knowing that 80 percent of potential American college students are non-traditional (not campus residents, not ages 18–22) should signal a need to re-examine traditional educational arrangements (Stahl, 2001).

How does academic complexity play out in practical terms? Consider these questions. Is it appropriate to work toward quality assurance for the entire institution or for each of its many parts and processes? Which is more important – quality of process or quality of product? Is *quality* an average or should it be assessed department by department? Some institutions already have moved toward *branding* their roster of programs and services, allowing secondary programs to ride on the reputation of the high quality of a hallmarked program. The Wharton School (PA) has been accused of just that with a new initiative in California, Wharton West (Mangan, 2001).

Using a computer graphics analogy, any institution is in reality *animated* in *millions of colors*, but often it is sketched in charcoal black on white for the public. Quality assurance strategies can help strengthen an institution on its own terms; nevertheless, the external constituencies still want a simple bottom-line descriptor. Funding sources, the media, legislators, the public, and prospective students all love sound-bite summative assessments of institutional quality. The public preferences for information about institutions in higher education, if fulfilled, might look similar to the investment bond ratings: AAA, AA, . . . B, C, D . . .

Traditionally, institutions have rejected comparison ratings because of their very real differences growing out of their statements of mission, purposes, size, location, history, and governance. The Integrated Postsecondary Education Data System (IPEDS) information collected by the federal National Center for

Education Statistics (NCES) "consists of institution-level data that can be used to describe trends in postsecondary education at the institution, state and/or national levels" (National Center, 2001, on-line). Such a database is tempting to use for comparison rankings; nevertheless, institutional variations and local interpretations of the survey information requests make the voluntarily-supplied IPEDS data just quirky enough to negate its use in institutional comparison studies. As a consequence, to fill that information void, public constituencies have invented their own rating systems, often based on limited or erroneous data. Consider a list of the "Ten Best Party Schools in America" or the controversial annual ratings given colleges and universities by the *U.S. News and World Report*. In like fashion, *Asiaweek* magazine has been rating Asian universities for 20 years, using the criteria of fees, student-teacher ratios, salaries, faculty qualifications, and reputations (Cohen, 1999). Some institutions have objected to this. For instance, the top-ranked University of Tokyo was pulled from the *Asiaweek* survey process in 1999 because its president Hasumi Shigehiko said that education and research "cannot be compared with that of other universities ... Such characteristics are profoundly individual and extremely difficult to quantify" (Cohen, 1999, On-Line). However, lists of this sort are still influential.

A recent counter-trend to media rankings of academe is to develop nationally normed student surveys. These surveys developed by the Pew Forum on Undergraduate Education and the Carnegie Foundation for the Advancement of Teaching are designed to "assist students in choosing a college" (Selingo, 2001). (These two foundations have had long-standing, significant influence on changes in higher education; Mulhern, 2001). The National Survey of Student Engagement (NSSE) is a 40-question research instrument available to paying volunteer client institutions to help them determine how deeply involved their students are with their own educations (Pew Forum, 2000). Pew claims that the survey gauges the extent to which "colleges encourage actual learning" (Selingo, 2001) and results are publicized. Antioch College issued a press release celebrating its high scores on the 2000 NSSE ("Antioch receives some of highest marks in nation," 2001) and has placed its own results online (Antioch, 2001). Examples of other institutions releasing their NSSE results on their institutional websites include Macalester College (MN), University of Colorado-Boulder, and Longwood College (VA).

In 2002, 100 community colleges will participate in a similar Pew survey seen as "a potential alternative to college rankings" (Selingo, 2001). Academic libraries are working to develop a similar instrument, a nationally normed LIBQUAL+ survey (Cook, Heath, Thompson & Thompson, 2001). It remains to be seen whether these types of national survey instruments will be used to improve quality or to confirm reputations (and dodge media rankings). Critics will charge that the NSSE and the LIBQUAL+ survey questions are based on existing institutional practices, thus implying that traditional institutions (and services) are the gold standard for definitions of high quality.

The second constraining issue is the tension generated in these hard-working organizations as they decide whether to evolve proactive internally motivated quality assurance or to give priority to the pressure for externally driven strategies for quality assurance. Internal motivation to improve institutional quality is entangled with internal struggles for power, particularly when a clumsy move to improve and assure institutional quality by the president or academic dean results in an insulted faculty. The strongest external pressures are coming from regional agencies for institutional accreditation (by far) (Peterson & Augustine, 2000), federal and state government oversight agencies, legislative processes, and national policy think-tanks (like the Pew Trusts groups). These external pressures are easier for administrators to *sell* to internal factions on the basis of institution survival. The new president of Voorhees College in South Carolina, an institution on probation by SACS for poor quality distance-learning programs, will have no trouble instituting program quality-assurance (McMurtrie, 2001). Knowing that SACS has withdrawn accreditation from other members previously on probation and that unaccredited schools have closed is a powerful incentive to attend to increasing quality in existing programs.

A third constraining issue is the need to assign appropriate weights to problem-driven quality assurance (responding to problems as they emerge) versus theory-driven quality assurance (developing the highest impact factors with research-verified strategies). McDonald and Micikas (1994) assert that the theory knowledge base is too weak and broad to provide guidance on specific quality assurance strategies, other than to verify that attention to quality issues is found in the strongest and most effective organizations. Practically speaking, institutions are likely to first develop limited quality assurance strategies to address "active bleeders" such as poor student retention rates, union actions, or crumbling buildings and to counter the competition coming from post-secondary education alternatives.

As an example, in the early 1990s, Central State University in Ohio intentionally focused extensive campus resources and attention on the quality factor relating to intercollegiate athletics (one of three prestige builders cited in Goldman, Gates & Brewer, 2001). Having top-rated sports teams was selected as a high-priority strategy to attract potential students and donors to a very visible institution. The outcome was a nationally ranked football team and exciting public relations exposure; the unintended effect was that dorms and campus services deteriorated, leading the State of Ohio to require the university to reorder its resource priorities (and thus redefine its definition of institutional quality). Central State responded appropriately to this "problem-driven" crisis with increased attention to quality assurance issues in the areas of financial management, facilities maintenance, and resource allocation.

Keeping Up with Research and Theory

A fourth constraining factor related to quality assurance is the task of staying connected with the strong yet evolving theoretical basis for management planning. Steering institutions of higher education toward increasingly sophisticated institutional planning processes, fundamental to quality assurance, comes most directly from the regional accrediting agencies. NCA, for instance, has emphasized strategic planning since the early 1980s and has required a student learning assessment and planning process since 1995. These emphases were developed collaboratively with members to improve their educational effectiveness and institutional efficiencies in ways understood by their constituencies. The requirements for institutional accreditation also reflect very generally the best practices of institutions known to be thriving.

The strategies for quality assurance used by the regional accrediting agencies are not without critics. One example is conservative critic Jane Wellman (2000), senior associate with the Institute for Higher Education Policy, having researched and written extensively on accreditation issues for 20 years. Wellman argues that the traditional "wide range of commonly shared measures of quality, including the number of full-time faculty members, the amount of time that students are in class, and the size of the library" (On-Line) should not be abandoned in favor of learning-outcomes assessments. Wellman asserts that assessment and accountability are sufficiently different in concept that regional accreditors should develop "two types of evaluations – one for improvement within an institution and another for accountability to those outside that institution" (On-Line).

In the past decade, some institutions have engaged in internally driven, proactive planning to assure quality. They have tried out the various quality management strategies and models, yet (not unusual for education research) have inconclusive results (McDonald & Micikas, 1994). As mentioned, results of quality assurance in academe thus far are inconclusive and defy replication. Cameron (cited by McDonald & Micikas, 1994) summed up just why these quality assurance initiatives likely are so unsatisfying. Both the planners and the researchers make similar errors. Cameron notes that:

(1) Planners (and researchers) of quality assurance processes often select models and criteria arbitrarily, relying primarily on convenience.

(2) Indicators of effectiveness selected by planners or researchers are often too narrowly or too broadly defined, or they do not relate to organizational performance.

(3) Outcomes are the dominant type of criteria used to assess effectiveness, whereas effects [impacts] are most frequently used in policy decisions and by the public (1986, p. 30).

All three of Cameron's concerns relate to faulty quality assurance design, especially in the selection of factors seeming to impact quality.

Quality assurance processes in higher education must begin with identifying in detail the dynamics of factors at work in such targeted processes as student recruitment and retention or senior student placement. Further, fundamental questions need to be asked. Why are we doing this? Is there a better way? Assumptions and traditions must be examined. Choose any three factors from the list of a hundred campus topics (parking, retention, and morale, for example) and potential inter-relationships can be identified. Every factor exists on a continuum and varies by institution. Every factor on such a summary list affects the dynamics of institutional quality assurance.

Identifying the quality factors obviously in play in a particular institutional process may be easy but actually improving quality may require also seeking those factors flying "below the radar."

To illustrate a sub-radar quality factor in higher education, a small rural college may devote considerable effort and resources toward improving students' persistence with emphasis on such "best practices" as more financial aid, more tutoring options, improved housing, and astute faculty advising. Nevertheless, an important factor in retention of their students may relate more directly to how many students are recruited from a single high school and how many have cars. Cohort support and transportation home are significant factors in decisions to stay in that particular college.

TRENDS IN QUALITY ASSURANCE IN ACADEME

Higher education in general does present special challenges to quality assurance. Despite these challenges, some institutions have embraced quality assurance, and several trends have emerged from their experiences. These trends include niche marketing and alternative delivery systems as strategies to re-engineer higher education. There is also evidence of an increasing emphasis on tracking student learning achievement (steered by the regional accrediting agencies) and streamlining management and planning practices (interpreting business models such as the Baldrige Award, the Deming Award, and ISO 9000 registration).

Niche Marketing and Alternative Delivery Systems

Niche marketing and alternative delivery systems are prominent in the headlines of *The Chronicle of Higher Education*. Niche marketing describes the efforts of institutions to tailor their programs and services to a specific clientele. Privately-owned for-profit institutions such as the DeVry, Inc. have grown rapidly by using quality assurance feedback strategies to respond to the high employment demand for trained technical workers. DeVry, in particular, has been able design and implement academic programs quickly in response to emerging employer needs. Unlike traditional colleges or universities, it has a streamlined corporate structure, does not share decisions with faculty, hires practitioners rather than tenure-track faculty as instructors, and prunes unprofitable programs with impunity. Its focus is on planned growth and the corporate development of a standardized curriculum subject to modification to meet local employer needs (Borrego, 2001). Through these business-style methods of operation, DeVry is pioneering a new type of for-profit postsecondary education that poses a direct challenge to traditionally-governed non-profit institutions. In Ohio the DeVry Institute has aligned itself with 18 traditional private liberal arts colleges as an equal partner in a library shared computer catalog cooperative, Ohio Private Academic Libraries (OPAL), to bolster its library services through shared collections. It is building a reputation for successful job placement of its graduates that meets or exceeds the quality expectations of its increasing numbers of students. DeVry is building on this reputation by opening a group of graduate schools using the same business model (Borrego, 2001).

Distance education is an umbrella term encompassing the use of a variety of technologies and strategies to coordinate students with faculty across distance and time, even across international boundaries. Beyond audio or videotapes and cable television, distance education may use satellite transmission and Internet communication. In addition to alternative delivery, distance education is stimulating the development of alternative institutional structures. These include degree granting institutions offering only distance education (the University of Phoenix) as well as meta-institutions, granting degrees based on the combined selection of distance education courses from cooperating institutions. One example is the Great Plains Interactive Distance Education Alliance of six universities offering an online master's degree in family financial planning. (Carnevale, 2001).

Moving a step further away from traditional course-based higher education, Western Governors University (WGU) is a competency-based online university. "WGU was founded by the governors of several western states with a vision of making higher education more accessible and with degrees and certificates based on what a person actually knows and can demonstrate. By using information technologies to promote interstate cooperation between colleges and corporations, WGU distributes courses and programs to students wherever they are" (Western, 2001, On-Line).

A third type of alternative program in higher education is the addition of an entrepreneurial-style academic program to a traditional institution (such as the non-traditional degree completion program CLIMB at Wilberforce University in Ohio). Operating parallel to the traditional structure, such programs may hold classes only in the evenings or weekends, combine classroom and distance education, make extensive use of qualified non-tenure track practitioners as instructors, and use a uniform curriculum. In each case, these alternative delivery modes evolved from quality assurance mechanisms that identified unmet needs and unproductive service models at the local level. Ideally, quality assurance also will be a rigorous component in the operation of these newer education delivery methods.

Regional Accreditation Associations Increase the Pressure

The second trend evident in quality assurance is the incremental leverage being applied by regional accrediting agencies on their membership. These agencies, in turn, are reflecting the pressure for "a better product" coming from legislators and powerful foundation-led policy groups. All regional accreditors have embraced a requirement focusing attention on the quality of student learning. For example, in 1995 NCA added a requirement for planned assessment of student learning for the purpose of increasing student achievement, a quality assurance requirement. An exemplar of NCA's push toward quality assurance of student learning is Alverno College. Alverno engaged in an institution-wide effort to improve student learning and shared its experiences in the quality assurance process in a book-length case study (Mentkowski, 2000). Since overall response to the assessment of student learning has been uneven among NCA members, the agency staff, led by Cecilia Lopez, has issued several research papers and detailed guidelines to nudge members into line (North Central, 2001).

NCA received requests from a number of institutions for an accreditation process compatible with TQM and continuous quality improvement. In response, in 1999, NCA added an alternative route to accreditation called Academic

Quality Improvement Project (AQIP). It also issued guidelines demonstrating how AQIP was compatible with the Baldrige Award process. Institutions pioneering the Baldrige Award process are profiled as exemplars in *High Performing Colleges* (Seymour, 1996).

Inter-Institutional Cooperation

The third trend related to quality assurance is increasing productivity and efficiency through consortia, cooperatives, and sometimes, mergers. Where this cooperation to improve quality is driven by planning processes, more than just cash savings are at stake. An example is the development in Ohio of Ohio Private Academic Libraries (OPAL), a cooperative of 20 private colleges jointly owning a library computer system and employing necessary computer system personnel. The quality of library service offered in each of the participating small colleges increased greatly. Another example of cooperation involves joint degree programs in which students take courses from two different colleges with complementary strengths and receive two degrees upon completion of requirements. Articulation agreements also demonstrate intercollegiate coordination. Student learning increases, student career or education goals are met, and neither institution needs to develop extra cost-inefficient programs.

Very recent examples of inter-institutional cooperation relate to responding to the need for more K-12 teachers. Community colleges, taking advantage of their characteristic flexibility, have developed solutions to putting more students into the teacher training pipeline. This expansion in traditional mission fills a public need at a time when four-year teacher training institutions have limited enrollments and have placed other restrictions on their growth. In Maryland, community colleges now offer an associate of arts in teaching degree, coupled with a guaranteed full- credit transfer to a four-year institution (with a 2.75 GPA and a passing teacher test score). Other states have pushed further with their changes. Rio Salado College, a community college in Arizona, offers an online teacher preparation course to help those with bachelor's degrees gain certification. Pushing aside any curriculum restraints based on institutional type, Great Basin College, a community college in Nevada, offers a B.A. degree in teaching (Levinson, 2001).

International Standards

Finally, in a trend popular in Europe, educational institutions have followed closely the international development of corporate and international standards, designed to facilitate a confident global exchange of goods and services through uniform quality performance. Without reviewing the complex development and monitoring structure of the international standards, called ISO 9000, it suffices to say that it is functionally multi-level and international in scope. In 1992, the ISO 9002-4 standard was issued for quality assurance in service organizations, which could include a category in education. Since that time, a variety of organizations have applied ISO principles, which require thorough documentation of streamlined processes. Institutions have the option to enhance their reputation through official registration. Other organizations have selected ISO guidelines to use in conjunction with locally developed quality assurance strategies (Pricewaterhouse Coopers, 2001).

The quality assurance strategies just mentioned are not the only ones attracting attention in higher education. The University of Dayton is known to be exploring the Balanced Scorecard. Other quality assurance models in use in Europe include Investments in People and Charter Mark. In the United Kingdom public institutions are using the European Foundation for Quality Management (EFQM) Excellence Model (Pricewaterhouse Coopers, 2001). This EFQM Excellence Model is viewed as a comprehensive and rigorous quality model and can be used either as a diagnostic self-assessment tool or to develop submissions for regional, national and European quality awards. The key principles or 'core values' for success are: leadership and consistency of purpose, people development, involvement and satisfaction, customer focus, supplier partnerships, processes and measurement, continuous improvement and innovation, public responsibility and results orientation. The EFQM Excellence Model divides the principles into *enablers* and *results* and each principle is weighted differently (Pricewaterhouse Coopers, 2001).

Use of Multiple Quality Assurance Strategies

Collaborating authors Izadi, Kashef and Stadt (1996) critiqued the usefulness in higher education of the three most prominent paradigms for quality assurance. They concluded as follows:

> Globalization of markets, heightened quality requirements, tough competition, and supplier pressures have led to three parallel and visible quality thrusts nationally and internationally. These thrusts are the Malcolm Baldrige National Quality Award in the United States, the Deming Application Prize in Japan (currently open to other countries), and ISO 9000 Registration, which originated in Europe and has expanded internationally.
>
> While ISO 9000 and MBNQA require support and some involvement by senior administration, the Deming Prize initiative requires substantial commitment of personal time and resources of senior administrators in implementing a quality system. In the latter initiative, quality cannot be just another aspect of business; it must become the way business is

conducted. These awards and preparation to achieve them support the broader goal of TQM. Many times, organizations apply for two or all three in order to achieve the highest degree of TQM (Izadi et al., 1996, On-line).

Izadi and his colleagues drew specific strengths from each of the three awards for application to quality improvement in higher education. They found the Baldrige process most promising for use in customer satisfaction and student retention. Deming was strong in statistical measures that could effectively track enrollment patterns, student progress, employee and faculty performance, recruitment and retention activities. The ISO 9000 emphasis on documentation and process analysis was helpful in curriculum, program, and facilities analysis (Izadi et al., 1996, On-line). NCA's accommodation of institutions following the Baldrige Award Criteria for Education (North Central, 2001) along with the AQIP accreditation process signals the likely trend of integrating multiple quality assurance models for a customized institution approach.

CONCLUSIONS

Two conclusions emerge from the recent experience of the academy with quality assurance. One is that, however higher education is delivered, those entities having success will be attentive to quality assurance based on self-monitoring against their own definitions of high standards. The second is that, because the delivery of postsecondary education is not monolithic and there is a public trust involved, there always will be oversight, trying to define quality and evaluate providers against general quality criteria (however defined).

Institutions Setting Internal Standards Will Thrive

Proponents of quality assurance are continuing their advocacy through research and practice. Some are leading traditional institutions of higher education; others are cheerleading for better postsecondary education practice or alternatives. Some try limited demonstrations of quality assurance management within a single department; others have led implementation in administrative areas only (Izadi et al., 1996). The current approaches to quality assurance do enable institution leaders to set the general tone and to "bundle" a variety of interpretations of quality assurance within an institution.

At the beginning of this new century, we are seeing a convergence of accreditation requirements for quality control, public expectations for accountability, emerging competitive alternatives, and government mandates. The setting for this convergence is not just the United States but the world. Those institutions that are able to achieve internal support for systems of quality assurance are likely to surge ahead of the pack in the race for students and dollars, particularly if they base changes on information provided by self-assessment and quality assurance processes. These same institutions, however, may not win also immediate high standing on traditional academic reputation lists where older definitions of quality will prevail (Keith, 2001).

Rather than relying on external models or benchmarking for direct imitation, quality assurance processes increase the advantage of an entity's own mix of unique factors. What one institution determines will thrust it ahead to meet a specified challenge might not be effective for another institution. The quality assurance approaches represented by learning assessment, Deming's TQM, Baldrige, or ISO 9000 (singly and in combination) can identify ways to strengthen an institution's competitive qualities. While some general *best practices* may emerge, institutions making internally informed decisions about how best to achieve their unique missions and purposes in unique environments will make the more exciting progress. They will proactively control their organizations for effectiveness and efficiency by coordinating, refining, and changing how they conduct higher education on their own terms. The emphasis is moving from effectiveness measurement toward effectiveness control.

Oversight Will Continue Apply Externally Set Criteria

Oversight agencies will be charged with interpreting performance in higher education to the general public. This oversight may come from the current accrediting agencies, education research foundations, commercial accrediting organizations, and government education offices although their oversight roles and activities will likely change as quality assurance evolves.

The future of traditional accrediting agencies is tied to trends in quality assurance. For over 100 years, membership-driven institutional accreditation agencies have been operating in the United States. By setting standards of operation, often using research results provided by the Carnegie Foundation, these agencies have been charged with discrediting diploma mills and helping colleges and universities strengthen their operations and programs. Lately, accrediting agencies also have been responding to changes in the national and global environment. They mounted a defense of traditional academe by adjusting and tightening their own criteria and processes and by inviting more public participation and understanding of accreditation processes. Accrediting agencies have addressed distance education, which crosses agency boundaries, by working together to produce cooperative guidelines. They expect their members to have fair policies dealing will many issues ranging from accommodation of those with disabilities to intellectual property rights (NCA, 2001, On-line).

Institutions running "tight ships" according to their own locally-developed quality assurance processes are much less likely to experience difficulty meeting regional accreditation expectations.

Transnational education is the latest challenge to intercollegiate quality assurance. Any standards developed in the United States would not necessarily be compatible with those of other countries. For example, most challenging will be issues of academic freedom, certainly not a uniform world concept. One alternative for assuring quality in international programs is through the United Nations or the World Trade Organization, which has issued a controversial draft policy concerning regulation of transnational education as an international commodity (Altbach, 2001).

A side issue in quality assurance of international initiatives in higher education is the controversy surrounding the formation of the Global Alliance for Transnational Education (GATE). An unknown number of unaccredited American educational institutions and businesses are offering distance education courses (and degrees) to international students. At the same time, American students are enrolling in educational programs offered through distance education by colleges, universities, and businesses in other countries. While American regional accrediting bodies are working together to evaluate their members' distance education programs which cross agency boundaries, they do not have oversight for institutions which eschew their services or for courses from other countries. To fill this quality assurance gap, Jones International Ltd., a commercial enterprise, formed GATE, a new international accreditation coordinating agency, which the founders describe as:

> dedicated to fostering access to quality higher education resources on a global basis, focusing on transnational education. Committed to developing and promoting transnational education as a viable means of delivering education to the world population, GATE plans to involve country accreditation bodies, college and university bodies, commercial institutions, multi-national corporations, and government agencies to face the challenge of evaluating degree programs and other academic standards from countries around the world. GATE is dedicated to identifying and disseminating these standards (GATE, 2001).

Although Jones International Ltd. formed GATE to address the pressing need to assure the quality of the burgeoning international education market, its commercial ties and the perceived conflict of interest with its own international distance education enterprise have crippled its efforts. Whether GATE is the answer or not, transnational higher education quality assurance certainly multiplies by several factors the challenges to quality assurance in American higher education.

Opponents of the quality assurance movement who stand behind the protective cloak of tradition, chanting "academe is not a business" miss the point. As John

Adams indicated, "All that part of Creation that lies within our observation is liable to change" (McCullough, 2001). Institutions of higher education can, do, and will change and not always for the better. Indifference to quality assurance likely will lead to some unnecessary negative outcomes for institutions or their stakeholders. Institutions could falter by simply ignoring their competition. Change, not quality assurance, is the real challenge. Fortunately for librarians, responding to change has become an attribute of the profession. Librarians are experienced change agents, able to advocate effectively on behalf of their clients for improved services and to interpret improved services to their clients. Reading the situation bifocally (ie. with a dual focus), librarians are intent on improving and assuring the quality of their traditional and neo-traditional (virtual) services while also shaping the vertical learning/teaching environments. They can make sure that the academic library (defined locally) is directly aligned with the local mission and strategies even when that means that the local library and its services become different from peer libraries. Quality assurance aims for enhanced success (however defined) by facilitating institution-specific responses to inevitable change in our complex, competitive global environment of higher education.

REFERENCES

Altbach, P. G. (2001). Why higher education is not a global commodity. *The Chronicle of Higher Education, 47*(35), B20.

Antioch College NSSE 2000 report (2001). [On-Line]. Antioch College. Available: http://www.antioch-college.edu/NSSE/nsse_report.html [2001, July 25].

Antioch receives some of highest marks in nation (2001, July 26). *Xenia Daily Gazette*, pp. 5B.

Borrego, A. M. (2001). The duo that leads DeVry: Different as they are, Dennis Keller and Ron Taylor share a vision for their thriving company. *The Chronicle of Higher Education, 47*(2), June 29.

Brubacher, J. S., & Rudy, W. (1997). *Higher education in transition: A history of American colleges and universities* (4th ed.). New Brunswick, NJ: Transaction.

Callan, P. (2001). Rating the states: On higher education [On-line]. Available: http://www.highereducation.org/commentary/ratingthestates.shtml (2001, Nov. 1).

Carnevale, D. (2001). Universities cross state lines for online degree. *The Chronicle of Higher Education, 47*(27, March 16), A38.

Cohen, D. (1999). Magazine's rankings of Asian universities are popular with readers, not academics, [On-Line]. The Chronicle of Higher Education. Available: http://www.chronicle.com [2001, July 25].

Connell, C. (2001, January). Grades that get attention (On-line). *Trust Magazine, 4*(1)(winter). Available: http://www.pewtrusts.org/pubs/

Cook, C., Heath, F., Thompson, B., & Thompson, R. (2001). The search for new measures: The ARL LIBQUAL+ project – a preliminary report. *Portal: Libraries and the Academy, 1*(1), 103–112.

Council for Higher Education Accreditation (CHEA). (2001). [On-Line]. Available: http://www.chea.org [2001, July 19].

Deming, W. E. (1982). *Quality, productivity, and competitive position.* Cambridge, MA: Massachusetts Institute of Technology, Center for Advanced Engineering Study.

Ewell, P. (2000) Grading Student Learning: Better Luck Next Time [On-Line]. National Policy Center for Public Policy and Higher Education. Available: http://measuringup2000. highereducation.org/PeterEwell.cfm [2001, July 25]

Global Accreditation for Transnational Education (GATE) (2001). [On-Line]. Jones International, Ltd. Available: http://www.edugate.org [2001, July 15].

Goldman, C. A., Gates, S. M., & Brewer, D. J. (2001). Prestige or reputation: Which is a sound investment? *The Chronicle of Higher Education, 48*(6), B13–B15. [Article adapted from In Pursuit of Prestige: Strategy and Competition in U.S. Higher Education. (2001). Transaction Pub.]

Hebel, S. (2001). Public colleges feel impact of the economic downturn. *The Chronicle of Higher Education, 47*(45), A21–A22.

Institute for Telecommunication Sciences, United State Department of Commerce (2001). Quality assurance, [On-Line]. Available: http://www.its.bldrdoc.gov/fs-1037/dir-029/_4291.htm [2001, July 20].

Izadi, M., Kashef, A. E., & Stadt, R. W. (1996). Quality in higher education: Lessons learned from the Baldrige Award, Deming prize, and ISO 9000 registration. *Journal of Industrial Teacher Education, 33*(2), 60–76.

Jauch, L. R., & Orwig, R. A. (1997). A violation of assumptions: Why TQM won't work in the ivory tower. *Journal of Quality Management, 2*(2), 279–292.

Keith, B. (2001). Organizational contexts and university performance outcomes. *Research in Higher Education, 42*(5), 493–516.

Levinson, A. (2001). Two-year colleges to train teachers. *Dayton Daily News,* August 1, p. 4A.

Lysons, A., Hatherly, D., & Mitchell, D. A. (1998). Comparison of measures of organisational effectiveness in U.K. higher education. *Higher Education, 36,* 1–19.

McCullough, D. (2001). *John Adams.* New York: Simon & Schuster.

McMurtrie, B. (2001). Accreditor cites auditing problems in criticism of 2 Louisiana universities. *The Chronicle of Higher Education, 47*(44), A26.

Mangan, K. S. (2001). Top business schools try collaboration over competition. *The Chronicle of Higher Education, 47*(43), A23–A24.

Mentkowski, M. (2000). *Learning that lasts: Integrating learning, development, and performance in college and beyond.* San Francisco: Jossey-Bass.

Mulhern, J. (2001). Liberal arts college libraries and the quest for the grail of library goodness: A literature review (Unpublished Paper). Dayton, OH: University of Dayton.

Mullin, R. F., & Wilson, G. W. (1998). A violation of assumptions about TQM: A response to Jauch And Orwig. *Journal of Quality Management, 3*(2), 293–308.

National Center for Education Statistics (2001). About IPEDS, [On-Line]. NCES. Available: http://nces.ed.gov/ipeds/AboutIPEDS.html [2001, July 29].

National Center for Public Policy and Higher Education. (2000). Measuring Up 2000 [On-line]. Available: http://measuringup2000.highereducation.org/ (2001, Nov. 1).

North Central Association of Colleges and Schools, Council on Institutions of Higher Education (1997). *Handbook of Accreditation* (2nd ed.). Chicago: NCA-CIHE.

North Central Association of Colleges and Schools, Higher Learning Commission. (2001). [On-Line]. Association website. Available: http://www.ncahigherlearningcommission.org [2001, July 18].

North Central Association of Colleges and Schools, Higher Learning Commission (2001). [On-Line]. AQIP. Available: http://www.AQIP.org/AQIPparticipants.html [2001, Nov. 1].

Peterson, M. W., & Augustine, C. H. (2000). External and internal influences on institutional approaches to student assessment: Accountability or improvement. *Research in Higher Education, 41*(3), 443–479.

Pew Forum on Undergraduate Learning, the Carnegie Foundation for the Advancement of Teaching (2000). National survey of student engagement: The college student report, September 2000, [On-Line]. Available: http://www.pewtrusts.org/pdf/edu_student_engagement.pdf [2001, July 25].

Pew Trusts (2001). Publications of the Center For Higher Education Policy Analysis, [On-Line]. Available: http://www.pewtrusts.org [2001, July 29].

Pricewaterhouse Coopers (2001). EFQM excellence model, [On-Line]. Available: http://www.excelsior. pwcglobal.com/tools/efqm/efqm.htm [2001, July 27].

Procter & Gamble (2001). [On-line]. Available: http://www.pg.com/news/sectionmain.jhtml [2001, July 27]

Selingo, J. (2001, July 23). Survey of community-college students aims to gauge institutional quality, [On-Line]. The Chronicle of Higher Education. Available: http://www.chronicle.com [2001, July 24].

Seymour, D. (1996). *High performing colleges: The Malcolm Baldrige national quality award as a framework for improving higher education* (Vol. II: Case and Practice). Maryville, MO: Prescott.

Spangehl, S. D. (2001). Some words about the word quality [On-line]. AQIP, NCA-HLC. Available: http://www.AQIP.org/AQIPparticipants.html (2001, November 1).

Stahl, L. (2001). Sixty Minutes [television show]. CBS Television Network (viewed July 29, 7–7:15 p.m.).

Suggs, W. (2001). College presidents urged to take control of college sports. *The Chronicle of Higher Education, 47*(43), A35–A36.

U.S. Department of Education (2001). Student Guide, 2000–01, Important Terms [On-line]. Available: http://www.ed.gov/prog_info/SFA/StudentGuide/2000-1/terms.html (2001, Nov. 1).

Western Governors University (2001) About WGU (On-Line). Available: http://www.wgu.edu/wgu/about/index.html (2001, Nov. 1).

A MODEL TO INCREASE THE EFFECTIVENESS OF UNDERGRADUATE INTERNET USE: THE HAMPTON UNIVERSITY EXPERIENCE

Anne Pierce

There is little research to tell us who may or may not use the Internet success-fully in the process of instruction (Poole, 2000). Identified here are the relationships between the availability of sources of information to support the preparation of preservice teachers on the Hampton University campus, and undergraduate's self-efficacy for instructional and research activities conducted through the Internet, specifically in an introductory course using the Blackboard web-based courseware environment.

The premise for the described study comes from Albert Bandura's definition of self-efficacy: "people's judgements of their capabilities to organize and execute courses of action required to attain designated types of performances" (Bandura, 1986, p. 391). By drawing on symbolic capabilities, people can comprehend their environment, construct guides for action, solve problems cognitively, support thoughtful courses of action, gain new knowledge by reflec-tion, and communicate with others at any distance in time and space. Bandura (1986) identified four sources of information in learning environments that participants use to judge self-efficacy: previous experience through performance exposure and self-instructed performance; vicarious learning through live or symbolic modeling; verbal persuasion through suggestion, exhortation, or

Advances in Library Administration and Organization, Volume 19, pages 165–170.
Copyright © 2002 by Elsevier Science Ltd.
All rights of reproduction in any form reserved.
ISBN: 0-7623-0868-0

interpretation; and physiological arousal, which contributes to strength and vulnerability (p. 126).

The author delivers instruction with Blackboard in the Foundations of Education (FE) course, an introductory course offered nationwide, which students in any major must pass in order to proceed through the Education Department's degree programs. At Hampton University students may choose between off-line and on-line versions of this course taught by different instructors. Some of the text's (McNergney & Herbert, 2000) accompanying web-based materials have been uploaded to Blackboard along with other resources that students will be using throughout the course. Students are allowed to pace their reading and assessment through online quizzes and can be fairly self directed as to how they attack the assignments which have a specific assessment rubric. While individual achievement is as important as group work, this course emphasizes the best characteristics of inquiry based learning: (1) involvement of students in instructional activities both online and on campus; (2) presentation of key questions through three strategies – identification, clarification, and interpretation of data; (3) activation of prior knowledge through group discussion; and (4) identification of sources of information available to support exploration of solutions.

A model (Fig. 1) has emerged to increase the effectiveness of Hampton University undergraduate Internet use in on-line classroom instruction and research required for those classes. This model attempts to distinguish how the quality of teaching and learning changes with the use of Internet resources due to the significant differences in computer self-efficacy between science and nonscience majors and the unique characteristics of the Web: interactivity, immediacy, networkability, information quality, and directness; and the web-based Blackboard environment in which activities occur.

The model visualized in Fig. 1. requires understanding the fundamental differences between learners. The instructor needs to understand that undergraduates in science and nonscience academic majors relate to sources of information differently (Shatkin, 1998). In Table 1 science majors have been shown to exhibit higher levels of manual dexterity and three-dimensional visualization. They work well under pressure, like to organize objects and know how things work. Science majors plan how they work, in essence they form a system. These characteristics shape beliefs about a student's own ability to perform a task on the Internet – their computer efficacy beliefs which determine the behaviors that result in successful outcomes.

Bandura (1986) indicates that efficacy beliefs have three dimensions: generality, strength, and magnitude. When using the Internet these are manifested as:

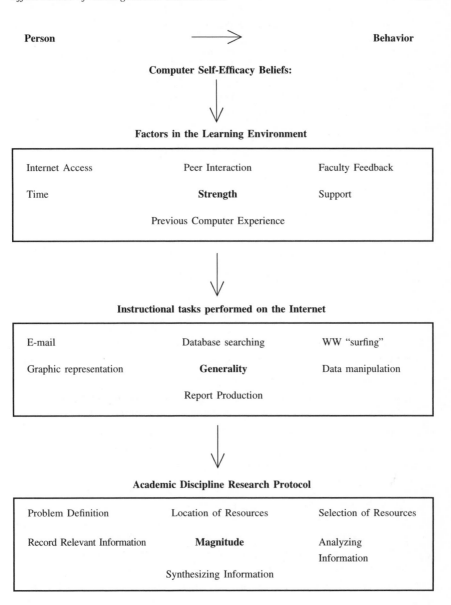

Fig. 1. Model of the Impact of Undergraduate Computer Self-efficacy on Blackboard-Based Instruction.

Table 1. Sample Description Statistics ($n = 30$).

	Science Major			Non-Science Major		
	L/H	M	SD	L/H	M	SD
Total Learning Environment	26/56	41.25	6.48	26/56	41.40	6.08
Hours spent	1/5	3.41	1.23	1/5	3.41	1.28
Exhibit Manual Dexterity	1/5	3.98	0.91	1/5	3.70	1.27
Exhibit 3-dimensional Visualization	1/5	4.00	0.96	1/5	3.55	1.29
Work Well Under Pressure	1/5	3.89	1.14	1/5	3.86	1.24
Like To Know How Things Work	1/5	4.18	1.12	1/5	4.16	1.09
Like To Organize Objects	1/5	4.25	0.83	1/5	4.00	1.16
Like to Plan How to Perform Activities	1/5	4.04	1.08	1/5	4.04	1.14
Like To Develop A System For Performing An Activity	1/5	4.02	1.03	1/5	3.82	1.17
Recover From Errors Easily	1/5	3.54	1.13	1/5	3.38	1.22

Abreviations: L/H = Low/High Score; M = Mean; SD = standard deviation.
Scale: 1 = Strongly Disagree 2 = Slightly Disagree 3 = Disagree 4 = Agree 5 = Strongly Agree.

- Generality – the ability to apply one set of skills in a similar context. If a student successfully e-mails they will be successful in a threaded discussion.

- Strength – the belief that a task can be successfully performed due to previous experience. If a student has successfully produced the information they sought on the World Wide Web, they will use the same search strategy again.

- Magnitude – The number of steps the student believes they will need to perform successfully to find the answer. If the student feels confident that they have defined the problem appropriately, they will believe that fewer steps are required to find a solution.

The author investigated the sources of information in the learning environment, the academic discipline, and the Internet tasks themselves that may shape computer efficacy beliefs and learner success (Table 2) With the lack of visual and verbal cues in the learning environment, organizational issues preoccupy students. They resist the idea that the class does not physically meet, that they must use a "professional" or standard university e-mail account, and that they must question directions which may not be very explicit. Consequently, students need more time to organize themselves to complete group assignments.

It was not anticipated that students would find focusing on the computer screen for reading tedious, either because the screen was not lit correctly or

Table 2. Sample Computer Self-efficacy Statistics (*n* = 30).

	Science Major			Non-Science Major		
	L/H	M	SD	L/H	M	SD
Total Computer Self-efficacy	30/143	82.82	27.54	30/143	75.02	25.22
Total Conversation Self-efficacy	7/40	28.55	7.21	8/40	25.99	8.54
email self-efficacy	1/5	4.61	0.80	1/5	4.28	1.24
thread self-efficacy	1/5	3.17	1.46	1/5	2.98	1.53
filter self-efficacy	1/5	3.24	1.50	1/5	3.34	1.55
address self-efficacy	1/5	4.01	1.16	1/5	3.81	1.45
attachment self-efficacy	1/5	4.02	1.32	1/5	3.44	1.54
mailgroup self-efficacy	1/5	3.03	1.59	1/5	2.83	1.62
chat self-efficacy	1/5	3.24	1.59	1/5	2.58	1.67
Total Data Creation Self-efficacy	8/35	17.32	7.48	8/35	16.02	5.42
Total Data Conversion Self-efficacy	8/40	22.91	12.21	8/40	20.04	11.36
Total Data Distribution Self-efficacy	6/30	14.03	7.91	6/30	13.83	7.20

Abreviations: L/H = Low/High Score; M = Mean; SD = standard deviation.
Scale: 1 = Strongly Disagree 2 = Slightly Disagree 3 = Disagree 4 = Agree 5 = Strongly Agree.

because they are not accustomed to maintaining one physical position for an extended period of time. FE texts are in the traditional printed form, however ancillary readings and graphics were available online and therefore students spent time printing them out. The FE course allows the student much freedom to choose the study strategy they will pursue. While it was hoped that a student moderator would take control of the class threaded discussions, providing the intellectual impetus and ideological framework (Tagg, 1994) from which peer interaction would progress, this did not happen. Assessment criteria and faculty feedback, regardless of major seem to be the most important.

Second in importance is the student's technical proficiency with the task to be performed. While the same faculty member does not usually offer both a content course and computer instruction, they rapidly judge a student's proficiency based on written assignments and recommend tutoring or suggest a software package that will increase the student's ability to research and write papers. In FE, without exception, when each assignment is given, students need to be reminded to bookmark web pages. E-mail is the easiest for all majors, uploading and downloading attachments more difficult for nonscience majors and manipulating data received from another researcher seems the most difficult for all majors. Students seem to be less willing to critically review each other's work so that they will not be viewed as rude or disrespectful. While a command of factual information is required for threaded discussions, the expression of opinion was more lively where controversial U.S. Supreme Court cases were referenced.

Finally the discipline's research protocol, passed from faculty member to student, has a decided influence on the successful outcome for each major. Science majors have little trouble defining the problem to be solved, recording the relevant data on a spreadsheet or representing it graphically; the generality dimension is evident. However, nonscience majors exhibit strength dimensions as they draw on prior experience to experiment in the location of resources as supporting evidence and are more thoughtful in their selection of the most useful resources. Analysis and synthesis of the selected information is still a challenge for both majors indicating the small magnitude of their computer efficacy.

When the idea of taking an on-line course is initially introduced with under-graduates there are two reactions: "This will be easy because I won't have to go to class"; or "I'm not getting my money's worth because you won't physically be in class with me every class meeting". The students soon realize that the on-line course requires 40% more work because no single source of information limits their search for solutions and they have to take time to write clearly in order to be understood. They are not simply reacting to knowledge, they are constructing it.

REFERENCES

Bandura, A. (1986). The explanatory and predictive scope of self-efficacy theory. Special issue: Self-efficacy theory in contemporary psychology. *Journal of Social and Clinical Psychology, 4*, 359–373.

McNergney, R. F., & Herbert, J. (2000). *Foundations of Education*. NY: Allyn and Bacon.

Poole, D. M. (2000). Student Participation in a Discussion-oriented Online Course:a case study. *Journal of Research on Computing in Education, 33*(2), 162–178.

Shatkin, L. (1998). Differentiating characteristics of college majors. Princeton, NJ: Educational Testing Service (http://www.ets.org/research).

Tagg, A. C. (1994). Leadership from within: student moderation of computer conferences. *The American Journal of Distance Education, 8*(3), 40–50.

UNDERGRADUATES, INSTITUTION TYPE, AND LIBRARY USE: IMPACT AND INSIGHT FROM THE OHIOLINK EXPERIENCE

Kathy Schulz

A number of previous articles have described the creation and success of OhioLINK, Ohio's consortial system of academic libraries (Hirshon, 1995; Kohl, 1994, 1997, 1998; O'Connor et al., 1995; Sanville, 1995a, b; Sessions et al., 1995). However, many of these articles were written in the early days of OhioLINK prior to growth and composition changes that have since occurred. Originally established for the state's public institutions, OhioLINK in its early years was dominated by large universities. Nine universities participated in the launching of patron-initiated borrowing in early 1994; other universities and two-year schools were soon added. Private institutions were first permitted to join in 1996. Because private colleges had no unified statewide administration and no public funds, they joined in a slow trickle over several years as their individual budgets and conditions allowed. These nonpublic institutions had a choice between two avenues toward OhioLINK membership: some joined through direct memberships, others banded together to form sub-consortia in order to join OhioLINK as unified groups. There are two such sub-consortia within OhioLINK: Consort, composed of four schools, joined OhioLINK in late 1996, and OPAL, composed of seventeen schools, joined at the start of 1999. In between these dates many other private colleges joined as single entities. (Throughout the remainder of this article the terms "direct member colleges" and "sub-consortial" will be used to distinguish between these two types of

Advances in Library Administration and Organization, Volume 19, pages 171–190.
Copyright © 2002 by Elsevier Science Ltd.
All rights of reproduction in any form reserved.
ISBN: 0-7623-0868-0

membership. "Private colleges" will denote all nonpublic schools regardless of membership type.)

Nineteen ninety-nine was a watershed year for OhioLINK. With the addition of OPAL, OhioLINK was nearing maturity from the standpoint of membership with thirty-five public institutions and thirty-four private colleges. The OPAL influx marked the point at which the vast majority of Ohio's institutions of higher education had become members, leaving only a very few schools that could potentially be added in future. Adding the private colleges increased the size of OhioLINK, but perhaps more important was the fact that these additions were gradually changing OhioLINK's population mix in terms of graduate students, undergraduates, and faculty. Each of the private colleges is either exclusively or predominately a four-year institution, and though each may be small, as a group, private colleges introduced a significant number of undergraduates into the OhioLINK community. During 1999 OhioLINK patron types were apportioned as shown in Table 1.

OhioLINK currently offers a wide range of electronic resources and services to its members, but its core feature has always been the Central Catalog, an integrated catalog combining the holdings records of all its member schools. Patrons may place electronic requests for items in this catalog; a delivery system is in place to promptly fill such requests. Snapshot data from 1999 indicated that at that time there were more than twenty-one million items in the Central Catalog representing seven million unique titles. All types of library holdings typically display in the Central Catalog, though in 1999 only books were available for OhioLINK circulation (media materials and microform have since been added as eligible categories). There were 480,282 OhioLINK interlibrary transactions generated in 1999.

The specific goals of this study were to assess OhioLINK book borrowing patterns resulting from the newly altered 1999 population mix and to gain knowledge about undergraduates' use of the system. The findings, however, yield further insights into undergraduates' library habits in general. This broader view was a natural outgrowth of the investigation, particularly because Ohio, with its many universities, colleges, and two-year schools joined in a single

Table 1. OhioLINK Student Population, 1999.

	No.	Undergraduate	%	Graduate	%	TOTAL
University	18	217,841	84.0	41,772	16.1	259,613
Two Year	17	67,063	100	0	0	67,063
College	34	58,928	89.3	7,033	10.7	65,961
TOTAL	69	343,832	87.6	48,805	12.4	392,637

system that facilitates coordinated data gathering, offers a unique opportunity to study students' library use.

Prior to the present study, Ohio librarians had anecdotal evidence and conjecture concerning undergraduates' need for the OhioLINK book distribution system but limited empirical data to back up their beliefs. There had been uncertainty about the role to be played in OhioLINK by undergraduates and, by extension, by the four-year schools. When OhioLINK was originally conceived, some individuals reasoned that the libraries of smaller schools would be dwarfed by large research libraries and would, therefore, offer little of substance to the Central Catalog. Those who held this view assumed that students and faculty at the smaller schools were likely to create a drain on the proposed statewide resource sharing system. These fears soon proved to be unfounded, as private colleges generally became net lenders into the system. This circumstance was driven by at least two factors: (1) Most private colleges, particularly those which joined early, held a wealth of unique library resources that were in fact very beneficial additions to the Central Catalog. (2) These materials were attractive to graduate students and faculty, many of whom were at the large research universities. This scholarly group tends to conduct library research and use OhioLINK at a much higher rate than do typical undergraduates; thus the flow of books tended to go from small schools, dominated by undergraduates, to big universities, where more scholars worked and studied. To their credit, some of the wiser minds influential in developing OhioLINK had predicted this pattern all along.

This imbalance eventually became part of a larger general concern over lending equity throughout OhioLINK prompting a lending algorithm to be instituted in 1997. When an OhioLINK user places a book request there are often several institutions that could potentially supply the title. In most cases the requester is not given the opportunity to select the supplying school; instead, a computer-driven algorithm now dictates which library will be tapped to lend the item. This algorithm employs a priority system based on the number of previous requests emanating from that school; the more items the patrons of an individual school request, the more that school is asked to supply. The goal, approached but never fully achieved, is to get each school to a 1:1 lending to borrowing ratio. At the time of the present study, which was conducted using 1999 data, this algorithm system was in place; the findings thus need to be viewed with this understanding.

LITERATURE REVIEW

As indicated above, various articles have been written that describe OhioLINK; additional articles exist describing other state consortial systems. However, as the phenomenon of patron-initiated borrowing within a statewide system is still relatively recent, there is a paucity of articles offering deeper analysis. A notable exception is work done by Prabha et al. (1998). Their research on the characteristics of books requested via OhioLINK was influential to the present study and will be referred to later in this paper. Also interesting is work done by Henderson (2000) which measures interlibrary borrowing rates of ARL libraries against collection size in order to compute a "Collection Failure Quotient." Though pertinent to the present study, Henderson's word choice is telling: he views interlibrary borrowing as a failure, not an opportunity, and argues for the comprehensive collection instead of mere access. These views are inimical to the OhioLINK way of thinking, where resource sharing is the raison d'etre and even the term "interlibrary loan" has been banished from the lexicon as non-applicable to the use of resources from a combined Central Catalog.[1]

Other germane articles do not deal specifically with patron-initiated borrowing but with undergraduate use of library material in general. Unfortunately, a number of these studies are quite dated; the most recent such work located was done by Mays (1986). Mays' study was conducted in Australia where conditions may differ from those in the United States; however, his research was influenced by the earlier American studies which he very helpfully and succinctly summarizes. Interestingly, most of these studies, as well as Mays' own work, yield the conclusion that undergraduates have only a weak reliance on their library collections and that their use of library materials has little relation to their academic success. By contrast, Mays further points out that undergraduates do value the library as a place and that its "study hall" function should not be overlooked when formulating library mission and services.

While these previous studies on undergraduate library use helped form a starting point for the present research, they have limited relevance for institutions other than those where the research was conducted. This is especially true when different types of schools are involved. This paper will show that undergraduate library habits can differ markedly from school to school so that librarians must use caution when attempting to draw universal conclusions about them.

OHIOLINK BOOK MOVEMENT PATTERNS

The first step in this multi-part study was the examination of data on book movement between all institution types within OhioLINK during calendar year 1999. To accomplish this, statistics on the OhioLINK lending and borrowing of each individual school needed to be coded as to school type and then totaled. Additionally, book movement data was acquired from Consort and OPAL, the two sub-consortia within OhioLINK. These sub-consortia are organized to facilitate two levels of book movement: one for items borrowed within a sub-consortium, a second for items borrowed from the regular OhioLINK Central Catalog. The same delivery system is used for both types of transactions. The opportunity to borrow on a sub-consortial track lessens the likelihood that library users will make requests from the full Central Catalog; moreover, in the end, transactions from either the OhioLINK Central Catalog or from the sub-consortium are "extra-library" and appear to be similar, if not identical, to the requester. Thus the author decided that data from Consort and OPAL should be included with the regular OhioLINK book movement data and considered part of the same unified picture.

Table 2 contains a summary of 1999 holdings and overall lending patterns. This book movement is not completely laissez faire but is influenced by the lending algorithm previously described; the reader is further reminded that sub-consortial data is included in Table 2. With those caveats in mind, note that colleges and two-year schools both lent their holdings in greater proportion than expected from their existence in the Central Catalog. Additionally, both of these institution types achieved a fairly high OhioLINK circulation rate, sending close to 4% of their holdings out to the system compared with the 2.2% supplied by universities. Two-year schools circulate a very impressive amount of material given the relatively slight holdings they contribute to the Central Catalog. Colleges are able to achieve a similar circulation rate due, in part, to the existence of the two sub-consortia within their ranks. Participation in the extra track of either Consort or OPAL helps to maximize the efficiency of the OhioLINK distribution system for those colleges who are members of one of these two-track systems.

Table 2 can be viewed as the supply side of 1999 OhioLINK book movement; Table 3 represents the demand side, showing data on the people/transaction portion of that year's OhioLINK activity. Unlike the supply side of the lending/borrowing equation, the demand side is unaffected by the algorithm; thus Table 3 gives an unmodulated view of requesting patterns. Note that universities request about what would be expected from their representation in the system; two-year schools, somewhat less; colleges, more.

Table 2. OhioLINK Library Holdings and Lending, 1999.

	% Bib records	% of all items lent	% of local holdings lent
University	73.6	63.1	2.2
Two Year	3.5	5.3	3.9
College	20.6	31.2	3.8
*CRL	2.4	0.4	0.4

* Center for Research Libraries, a scholarly book repository with no associated student body.

Table 3. OhioLINK Student Population and Borrowing, 1999.

	% FTE (all types)	% books borrowed	Books borrowed/FTE
University	66.1	65.6	1.36
Two Year	17.1	5.7	0.46
College	16.8	28.7	2.35

UNDERGRADUATES IN OHIOLINK

As previously noted, there had been some early doubt about OhioLINK's importance to undergraduates. OhioLINK is an egalitarian system with all borrowers of all patron types expected to abide by the same loan rules. Undergraduates are therefore offered the same opportunities to place requests as are graduate students and faculty; this is a new concept for some schools, particularly the large universities, where undergraduates had not previously been permitted to use interlibrary loan services. Statistics from OhioLINK's first year of operation show that undergraduates placed about 30% of the requests (Sanville, 1995b); by 1998, Prabha et al. noted that undergraduate requests had increased to 42% of the total despite the fact that, in the view of these authors, undergraduates represented a constituency with little previous experience or familiarity with interlibrary loan services. Apparently unknown to Prabha et al., undergraduates had been successfully using traditional interlibrary loan services in many college libraries long before the advent of OhioLINK; however, their extra-library requests undoubtedly ballooned with the easy, self-initiated borrowing opportunities OhioLINK offered. Prabha et al. concluded that OhioLINK's three-day delivery times, coupled with its significant undergraduate use rate, "compels us to reassess a prevailing notion that undergraduate needs are usually so immediate that interlibrary loans cannot effectively serve them" (p. 3).

Though the percentage of OhioLINK transactions initiated by undergraduates has become significant, undergraduates as a group request at a disproportionately lower rate than do either graduate students or faculty. Nonetheless, some individual schools dominated by undergraduates have outpaced the whole state in their rate of OhioLINK use per capita. From July 1998 through June 1999, six of the top eight institutions in the state in terms of requests made per student were either private colleges or, in the case of Consort, a group of private colleges (Ohiolink, 2000). Clearly this was an anomaly. The Prabha study had determined that students at colleges, compared to those at universities, were indeed placing an inordinately high number of requests; this in spite of the fact that the same study indicated that college library collections offered more bibliographic records per student than did university collections. These authors seemed somewhat surprised by their findings noting that "it is not clear that four year colleges should require interlibrary loan services more than students in research universities" (Prabha et al., 1998, p. 6).

All of the nonuniform evidence above suggests a diversity of educational experience in Ohio, and, unfortunately, the means of examining its multiple facets have been limited. Existing data from OhioLINK and from previous studies compared undergraduates with graduate students but did not distinguish between their resident institution types. Other data measured the OhioLINK transactions of two-year institutions, colleges, and universities but did not further distinguish between patron types within these categories. No study attempted to mix these variables to focus on the library activities of undergraduates at colleges versus the library activities of undergraduates at universities. The remainder of this paper will describe such an attempt to look more closely at these multiple factors in order to draw a more refined picture of the OhioLINK activities of undergraduates.

One reason this type of study had not been undertaken previously was that data of this specificity were not available centrally from OhioLINK and had to be obtained individually from each of the sixty-nine schools that were members in 1999. With assistance from OhioLINK staff, two different reports were requested from all OhioLINK libraries: (1) Regular Checkouts by patron type and (2) OhioLINK Checkouts by patron type. Again, calendar year 1999 was the focus of the investigation. Since all OhioLINK libraries have Innovative Interfaces catalogs, it was assumed that the requested reports could be uniformly and easily produced at all schools. However, it turned out to be more difficult than anticipated to acquire the needed data, as some libraries had not set up the means to produce statistics specifically on their OhioLINK circulation. Both reports were therefore not supplied by all schools, though it is a testament to the cooperative spirit within OhioLINK that librarians in most locations promptly and graciously sent complete circulation data to the author, some working diligently to do so. In the end, data representing 87% of all university FTE and 68% of private college FTE were received. This was deemed a critical mass from both of these categories; however, sufficient data was not received from the two-year schools so they were, regrettably, excluded from this part of the study.

Besides the local and OhioLINK circulation reports, data were also acquired on all intra-Consort and intra-OPAL transactions. It was necessary to isolate and treat the schools of these two groups separately since they operate under somewhat different circumstances than do the schools with direct OhioLINK relationships.

Table 4.   OhioLINK Undergraduate Circulation Data, 1999.

	Aggregate mean	Median
Universities (10)		
Local collection checkouts per undergraduate	6.96	6.82
OhioLINK checkouts per undergraduate	0.36	0.39
Total checkouts per undergraduate	7.32	7.21
Percent of undergraduate checkouts that are non-local	5%	5%
Direct Member Colleges (8)		
Local collection checkouts per undergraduate	21.80	13.38
OhioLINK checkouts per undergraduate	1.89	1.75
Total checkouts per undergraduate	23.69	15.13
Percent of undergraduate checkouts that are non-local	8%	12%
Consort Colleges (4)		
Local collection checkouts per undergraduate	21.87	22.46
Consort checkouts per undergraduate	3.30	3.25
OhioLINK checkouts per undergraduate	1.94	2.03
Total checkouts per undergraduate	27.11	27.74
Percent of undergraduate checkouts that are non-local	19%	19%
OPAL Colleges (17)		
Local collection checkouts per undergraduate	7.60	6.05
OPAL checkouts per undergraduate (est.)	0.82	0.44
OhioLINK checkouts per undergraduate (est.)	0.28	0.15
Total checkouts per undergraduate	8.70	6.64
Percent of undergraduate checkouts that are non-local	13%	9%

A summary of the undergraduate checkout data is presented in Table 4. Both mean and median data are given; these are significantly different in the case of the private colleges. This discrepancy is due to the "Oberlin factor," meaning that Oberlin, one of the schools in this category, has a circulation rate per student that far exceeds that of others in its group as well as all other institutions in the state. Also note that some of Table 4's itemized figures for OPAL had to be estimated, since data supplied by that group reflected only the total of OPAL and OhioLINK interlibrary checkouts without distinguishing between these two types of transactions. Other information acquired by the author suggested the split between OPAL and OhioLINK checkouts to be approximately 75%–25%; consequently, these percentages were used to calculate estimates.

The statistics in Table 4 indicate that within Ohio there are wide variations in the degree to which undergraduates use both their home library collections and OhioLINK. This finding should be considered with the understanding that the data on local collection checkouts per undergraduate could not be limited to just books but included all items checked out at a library's circulation desk(s) other than OhioLINK/OPAL/Consort material. These statistics, though correct and numerically consistent for all libraries, cannot account for differences in circulation practices within those libraries. For example, periodicals may be checked out at one institution but not another, a circulating media collection may be located in the library or it may not, or an electronic reserve service may or may not be in place that reduces the physical circulation of reserve material for some institutions. This limitation in the data advises against the direct comparison of circulation rates of individual libraries; however, it is likely to have a relatively minor affect on the summaries by category given in Table 4.

INFLUENCES ON UNDERGRADUATE OHIOLINK USE

Table 3 and Table 4 both suggest differences in borrowing behaviors among the various school types. It seemed sensible to investigate these differences further. What were the factors that influenced undergraduates to use/not use OhioLINK and did these factors operate similarly at universities and at private colleges? To determine this, each school's rate of undergraduate OhioLINK usage (if it had been sent) was compared with four other factors: (1) circulation of the local collection by undergraduates, (2) size of the local collection measured in bibliographic records contributed to the OhioLINK Central Catalog, (3) undergraduate FTE, and (4) overall student FTE. Correlation coefficients were then calculated on the data by institution type as shown in Table 5.

As the data accumulated, it became apparent that the factors associated with high/low OhioLINK usage were indeed different for universities and private colleges. For the universities, there were strong negative correlations between undergraduate OhioLINK usage and all of the following: bibliographic records, undergraduate FTE, and overall FTE. In other words, as might be expected, the universities with the largest library collections and the largest student bodies showed relatively low undergraduate OhioLINK usage, while universities with smaller libraries and smaller student bodies experienced higher undergraduate OhioLINK usage. Undergraduate circulation of the local collection was not well correlated with undergraduate OhioLINK usage at the universities.

For the direct member colleges the situation was found to be the exact opposite. The factor most closely associated with college undergraduate OhioLINK usage was the rate at which those students used their local collection.

Table 5. Correlations between OhioLINK Undergrad Circ and Other Factors.

	University	Ind College	OPAL	Consort
Bib Records compared to OhioLINK Undergrad Circ	r = –0.84	r = 0.57	NA	NA
Undergrad FTE compared to OhioLINK Undergrad Circ	r = –0.80	r = –0.24	r = –0.36	r = 0.14
Total FTE compared to OhioLINK Undergrad Circ	r = –0.77	r = –0.40	r = –0.36	r = 0.14
Local Undergrad Circ compared to OhioLINK Undergrad Circ	r = 0.50	r = 0.80	r = 0.51	r = 0.70

Though the direct member colleges also vary in size according to undergraduate FTE and overall FTE, size did not correlate with undergraduate OhioLINK usage for these institutions. The number of bibliographic records contributed to the Central Catalog also did not strongly correlate with the rate of undergraduate OhioLINK usage, although what little correlation existed was positive, not negative as it was for the universities.

The above statements about direct member colleges apply somewhat to Consort and OPAL though to a lesser extent. Undergraduates' use of their local collections appeared to be correlated with OhioLINK/Consort interlibrary circulation, less so for OhioLINK/OPAL interlibrary circulation. As with the direct member colleges, undergraduate FTE was not well correlated with undergraduate OhioLINK usage for either group. Since the student makeup of both sub-consortial groups is exclusively undergraduate, there was no distinction between undergraduate FTE and total FTE. It was not possible to calculate correlation coefficients for bibliographic records contributed to the Central Catalog for Consort or OPAL since, as described previously, each of the sub-consortia contributes its records in a jointly combined database instead of individually.

DISCUSSION

One of the most intriguing findings indicated above is the existence of a clear inverse relationship at the universities between undergraduate OhioLINK use and both library size and student body size that is weak to lacking for the colleges. One might wonder if this points to a difference in scale between the universities and colleges, with the conclusion that only the smaller university libraries really *need* OhioLINK for their undergraduates, but that *all* college library collections fall under some minimal point and are thus small enough to make extra-library transactions desirable. This might fully explain the different rates of undergraduate OhioLINK use at colleges and universities were it not for two other facts: (1) In measures of size there is actually an overlap between the two groups, with the largest colleges and the largest college libraries exceeding the smallest universities and smallest university libraries. Moreover, Prabha et al. noted in 1998 that OhioLINK's colleges actually outranked universities in number of bibliographic records per student, and this college library material was selected with undergraduate needs firmly in mind. So if it were size alone that mattered, college libraries ought to be big enough to meet undergraduate needs in the same way that most university libraries do. (2) The contention about a difference in scale would make more sense if all undergraduates used library material at about the same rate, but clearly they do not. As demonstrated in Table 4 there are actually wide variations in library use; for example, at both the direct member colleges and the Consort colleges, undergraduates circulate library materials at two to three times the rate of their counterparts at the universities. Therefore a difference in scale, even if it did exist, may not be the point; the key difference between universities and colleges appears to center, not so much on supply, but on demand.

At the colleges, undergraduate demands on the local collection are strongly correlated with their rate of OhioLINK use. Though this statement is somewhat less applicable to OPAL than to the direct member colleges or to Consort, for all three of these groups, circulation of the local collection is the best predictor found for the rate of undergraduate OhioLINK use; for the universities it was the weakest predictor. If undergraduates at a college check a lot of material out of their local library, they are also likely to use OhioLINK. Undergraduates at the universities use their home collections at varying rates, but this use does not necessarily spur them on to request OhioLINK material.

The explanation for this difference in behavior may lie somewhere in the measure of bibliographic records compared to OhioLINK use. It is interesting to consider why this correlation is a negative one for the universities but a positive, if weaker one, for the colleges. This seems to suggest a key difference between the two groups. Among colleges, ample resources in the academic library are apparently associated with a demanding curriculum, assiduous undergraduate study habits, and high undergraduate library circulation. For this group extensive resources, talented students, and a strong curriculum are all part of the same calculus. For the universities, ample library resources result from different factors: advanced study by scholars and funding that has built research collections in various specialized fields. Library size among universities says little or nothing about the quality of the undergraduate program; moreover, in this category large libraries operate as a deterrent to undergraduate OhioLINK use. At the college level, large libraries are more indicative of quality in the undergraduate program and, therefore, do not function as a deterrent to OhioLINK use, but as a predictor of it. Undergraduates at colleges use OhioLINK not necessarily due to deficiencies in their home collections but due to the emphasis on student research found at their schools.

The above does not suggest that private colleges always exceed universities in the quality of their undergraduate education; indeed, there is actually a large range of quality variance, as indicated by library circulation, among both groups. It does suggest, however, that there is a difference in focus between the two institution types, with undergraduate needs driving library development for the colleges and higher level academic pursuits driving library development at the universities.

STUDENT VIEWS OF OHIOLINK AT WITTENBERG

A final part of this study was a survey of OhioLINK users conducted at Wittenberg University. This direct member college offered a convenient environment from which to gain further insight into the use of and attitudes toward OhioLINK by college undergraduates. As well as being well known to the author, Wittenberg is fairly typical of colleges: in 1999, its undergraduates checked out 2.14 OhioLINK items per person, just slightly more than the means and medians shown in Table 4. Moreover, on the correlation coefficient calculations, Wittenberg fell somewhere near the middle range for all measures studied and appears to be, therefore, a fairly representative private college.

To support this part of the study a two-page survey was designed; all OhioLINK books that were checked out by Wittenberg library users in the months of February and March, 2000, were accompanied by this survey. There were 1531 such transactions in these two months; 300 surveys were returned for a return rate of 19.6%. Nearly all of Wittenberg's OhioLINK users are either students or faculty members; though the focus of this article is on students, survey tallies for both of these patron classes are shown in the Appendix.

In general, the students who returned surveys appear to be competent, realistic, and satisfied OhioLINK users. They exhibit very little recreational use of OhioLINK. An overwhelming majority of student OhioLINK transactions result from work related to a class; most of that use revolves around the academic major. The survey revealed a fairly even split between books ordered because the requester had a specific title in mind (such as from a bibliography or professor suggestion) and those that the requester found as a result of a investigative search in the Central Catalog (such as a subject search). The majority of students report attempting to find material locally before requesting items through OhioLINK; many of these did succeed in finding relevant material but "wanted/needed more."

Most books arrived in a time frame that satisfied the requester and also appeared to fulfill expectations regarding content; only 5% of student respondents reported that once a book arrived it appeared to be "not at all helpful." These particular responses were cross-checked with the question about timeliness to determine if the books were deemed not helpful because they arrived too late. But since reported delivery times for the "not helpful" books differed little from overall responses to this question, late arrival did not appear to be the problem. Content did.

Few Wittenberg students order a single OhioLINK book at time. Fully 74% of student respondents report ordering two or more books at a clip, with 39% ordering four or more. When this question was cross-checked by class, it became apparent that seniors were particularly likely to order multiple books at a sitting, with 43% ordering four or more and only 20% ordering just one. By contrast, 24% of first-year students claimed to order four or more and 35% reported ordering one.

This finding about multiple book requests, combined with responses to the final question about amount of past OhioLINK use, yields some important insight into the pattern of OhioLINK use. Wittenberg's annual rate of OhioLINK requests per student is 2.14; however, most survey respondents were meeting, exceeding, or even doubling this average in one sitting! When asked to estimate the total number of books they had ever requested through OhioLINK, the reported overall average was just a hair under fourteen books per student. These two questions seem to corroborate each other and suggest that, rather than being used somewhat equally by nearly all students, OhioLINK usage is concentrated among less than half of Wittenberg's student body (very likely between a quarter to a third).[2] If all Wittenberg students used OhioLINK equally, each would be getting just over two OhioLINK books per year. Because of a cumulative effect going back to January 1998 for the upperclassmen, an expected reported total would be three to four OhioLINK books per student, not fourteen. Several things may be going on here that explain this discrepancy. Perhaps the heaviest OhioLINK users were the most interested in and responsive to the survey, or perhaps students simply tend to overestimate their past OhioLINK usage.[3] However, in spite of those possible explanations, it does appear that a portion of Wittenberg's student body uses OhioLINK heavily but that a larger percentage may not use it at all. By contrast, the total number of OhioLINK transactions faculty reported is somewhat closer to what would be mathematically expected, suggesting that OhioLINK usage is distributed among a majority of faculty.

No matter how studious the undergraduate or how demanding the course of study, a student cannot use OhioLINK if she is not aware of it. It is therefore important to consider how Wittenberg's students report learning of the service. There are a variety of ways this happens but two stand out ahead of the pack, together accounting for 62% of the responses. By far the most commonly reported way was from "a librarian who was talking to my class." An active library instruction program would therefore seem to have a strong relationship to student OhioLINK use. The second most commonly reported method of discovering OhioLINK was through "my professor." The latter is noteworthy since it shows faculty endorsement to be a potent impetus for student OhioLINK use. Highly enthusiastic faculty support for OhioLINK may be more prevalent at Ohio's smaller schools, giving them the advantage over large universities on this factor. College librarians have noticed that faculty scholars, used to laboring in library collections of limited size which were assembled for the needs of undergraduates, find OhioLINK to be a joyous boon and readily turn into vocal proponents of the system. This may create built-in encouragement for student OhioLINK use at the private colleges that is lacking at the universities.

Student respondents to the Wittenberg survey represented the four classes in the following percentages: first-year, 23%; sophomore, 19%; junior, 28%; senior, 31%. This spread is less balanced than it first appears, because classes normally decrease as they matriculate for four years; in addition, the Wittenberg class of 2000 was particularly small due to additional circumstances. Thus respondents per enrollment in each class were as follows: first-year: 2.7%, sophomore: 2.9%, junior: 4.0% and senior: 6.0%. This and other data available to the author indicate that seniors are more than twice as likely to use OhioLINK than are first-year students or sophomores.

CONCLUSIONS

All portions of this study clearly establish that there are important differences between undergraduates from school to school; they are simply not a homogeneous and like-behaving group. These findings underscore the diversity of educational experience in Ohio and suggest that, contrary to the studies cited by Mays, there may be schools where library use is indeed important to undergraduates and may in fact be associated with academic success. It appears that this is more likely to be true at private colleges than at large universities and that the libraries of these two institution types differ in significant ways. The disparate experiences on various campuses mean that any study of undergraduate behavior conducted at a single institution, including the Wittenberg survey, can be applied only with caution to other institutions. Planning for patron-initiated borrowing, as with most other library services, must be done at the individual school based on individual conditions. However, among the multiplicity of factors affecting undergraduates' use of such a system, local circulation rate appears to be primary for colleges while size of the library collection and student body are most important for universities.

Despite these differences, it seems safe to make the generalization that OhioLINK is a tremendous success for institutions of all sizes in the state. Through their lending rates, smaller institutions (both four-year and two-year) demonstrate themselves to be worthy participants in Ohio's statewide resource sharing system. Through their borrowing rates, private colleges in particular find that membership is a highly worthwhile investment; the benefits are further extended for those colleges participating in one of the state's two-track systems, Consort or OPAL. By comparison, the cost of administering OhioLINK for the universities may not be justified as much by undergraduate use as it is by service to graduate students and faculty.

The very high rate of OhioLINK use on some college campuses makes it likely that patron-initiated borrowing has built upon itself and become part of the campus culture at those locations. For example, patron-initiated borrowing is strongly encouraged at sub-consortial colleges where the online catalog users see by default is the OPAL or Consort catalog. Students at some of these schools have apparently become attuned to extra-library circulation and have learned to allow time for it. In addition, there are other factors not included in the present study, such as school selectivity, student to faculty ratio, and required senior research, that may account for high OhioLINK usage rates at some colleges.

Investment in a patron-initiated borrowing system is certainly worthwhile though it often needs to be accompanied by additional investment in staff. OhioLINK transactions are more labor intensive than regular library circulation given that library staff must retrieve requested items from the stacks and prepare them for shipment on the lending end, unpack, pre-process items, and notify requesters on the receiving end. For colleges, the data suggest that OhioLINK offers no relief to an already busy circulation staff. A taxed college library circulation staff will become that much busier after membership in a patron-initiated borrowing system, whereas college libraries with lower circulation rates may not see a significant change. Circulation/interlibrary loan is not the only department that should be considered, however. The fact that Wittenberg students most often learn of OhioLINK "through a librarian talking to my class" points to the need for sufficient instruction librarians if an institution is to reap full benefits from a resource sharing system. At the same time, it is doubtful that an expanded instruction program would boost OhioLINK circulation at institutions where library use is not a valued component of the educational program.

Finally, there are implications to be gleaned from this study for coordinated collection development. Ohio college and university library administrators have been considering if, when, and how book buying within OhioLINK might be better managed in order to extend overall buying power to more titles and prevent a glut of copies of some titles. While this proposal is not without merit, the findings reported herein suggest that coordinated collection development may have limited applicability to undergraduates, at least for the present. University undergraduates and students at two-year institutions seldom use OhioLINK. College undergraduates have demonstrated a greater willingness to request items from other libraries; however, if the pattern at Wittenberg is any indication, OhioLINK use is concentrated among a minority of students, primarily upperclassmen working within their academic majors. Therefore, even where undergraduate OhioLINK usage is strong, it appears necessary to maintain a broad, general collection on site to support first and second year work, and perhaps much of third and fourth year work as well. The OhioLINK Central Catalog expands the research opportunities for students of all levels but is no substitute for a well-balanced library collection that meets basic undergraduate book needs. It is unclear that undergraduates would order more books from OhioLINK if their local collections ceased to be kept up-to-date in selected areas. One imagines that at present the immediacy of undergraduate needs forces the use of the home collection for many assignments and that OhioLINK use is generally reserved for the more extensive college research assignments. It is unlikely that all undergraduates would readily alter these habits; it therefore seems prudent to focus on advanced materials when envisioning a coordinated collection development plan. This minor limitation in no way detracts from OhioLINK, which is in all ways a very successful venture. The spirit of cooperation and innovation in Ohio has wrought a system with stunning benefits for higher education throughout the state.

The author wishes to thank Tom Sanville of OhioLINK for his unerring wisdom and guidance, along with Anita Cook of OhioLINK and Hollis Wolfe and Nicole Atkisson of Wittenberg University for their helpful assistance.

NOTES

1. In his 1997 article "Resource Sharing in a Changing Environment," Kohl makes the case that the term "interlibrary loan" no longer applies "because the transaction is

no longer a library-to-library transaction in any significant sense but simply a patron requesting a known item from a known location within a single system" much like a request for material from closed stacks.

2. This information cannot be derived from library records since details on past transactions are purged for reasons of confidentiality.

3. This possibility is supported by research done by Mays reported in "Do Undergraduates Need their Libraries?" *Australian Academic and Research Libraries*, *17*(1986), 51–62.

REFERENCES

Henderson, A. (2000). The library collection failure quotient: The ratio of interlibrary borrowing to collection size. *Journal of Academic Librarianship*, *26*(3), 159–170.

Hirshon, A. (1995). Library strategic alliances and the digital library in the 1990s: The OhioLINK experience. *Journal of Academic Librarianship*, *21*, 383–386.

Kohl, D. (1994). OhioLINK: A vision for the 21st century. *Library Hi Tech*, *12*(3), 29–34.

Kohl, D. (1997). Resource sharing in a changing Ohio environment. *Library Trends*, *45*(3), 435–447.

Kohl, D. (1998). How the virtual library transforms interlibrary loans – the OhioLink experience. *Interlending & Document Supply*, *26*(2), 65–69.

Mays, T. (1986). Do undergraduates need their libraries? *Australian Academic and Research Libraries*, *17*, 51–62.

O'Connor, P., Wehmeyer, S., & Weldon, S. (1995). The future using an integrated approach: The OhioLINK experience. *Journal of Library Administration*, *21*(1–2), 109–120.

OhioLINK. Patron online borrowing: Annual requests made per FTE as of August 1999. [staff restricted Web site]
    http://silver.ohiolink.edu/webstats/pcirc%20B%20per%20FTE.htm (26 Nov. 2000).

Prabha, C., & O'Neill, E. (1998). Interlibrary borrowing initiated by patrons: Some characteristics of books requested via OhioLINK. Annual Review of OCLC Research [Online], 8 pages.
    http://www.oclc.org/oclc/research/publications/review98/ (26 August 1999).

Sanville, T. J. (1995a). How a library network operates: The Ohio model. *Logos*, *6*(2), 79–82.

Sanville, T. J. (1995b). Moving toward the statewide virtual library. *Catholic Library World*, *66*(1), 22–24.

Sessions, J. A., Pettitt, R. N., & Van Dam, S. (1995). OhioLINK inter-institutional lending online: The Miami University experience. *Library Hi Tech*, *3*(3), 11–24.

APPENDIX

Thomas Library, Wittenberg University OhioLINK Survey Results,
Spring 2000.

Question	Student	Faculty
Which best describes your purpose in borrowing this book?		
__Recreational purposes or general interest	3%	26%
__Faculty research/teaching	0.5%	74%
__Student assignment/research for a class you are taking	96%	0%
If for student assignment/research, answer the following		
__Class relates to my declared or probable major	75%	0%
__Class does **not** relate to my declared or probable major	15%	0%
__Not sure	6%	0%
Why did you order this particular book?		
__ Knew I wanted this exact title	42%	80%
__ Did **not** start off knowing I wanted this exact title, but I did a search and this book seemed OK	58%	20%
Describe how you chose the book.		
__ By myself	93%	96%
__ With study partner/friend	1%	1%
__ With a faculty member, librarian, or some other "expert"	6%	3%
Where were you when you ordered the book?		
__ In the library	76%	27%
__ Someplace other than the library	24%	73%
**Did you request other OhioLINK books on the same day?		
__ No	27%	36%
__ Yes, I ordered a total of 2 or 3 books	35%	54%
__ Yes, I ordered a total of 4 or more books	39%	11%
Describe the delivery time		
__ Shorter than expected	22%	18%
__ About what I expected	62%	80%
__ Longer than expected	15%	1%
Now that you have the book in hand, how helpful do you think it will be?		
__ Very helpful	53%	66%
__ Possibly helpful	43%	32%
__ Not at all helpful	5%	1%

Question	Student	Faculty
Before requesting this book, did you attempt to find an appropriate book in Thomas Library? Note: Thomas Library includes the Science Library.		
__ No	21%	39%
__ Yes	78%	57%
If yes, answer the following:		
__ Thomas Library had nothing that looked suitable	41%	50%
__ Thomas Library had some material but I wanted/needed more	54%	49%
__ Thomas Library had suitable material but it was checked out	4%	0%
__Blank	0.5%	1%
**How do you usually look for books in Thomas Library?		
__ Carefully searching in EZRA	57%	82%
__ Doing a quick search in EZRA to determine a call number area, then browsing the stacks	39%	7%
__ Going directly to the stacks and browsing	4%	4%
__ Mixed	0%	7%
**What is your opinion of the book collection in Thomas Library?		
__ Excellent	3%	11%
__ Good	51%	64%
__ Fair	31%	18%
__ Poor	13%	7%
__ Terrible	3%	0%
**What is your opinion of the overall services of Thomas Library?		
__Excellent	20%	46%
__ Good	57%	54%
__ Fair	21%	0%
__ Poor	0%	0%
__ Terrible	1%	0%
**OhioLINK provides online tables of contents for many of its books. Did you know that this information was available?		
__ No	44%	21%
__ Yes	56%	79%
If yes, answer the following: Do you ever look at the online table of contents?		
__ Usually	48%	45%
__ Sometimes	38%	55%
__ Never	14%	0%

Question	Student	Faculty
**Who/what first told you about OhioLINK?		
__ A sign	5%	4%
__ A computer screen	6%	4%
__ A mailing	5%	25%
__ My professor	23%	0%
__ A librarian who was talking to my class	39%	4%
__ Someone who was working in the library	9%	21%
__ A friend or acquaintance	9%	0%
__ Other	11%	28%
__ Blank (Some checked more than one)	0%	14%
**Please tell us who you are:		
Student (by year)		
__1	23%	0%
__2	19%	0%
__3	28%	0%
__4	31%	0%
__4+	0%	0%
__SCE	0%	0%
__Faculty		100%
__Other		0%
Estimate the **total** number of OhioLINK books you have ever requested	13.99	46.36
This is		
__ the first	75	28
__ not the first	143	46
OhioLINK survey you have filled out		

** First responses only were tallied.

INTERLIBRARY COOPERATION IN THE ERA OF ELECTRONIC LIBRARY – THE TAIWAN EXPERIENCE

Hao-Ren Ke

INTRODUCTION

Interlibrary cooperation is a concept of collaborative activities among libraries. By sharing resources in a cost-effective manner, it aims to supply better services to patrons, improve the efficiency of library operation, and utilize resources effectively. Cooperation among libraries is absolutely not a new concept, but it has undergone a series of revolutions in recent years under the influences of the cooperation model, the evolution of library services, and recent progress in information technology.

Interlibrary cooperation is often realized by establishing consortia (Knigma, 1997; Potter, 1997), like GALILEO (Potter et al., 1996), the Louisiana Library Network (Boe, 1996), OhioLINK (Kohl, 1997), TexShare (Martin, 1996; Rooks, 1996), and VIVA (Hurt, 1994; Perry, 1995). In the era when most libraries were print-based and when cooperation was getting its start (1960–1980, roughly speaking), library consortia principally focused on activities concerning inter-library loan, on-site reciprocal borrowing privileges, cooperative collection development, cooperative cataloging, and joint automation projects.

All that began to change as people ushered in the age of the *Electronic Library* beginning in the mid-1990s, by virtue of the development of computer, multimedia, and telecommunication technologies. The concept of the electronic library has had an imposing significant impact on the operation and service

Advances in Library Administration and Organization, Volume 19, pages 191–244.
Copyright © 2002 by Elsevier Science Ltd.
All rights of reproduction in any form reserved.
ISBN: 0-7623-0868-0

191

model of libraries. Undoubtedly, cooperation among libraries and the conse-
quent establishment of consortia are also influenced by the concept of the
electronic library: new kinds of activities may occur, and the implementation
of existing activities may be changed or improved.

Many definitions of electronic library exist in the literary. We in Taiwan have
chosen the seemingly most logical definition from the viewpoint of librarians,
which was proposed by Waters (1998):

> *Digital libraries are organizations that provide the resources, including the*
> *specialized staff, to select, structure, offer intellectual access to, interpret,*
> *distribute, preserve the integrity of, and ensure the persistence over time of*
> *collections of digital works so that they are readily and economically*
> *available for use by a defined community or set of communities.*

In this essay, the author considers that the two terms *electronic library* and
digital library have the same meaning. On the basis of the above definition,
Cleveland (1998) stated several characteristics of electronic library, including
the following one:

> *Digital libraries are the digital face of traditional libraries and include*
> *both electronic (digital) as well as print and other (e.g. film, sound)*
> *materials.*

In the author's opinion, an electronic library (or digital library) is a library that
can manipulate the newest computer and telecommunication technology to
engage in the selection, preservation, organization, presentation, access, dissemination, and sharing of electronic and non-electronic collections.

The purpose of this article is to elaborate on two recent endeavors of
Taiwanese libraries to actualize interlibrary cooperation in the era of the electronic library. The first is the establishment of a consortium to cope with the
issues raised by the emergence of WWW-based electronic resources; the second
is the development of a computerized workflow system to enhance the performance of interlibrary loan. But before dwelling on the main themes, a brief
introduction to the interlibrary cooperation organizations in Taiwan is required.

Interlibrary-Cooperation Organizations in Taiwan

Taiwanese libraries have been implementing interlibrary cooperation for nearly
thirty years. Many organizations for interlibrary cooperation have been
established in that period. Generally, these organizations can be grouped
into three categories: nationwide organizations, regional organizations, and
organizations with single-type libraries.

Nationwide Organizations

Sci-Tech Interlibrary Cooperation Association (est. in 1975) and *Library Consortium on Humanities and Social Sciences* (est. in 1981) were two primary nationwide organizations for interlibrary cooperation. Since September 1999, they have been consolidated into the *Interlibrary Cooperation Association* (ILCA). The principal missions of ILCA are

(1) Planning regular affairs and academic research activities related to interlibrary cooperation;
(2) Devising schemes for effectively making use of information resources;
(3) Publishing literatures concerning interlibrary cooperation, in order to advocate the significance of information literacy and enhance professional skills of librarians;
(4) Supporting the cultivation of specialists in information technology management;
(5) Assisting new libraries to acquire sufficient collections and facilities;
(6) Enhancing cross-strait and international cooperation.

To accomplish the above missions, ILCA sets up seven functional and four district committees. The seven functional committees deal with business planning, academic activities, financial affairs, interlibrary cooperation, publication, cross-strait information communication, and cooperative collection development for the publications of Mainland China. One district committee each has also been established for North, Middle, South, and East Taiwan.

To date, ILCA has 450+ member libraries including governmental, academic, research, public, and military libraries. Perhaps the most remarkable achievement of ILCA is the establishment of a standard set of rules for guiding interlibrary loan between member libraries. These rules explicitly state rights and obligations of members in interlibrary loan and have to be obeyed by every member. In addition, many programs sponsored by the Government are discussed initially in ILCA. These programs include the Consortium on Core Electronic Resources in Taiwan (CONCERT) and the Interlibrary Loan Networking System for Taiwanese Libraries, both of which are central themes of this article.

ILCA devotes itself to many activities every year. For example, it encourages libraries to exchange or donate duplicate materials; hold or sponsor conferences and meetings related to interlibrary cooperation; publish news-letters; arrange visits to libraries or information centers located in Mainland China and other countries.

Regional Organizations
Libraries located within the same or neighboring regions may found formal or informal organizations to share resources effectively and efficiently. Taiwan has many regional organizations. The programs implemented by regional organizations encompass on-site reciprocal borrowing, interchanging library cards, and cooperative collection development.

Organizations With Single-Type Libraries
The *Consortium of Taiwanese Technical-School Libraries* and the *Consortium of Medical Libraries* are the two prominent organizations that bring together single-type libraries. This kind of organization comprises members with similar characteristics (like technical schools) and/or subject coverage (like medical science), as they can cooperate more closely and fittingly than libraries with disparate characteristics and/or subject coverage. The major programs contain cooperative reference services, reciprocal borrowing, interchanging library cards, and cooperative collection development.

CONSORTIUM ON CORE ELECTROIC RESOURCES IN TAIWAN (CONCERT)

Researchers need up-to-update information for advancing their research. From the mid-1990s, the World Wide Web (WWW) has been offering many opportunities for researchers to rapidly obtain and exchange information. The proliferation of WWW-based abstracting and indexing (A&I) databases and electronic journals is especially effective in revolutionizing the way researchers communicate their research results. The challenge is that many new issues come up, and these cannot be tackled by any single library; consequently, libraries organize consortia for surviving in these circumstances. This part of the article focuses on a Taiwanese library consortium named *CONCERT* that makes electronic resources available to the research and academic community. From now on, the terms *WWW-based reference databases and electronic journals*, *WWW-based electronic resources*, *databases*, or just *electronic resources* are used interchangeably.

Background – The InfoSpring Project

Introduction
The *InfoSpring Project* is described first to give the background of CONCERT. The InfoSpring Project is an experimental project conducted by the National Chiao Tung University (NCTU). Many valuable experiences of this project have

been transferred to CONCERT. NCTU is regarded as the cradle of Taiwan's high-tech industry and development. The first TV transmitter, transistor, IC, laser, computer, and telephone switching system in Taiwan were all developed by NCTU. In addition, NCTU always takes the lead among Taiwanese universities in network infrastructure and application. In 1988 NCTU connected to the BITNET (Because It's Time Network); in 1990 NCTU connected to the TANet (Taiwan Academic Network)[1] and built an FDDI campus network; in 1991 NCTU linked all its buildings to this campus network, including its student dormitories. In the mid 1990s, NCTU maintained the largest FTP server in the Asia-Pacific region.

As a distinguished research-oriented university, NCTU needs to provide easy access to the most up-to-date research information for its faculties and students. In 1995, NCTU observed that WWW-based electronic resources would become the most important information sources, and decided to offer its patrons access to WWW-based electronic resources. At that time, the TANet had only two T1 lines to the United States, where most WWW-based electronic resources were located, and the access speed to these resources was unacceptable. To overcome this obstacle, mirror sites of several electronic resources were installed locally at NCTU. The mirror-site approach installs the same kind of computer hardware and software (such as indexing engines, information retrieval systems, and user interfaces) as that in the original site at a mirror site. More than $250,000 were invested by NCTU for the related hardware, software, and work force. The mirror sites installed included systems designated to support CSA, Elsevier, Ei, ISI, and OVID.

The original intention was for NCTU to act as an electronic-resource host for its patrons. However, NCTU recognized from the experience of managing these resources for in-house needs that it would be difficult for many Taiwanese organizations to follow the same model. Two factors emerged as particular problems in this regard: (1) expensive server, storage, and maintenance costs, and (2) insufficient technical staffs for managing mirror sites and solving network- and computer-related problems. To help Taiwanese academic institutions speedily access electronic resources and cope with these two problems, NCTU implemented resource sharing. The mirror sites maintained by NCTU were shared among 20+ Taiwanese academic subscribers with permission from information providers. The InfoSpring Project was born (Ke & Chang 2000).

Impacts

As a pilot project with the goal of providing fast access to electronic resources, the InfoSpring Project had many impacts on Taiwanese libraries, to include:

1. Expediting a shift in research information services
In the mid 1990s, web-based electronic resources were just in their inception. Libraries in many countries began catching the electronic-resource bandwagon; however, Taiwanese libraries hesitated to offer this kind of service to their users. Slow access speed and expensive subscription prices were and are their main concerns. The InfoSpring Project worked around this conservatism and built mirror sites so that the access speed could be improved significantly, thereby giving Taiwanese libraries more motivation to join the Web trend. In addition, trial access also enabled them to collect enough usage information to evaluate the cost-effectiveness of offering this service.

2. Exploring the possibility of resource sharing
The InfoSpring Project was a large-scale project that realized resource sharing. The organizations participating in the project could offer their users a more efficient information services without significant investment. Its success confirmed the effectiveness of resource sharing and encouraged Taiwanese libraries to launch many more large-scale collaborative projects. Furthermore, traditional interlibrary cooperation in Taiwan was confined to collection sharing (by interlibrary loan or open access), but the InfoSpring Project broadened it to sharing of hardware, software, work force, and expertise.

3. Integrating library and computer sciences
For the last two decades, library services have been revolutionized by computer technology. Except for library automation systems, Taiwanese libraries made little use of computer technology for improving their operation and service. The professionals of computer and library sciences had little interaction. The InfoSpring Project demonstrated the effectiveness of integrating the expertise of the two fields.

4. Establishing a resource-sharing consortium model for research information
One side benefit of the InfoSpring Project was the establishment of an informal library consortium that leveraged union strength to negotiate with information providers for favorable pricing and licensing agreements.

5. Initiating government support
In the beginning, NCTU supported all servers, storage capacity, and workers for mirror sites from its own budget. In three years, the value of this project has been verified, especially with regard to Taiwan's research activities; consequently, Taiwan's National Information Infrastructure (NII) began granting

funds to the InfoSpring Project and other activities concerning the provision of electronic resources, particularly through the Scientific and Technical information Center of Taiwan's National Science Council.

InfoSpring and CONCERT

The InfoSpring Project only dealt with one issue related to the provision of WWW-based electronic resources – the access speed and the cost of hardware, software, labor, and expertise. When academic libraries in Taiwan attempted offering electronic resources to their patrons, several additional issues were raised, including (1) expensive subscription fees, (2) complicated licensing agreements, and (3) scarce technical staffs for solving network- and computer-related problems. Obviously, any single library could not solve these alone. Inspired by the informal consortium for accessing the resources hosted by the InfoSpring Project, Taiwanese academic libraries started thinking about the possibility of organizing a consortium for handling the issues. The experiences of many consortia around the world also showed that a consortium should be supported by its government for the sake of its long-term and stable operation.

In September 1998, the Science and Technology Center (STIC), which works under the jurisdiction of the National Science Council (NSC), made a decision to develop CONCERT (CONsortium on Core Electronic Resources in Taiwan). In order to integrate resources of the whole country, NCTU transferred all the skills and experiences obtained from the InfoSpring Project to CONCERT. The InfoSpring Project had achieved its aims and ended successfully.

Establishment

STIC is a national information center of Taiwan. One of its missions is to integrate national information resources and introduce international information resources to foster the domestic research activities. Since the establishment of its STICNET in 1988, STIC has been playing an important role in the provision of major domestic and international databases for the Taiwanese academic and R&D community. STIC made a decision to organize a library consortium in September 1998 and assumed responsibility for the management of this consortium, ushering in the era of the electronic library and responding to the expectation of academic libraries. This consortium is called the Consortium On Core Electronic Resources in Taiwan, better known as CONCERT. The experiences of the InfoSpring Project laid a good groundwork for CONCERT. The primary goal of CONCERT is to bring in electronic resources cost-effectively. To fulfill this goal, CONCERT adopts the following strategies:

(1) Implement a resource sharing policy by integrating national resources, including funding, work force, hardware, software, and technical knowledge.
(2) Assist members to improve network infrastructure so that members can use electronic resources at satisfactory connection speed.
(3) Enable a collective purchasing mechanism in order to acquire electronic resources in a cost-effective manner.
(4) Collaborate with members to negotiate with information providers about pricing and licensing agreements; in this manner, individual member's time and effort spent on negotiation and review of licenses can be saved.
(5) Establish a long-term and stable mechanism for using foreign databases.
(6) Catch and understand the requirements of academic research; evaluate and make available required electronic resources promptly.

CONCERT is a multi-type library consortium. The members of CONCERT are mainly libraries of universities, colleges, but also includes some serving research institutes and non-profit organizations. As of May 2001, CONCERT has 182 members.

Core Program

Offering foreign electronic resources cost-effectively is the core program of CONCERT. Initially, databases were chosen as *core* collections of CONCERT based mainly on the investigation of Wu (1997) and the usage statistics of several foreign databases served by STIC in the past decade. After two years in operation, CONCERT has drawn up a selection principle recently, which is presented later.

Table 1 lists the database systems made available by CONCERT from 1999 to 2001. It also shows the number of members licensing each system. Each system may contain more than one database. It can be seen from Table 1 that the number of systems available in CONCERT increases from eight, fifteen to twenty-one in the three years. NAL in Table 1 stands for *National Academic Licensing*, which is described below.

Licensing Model
CONCERT adopts two models to acquire electronic resources – *group purchasing* and *national-academic licensing*. For a database acquired via the group-purchasing model, CONCERT exercises group purchasing power to bargain with information providers to get the best possible prices and rights. Members subscribe to this kind of electronic resource according to their

Table 1. Database Systems of CONCERT (NAL: National-Academic Licensing).

Name of Database Systems		Members		
		1999	2000	2001
1	Chadwyck-healey	NA	NA	3
2	eShaman.com	NA	NA	22
3	CSA IDS	NA	34	34
4	EBSCOhost	NAL	37	54
5	Ei Engineering Village	21	38	50
6	GaleNet	NA	16	7
7	IEL Online	21	29	32
8	JCR Web	NA	NA	19
9	JSTOR	NA	NA	14
10	Lexis-Nexis	NA	NA	17
11	Ovid Databases@Ovid	NA	44	36
12	ProQuest	NA	73	94
13	ScienceDirect OnSite	37	52	67
14	SilverPlatter WebSpirs	NA	NA	59
15	Web of Science	5	15	20
16	Grolier	NA	NAL	NAL (170)
17	IDEAL	62	61	61
18	LINK	NA	NAL	NAL (178)
19	OCLC FirstSearch	NAL	NAL	NAL (164)
20	PQDD	NA	NAL	NAL (167)
21	SwetsnetNavigator	NAL	NAL	NAL (163)

individual needs and pay the subscription fee mostly from their own budget though a portion of the subscription fee is subsidized by the Ministry Of Education (MOE) in Years 2000–2001.

For a database acquired via the national-academic licensing model, STIC or MOE pays the subscription fee. All academic members are allowed to use this kind of database without paying. However, research institutes and non-profit organizations may need to pay money for using this kind of database, depending on information providers. As this licensing model is beneficial to construct a level playing field for the domestic research environment, STIC and MOE prefer this model when pricing is affordable and reasonable.

Selection Policy
After nearly three years of work, the database systems procured by CONCERT have risen to 21. Notwithstanding this significant achievement, CONCERT has to continue acquiring new databases to meet the needs of members. To have a

systematic mechanism for purchasing new databases with limited budgets and staffs, the formulation of a selection policy is essential. In October 2000, the Selection Policy Of CONCERT was discussed in the *Information Resource Committee of STIC* and then approved by the *CONCERT Advisory Committee of MOE/NSC*. This policy comprises four parts: selection principles, reference information, selection timetable, and assessment criteria.

Selection principles
(1) CONCERT seeks to procure electronic resources highly demanded by many members.
(2) CONCERT inclines to acquire quality information resources.
(3) CONCERT gives higher priority to multi-disciplinary information resources.
(4) CONCERT aims to balance subject coverage.
(5) CONCERT prefers favorable consortia price for facilitating cost-effective acquisitions of information resources.

Reference information
Consistent with the above principles, CONCERT refers to the following information during the selection process:

(1) Recommendations from members;
(2) Members' responses to an annual questionnaire designed to establish a want list;
(3) Recommendation from the CONCERT Advisory Committee of MOE/NSC;
(4) Research reports on domestic needs;
(5) Resources acquired by the members of the *International Coalition of Library Consortia* (ICOLC).

Selection Timetable
Table 2 presents the timetable of the selection process. Five steps are taken to determine the electronic resources to be procured in the next year.

(1) *Collect a candidate list.* A member may fill out a form to recommend specific databases throughout the whole year. If five or more members recommend a database, it is included on a candidate list.

(2) *Send out an annual questionnaire.* Every April, STIC distributes an annual questionnaire to collect input on members' demand for new databases in the next year. The annual questionnaire contains the candidate list gathered in the preceding step; in addition, members can suggest other databases when responding the questionnaire.

Table 2.   Selection Timetable of CONCERT.

Item \ Month	1	2	3	4	5	6	7	8	9	10	11	12
Collect Candidate List	▬	▬	▬	▬	■	■	■	■	■	■	■	■
Send out Annual Questionnaire					▪							
Evaluate and Decide Final List (Committee)					▪							
Start Assessing and Licensing Procedure						▬	▬	▬	▬			
MOE/NSC Meeting										▬		

(3) *Evaluate and decide a final list.* Every May, STIC compiles a final list based on the responses of the annual questionnaire. If ten or more members recommend a database, it is included into the final list. The Information Resource Committee of STIC then confers on the final list, and determines how to distribute the load of assessing and licensing to the *International Resources Division of STIC* and member libraries.

(4) *Start assessing and licensing procedure.* From June to September of every year, the International Resources Division of STIC and the member libraries elected in the preceding step start the process of assessing and licensing for each database included in the final list. The International Resources Division of STIC collaborates with members to work out assessment criteria. The criteria are divided into the following five parts: (1) assessment of database systems, (2) assessment of electronic full text, (3) assessment of licensing agreements, (4) assessment of pricing, (5) assessment of vendors, and (6) overall assessment. For a detailed description of the assessment criteria, refer to the Appendix. The issues on pricing, licensing agreement, archiving, and so on are then negotiated with information providers. Members and information providers may meet several times to discuss and clarify related issues.

(5) *MOE/NSC meeting.* Every October, a list of databases on which CONCERT and information providers have reached an agreement is presented to the CONCERT Advisory Committee of MOE/NSC to finalize the list of electronic resources acquired by CONCERT and subsidized by MOE and STIC. Then CONCERT informs members of the contents of this list.

Assessment Criteria

Database Access Method

It is far from true that users can access electronic resources "any time, any place" because of the limited Internet bandwidth in the global Internet environment. To make effective use of the collections of CONCERT, it is very critical to offer members a speedy (at least acceptable) Internet connection for accessing them. Taking into consideration the Internet infrastructure in Taiwan, CONCERT adopts two kinds of database access approaches:

• Access Through Mirror Sites Locally in Taiwan

The Internet speed from Taiwan to information providers' original sites, most of which are located in USA or Europe, is not acceptable. To resolve this problem, with the permission and cooperation of information providers, CONCERT creates mirror sites locally in Taiwan for several electronic resources. At present, members access the databases from CSA, Ei, Elsevier, ISI, OVID, and Silver Platter via the corresponding mirror sites. STIC is the consortium host for Ei, ISI, and OVID; Academia Sinica is the consortium host for Elsevier and Silver Platter; NCTU is the consortium host for CSA.[2]

• Access Through Internet

This is an ordinary way to access databases. Libraries access these kinds of databases directly through Internet from sites maintained by information providers. The databases not mentioned in the preceding paragraph are accessed by means of this approach.

The two approaches have their pros and cons. CONCERT chooses an appropriate approach for a specific database based on the following factors (as shown in Table 3).

Table 3. Comparisons between the Mirror Site and the Internet Approaches.

Comparison	Mirror Site	Internet
Cost	Expensive	Cheap
Data Transmission Speed	Good	Bad to Fair
Value-Added Service	Many	Few
Policy (IPs' and CONCERT's)	Depends	Depends

- Setup and Maintenance Cost

CONCERT has to purchase servers and storage spaces for mirror sites and must meet the subsequent cost of maintenance. In comparison, CONCERT does not have to care the cost of setup and maintenance when choosing the Internet approach.

- Data Transmission Speed

Data transmission speed is the primary reason for CONCERT to employ the mirror site approach. If CONCERT builds the mirror site of a database, the speed to access it can be improved significantly. Information providers should propose a solution for ameliorating the situation of unsatisfactory Internet speed if the mirror-site approach is not allowed. A few information providers lease bandwidth to improve the data transmission speed; for other databases, CONCERT has to use proxy servers or other mechanisms to improve the speed.

- Value-Added Services

The mirror-site method, especially its generalization – the local-host method – is likely to incorporate value-added services. Using the local-host method, a consortium obtains raw data from information providers and loads the raw data into its own search engine. In this manner, the consortium does not have to use hardware and software identical to that used by information providers; furthermore, it is easier for the consortium to develop a system more closely fitting the requirements of its members. OhioLINK and a few other consortia adopt the local-host method to build their electronic-resource collections.

When a consortium employs the mirror-site or local-host method, the possible value-added services encompass: (1) an integrated authentication mechanism for remote access, (2) a uniform user interfaces for all electronic resources, (3) a customized linking to Web OPACs, full text and other local resources, and (4) a customized and thorough analysis of usage statistics and user behavior. In the case of CONCERT, NCTU Library has been conducting an in-depth analysis of the usage logs of Elsevier's SDOS by means of statistics and data mining, in the hope of better understanding user behavior.

- Policies of CONCERT and Information Providers

Information providers usually demand that the number of subscribers reaches a certain threshold before they allow for building mirror sites. Information providers also consider the technical maturity and complexity of their own systems to determine if the mirror-site method is feasible. In the case of the local-host method, many providers are reluctant to give raw data. On the other hand, CONCERT considers several technical and non-technical issues for building mirror sites. For example, CONCERT has to consider whether STIC or any of its members are willing to take charge of a specific mirror site.

The Internet connection from Taiwan to other countries has improved gradually over the last two years, especially after MOE reserved some bandwidth for electronic resources (described later). Notwithstanding this, many Taiwanese libraries still suffer from bad Internet connections. Before most members can enjoy appropriate Internet connection speed, it is necessary for CONCERT to establish mirror sites for a number of databases.

Funding and Governance

Figure 1 depicts the funding and governance organization of CONCERT. CONCERT's funding and administration agencies are NSC and MOE. As a governmental information center with the support of the technology development of the nation as its key mission, STIC, under the jurisdiction of NSC, allocates its budgets and staffs to support CONCERT. Specifically, STIC funds the acquisition of a number of national-academic databases and the purchase of several shared central servers, storage spaces and software for mirror sites. Two Divisions of STIC, the International Resources Division and the *Information Technology Management Division*, are closely involved in CONCERT. The International Resources Division performs the regular operation of CONCERT. The core responsibilities of this Division are to: (1) coordinate the selecting and licensing of electronic resources, (2) arrange training, promotion, annual conventions, and conferences, and (3) encourage technical enhancement of members. The Information Technology Management Division is responsible for the maintenance of the mirror sites of ISI, Ei, and OVID. STIC also organizes the Information Resource Committee. This Committee is consulted for the operation of CONCERT and is involved in the decisions leading to the development of the final list mentioned in the selection policy. In addition, for integrating the experiences and skills of the InfoSpring Project, STIC has granted NCTU a project (described later) to handle technique-related issues.

MOE started fostering CONCERT in the year 2000. To encourage the participation and reduce the fiscal load of participating academic libraries, MOE subsidizes a proportion of the subscription fee for every database acquired using

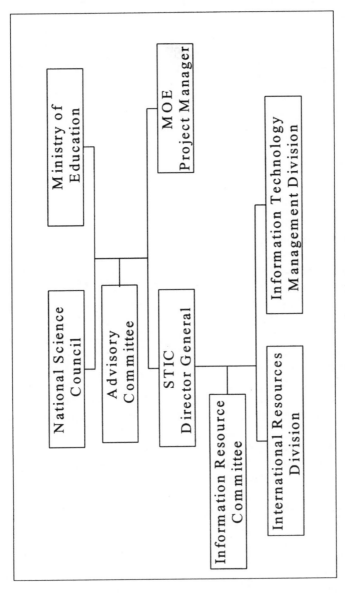

Fig. 1. Funding and Governance Organization of CONCERT.

the group-purchasing model. Moreover, a portion of MOE's funding is used for the acquisition of a number of national-academic databases.

To keep the policy and direction of CONCERT on the right track, NSC and MOE jointly organize the CONCERT Advisory Committee of MOE/NSC. The Committee is composed of directors from major Taiwanese libraries. The Committee has three primary tasks. First, determine the policy and direction of CONCERT. Second, it recommends and makes decisions about which electronic resources are acquired and subsidized. Third, it deliberates upon how to effectively use the funding supported by STIC and MOE. The Committee formulates a scheme to evaluate whether academic libraries fully use the electronic resources brought in by CONCERT. The evaluation is conducted by a project funded by MOE.

Other Programs

NSCDL Project

Strong technical support is essential for successfully offering the services that depend on electronic resources. The Information Technology Management Division of STIC and the NCTU Library are the two major technical partners undergirding CONCERT. For integrating the valuable experiences in carrying out the InfoSpring Project, CONCERT has created a seamless relationship with NCTU through the NSCDL Project (Ke & Hwang, 1999). The primary missions of this project are to help CONCERT: (1) assess the technical feasibility of access approaches of electronic resources, (2) install and maintain mirror sites, (3) assist in the promotion and training conducted by the International Resources Division of STIC, and (4) carry out related research and development. In practice, this project serves as a task force for CONCERT in related technical issues. The mirror sites maintained by this project once encompassed the databases from Ei, ISI, and OVID, but they have since been transferred back to the Information Technology Management Division of STIC.

The NSCDL Project is currently developing an electronic journal union list for the consortium. It will be described next.

The Electronic Journal Union List

CONCERT has made many Electronic journals (e-journals) available in Taiwan. Nevertheless, patrons do not have a convenient way to learn about the e-journals that they can access. Traditionally, libraries add MARC records for paper-based journals and provide access through their OPACs. In view of the emergence of electronic resources, the MARC format is amended to include URL-related information in Field 856; therefore, patrons can access electronic resources also through OPACs if libraries add these fields to their records and the underlying OPACs can support the linking of electronic resources from bibliographic records. But, in Taiwan, most libraries have not yet added URL-related information to the 856 field for e-journals for two primary reasons. First, many OPACs have not yet incorporated the linking through the 856 field; therefore, even if libraries add the TAG, patrons still cannot access e-journals through OPACs. Second, as the majority of information providers do not offer libraries MARC records of e-journals for free, Taiwanese libraries do not do the original cataloging because of inadequate staffing.

So, to provide patrons with a channel for accessing e-journals, a number of Taiwanese libraries make two types of web pages: a simple alphabetical list of e-journals held and a series of subject listings. Some even develop a simple search engine. Although this is a feasible alternative, not every library has the workers and skills to develop this kind of web page and search engine; furthermore, it is essential to have an overall understanding of the breadth and depth of e-journals acquired by Taiwanese libraries. As a result, the idea of developing an electronic journal union list has been raised. The development of this union list is guided by four principles:

(1) The e-journals gathered in this union list are all e-journals available to Taiwanese libraries, not limited to the e-journals acquired by CONCERT.
(2) In order to save the efforts of libraries for designing their own e-journal web pages and search engines, a special function is designed to list and search the list of e-journals acquired by each individual library.
(3) To realize resource sharing, the load of gathering lists of e-journals is distributed among members.
(4) In the short term, the records for e-journals are not in MARC format, but eventually the list may use MARC records for e-journals.

Gathering e-journal records is done in three stages:

Stage 1: STIC collectively gathers the records of CONCERT members' e-journals from information providers.
Stage 2: STIC coordinates efforts by several large libraries who share the load of gathering the records of e-journals not acquired by CONCERT.
Stage 3: Other libraries may supply the records of e-journals left out in the first two stages. An on-line interface is designed for libraries to manage their holdings.

STIC has finished the first stage, and the second and third stages are on going. The NSCDL Project takes charge of the system design. To identify which libraries own a specific e-journal, patrons can search the list via journal title,

ISSN, and database name, or browse an alphabetical list. The function to list and search for the e-journals belonging to each individual library is also available. The on-line interface to manage e-journal holdings is finished as well.

In our opinion, the development of this e-journal union list is a solid fulfillment of resource sharing. Libraries hang together to collect e-journals, and the centralized development of this list saves individual libraries a lot of time and effort.

Evaluate Utilization of Electronic Resources

The success of a consortium like CONCERT does not fully hinge on how many electronic resources it acquires. The utilization of the resources is also important. After all, an information resource is valuable only if it has heavy usage and greatly contributes to the research and study of patrons. In view of this, the CONCERT Advisory Committee of MOE/NSC has devised a scheme to address the following objectives. It expects to:

(1) Evaluate members' utilization of electronic resources.
(2) Understand the ability of members in the exploitation, promotion, and training on electronic resources.
(3) Measure the cost-effectiveness of subsidization supported by NSC and MOE.

The evaluation scheme takes into account six bases: (1) usage statistics; (2) characteristics of members, such as size, location, FTEs, students, and whether the institutions are research- or teaching-oriented; (3) efforts of members in promotion and training; (4) impact of resource sharing in walk-in use, promotion and training, and reference services; (5) database-related issues, like characteristics (A&I or full-text), licensing period, and pricing; (6) assistance and support provided to members as a result of CONCERT's operations.

In assessing its activities using the above criteria, CONCERT uses several pieces of information including: (1) self-evaluations of members in utilization, promotion, training, and resource sharing; (2) usage statistics; (3) on-site interview by the CONCERT Advisory Committee of MOE/NSC; (4) observations of medium- and long-term performance; (5) the amount of the subscription fees for content subsidized by MOE.

Strive for Dedicated Bandwidth

As mentioned previously, data transmission speed in Taiwan is a big issue. Either the mirror-site approach or bandwidth leased by information providers is used to offer users a satisfactory speed for accessing a few electronic resources. Since access to other databases is still slow, CONCERT and *MOE's*

Strategic Committee for Library Automation and Networking work together to reserve TANet bandwidth for the use of electronic resources. At present, 10 Mbps out of the OC3 (155Mbps) TANet bandwidth to the United States is reserved for this purpose.

Hold Conferences, Annual Conventions, User Group Meetings, and Training
In the era of the electronic library, librarians should play the role of interme-diary between patrons and electronic resources. To play this role more effectively, librarians have to keep pace with the newest trends and technology regarding the electronic library, and must understand the capabilities, current developments and future prospects of database systems. CONCERT helps librar-ians master the above topics by conducting conferences, annual conventions, user group meetings, and training.

The Conference on Electronic Resources Consortium was held in May 1999. The goal of this conference was to share the experiences of several consortia (including NERL, CARL, VIVA, OhioLINK, GALILEO, and CONCERT) and address issues related to electronic resources (licensing, fair use, archiving, and so on) and consortia (management, budgeting, leadership, and so forth). Member conventions are scheduled to take place annually. In these annual conventions, STIC reports to members about the status and future directions of CONCERT; information providers present their systems, and invited speakers give keynote speeches about the progress and tendencies of electronic library development. Information providers are welcome to host user group meetings for interacting with libraries. User group meetings are also suitable for sharing librarians' expe-riences in promotion and training on specific resources.

Members are also encouraged to host courses for training librarians regarding detailed functions of specific databases in cooperation with STIC and infor-mation providers. Around 160 site or district training courses have taken place within the last two years along with countless training courses targeting patrons that are individually held by members. In addition to the site or district training courses, STIC also creates a variety of training channels, to include news on Internet, WWW pages for each resource, discussion forums, user manuals in Chinese, and messages passed via E-mails.

Experiences

Many valuable experiences have been learned in developing CONCERT. Problems it has addressed related to the development of its pricing and archiving model, licensing negotiation, copyright, and the legal use of data files are ubiquitous to all consortia, and many articles related to them have been published (Allen & Hirshon,

1998; ICOLC, 1999, 1998a, b; Kopp, 1998; Okerson, 1999). The following elaborates on the specific experiences of CONCERT relating to these issues.

Governmental Support and Long Term Operation

Taiwanese libraries have been encountering restrained budgets in recent years. The emergence of electronic resources does not mitigate but worsens this situation. Constrained budgets provide an important reason why libraries do not move toward the provision of electronic resources. To release libraries from this plight, MOE subsidizes a portion of the subscription fee; furthermore, MOE and STIC procure databases via the national-academic licensing model.

Negotiating with information providers is time consuming. To have a smooth negotiation process, two points are essential. First, a consortium must be united. Second, experienced negotiators must be employed on behalf of the whole consortium. Thanks to enthusiastic and skillful colleagues at STIC, CONCERT members hang together to face information providers, and, as a result CONCERT can usually gain favorable pricing and licensing agreements.

In short, from the viewpoints of finance and administration, the Government plays a crucial role in the long term and stable operation of CONCERT. To make the Government draw up a long-term plan to bolster CONCERT, the members have to convince the Government that electronic resources are becoming the foremost information sources required to support scholarship and that sufficient provision of electronic resources is critical for strengthening research competitiveness.

Strong Cooperation between Members

The group purchasing mechanism of CONCERT allows members to reduce their expenditures on subscribing to electronic resources and save a lot of time and effort in bargaining with information providers. In return for this, members have to keep in mind that *there is no free lunch* and that they must participate in the growth of CONCERT more actively.

The success of a consortium relies heavily on the participation of its members. CONCERT members are strongly involved in the many activities required to fulfill the potential that grows out of collaboration and resource sharing, and which demonstrates very advantageous to the development of CONCERT. Members must work together to:

(1) Devise and enforce the selection policy.
(2) Recommend electronic resources for purchase.
(3) Lead or participate in the negotiation with information providers.

(4) Establish and enforce the evaluation scheme.
(5) Gather e-journal records for building the e-journal union list.
(6) Install and maintain mirror sites.
(7) Host training sessions and share experiences in conducting reference services.
(8) Translate user manuals and licensing agreements into Chinese.

Development of a Formal Administrative System

At the inception of CONCERT, its operation was empirical. From the experiences gained in running CONCERT over time, STIC and its members learned that a formal administrative system needed to be introduced for the efficient and proper operation of CONCERT. As a result, CONCERT has worked out systems concerning selection, evaluation, promotion, and training.

Reformation of Related Enactments

It is interesting that the emergence of electronic resources affects the enforcement of laws concerning procurement and property. By "procurement" or "property", the conventional laws mean purchasing (or owning) something tangible (touchable and visible). It is obvious that this definition cannot apply to the purchase or possession of electronic resources. In order to deal with this situation, the procurement, accounting, and property departments of a few members interpret the laws flexibly. On the other hand, those of other members interpret the laws literally; and, as a result, these members are obliged to request information providers to give them physical copies (like CDROM) to comply with the existing laws. This somewhat ridiculous situation has occurred frequently early in CONCERT's history, but, fortunately, this situation has been ameliorated as electronic resources have become more common and purchasing agents have gained experience dealing with them. Moreover, the procurement process stated in the conventional laws consists of a number of steps, including price negotiation. Even though CONCERT, on behalf of members, has reached into agreements with information providers about pricing, a number of members are still obliged to go through the whole procurement process.

Win-Win Strategy

The advent of new computer and telecommunication technology has been driving the provision of electronic resources over the Internet. In just a few years, the development of electronic resources has been imposing significant impacts on publishers, aggregators, agents, libraries, and patrons. Even now in the twenty-first century, all of the five parties are still learning how to handle the issues concerning the place of electronic resources in their professional lives. In our opinion, one necessary condition of a successful consortium is to be able to encourage the growth of all five parties.

In the 2000 annual convention, STIC summarized several requests that members expect information providers to fulfill. These requests include: (1) remote access (ID/PW) to e-resources, (2) free trials for new members and/or new resources, (3) the smooth transmission of data, (4) links to Web OPACs & full text, (5) a pay-per-view pricing model, (6) interlibrary loan service, and (7) the provision of records in MARC format. Two or three years ago, all expectations seemed impossible. Now, many of them have come true because of the change and growth in thought, technology and business model of information providers. Specifically, most providers allow remote access and free trial; many providers have offered acceptable connection bandwidth and linked their databases to Web OPACs & full text. However, few providers are currently willing to accept the pay-per-view or more flexible pricing models; furthermore, most providers are reluctant to allow interlibrary loan service and/or provide MARC records for electronic resources at no cost.

Similarly, libraries and local representative agents have evolved together with CONCERT. Libraries are more enthusiastic about taking part in the operation of CONCERT. Local representative agents have learned more about the expectations of members, and they are more proactive in providing customer services. At the same time, patrons are gradually becoming proficient in making use of electronic resources to support learning and to do research.

PATRON-INITIATED INTERLIBRARY LOAN

Background

According to the definition given in the Introduction, both electronic and paper materials coexist in a digital library. The U.K. Electronic Libraries (eLib) Programme even uses the term *hybrid library* to emphasize this reality (Rusbridge, 1998). An important issue in a hybrid library lies in facilitating resource discovery and information utilization by patrons in a variety of formats and from both local and remote sources. Without doubt, in a hybrid or electronic library, interlibrary loan (ILL) and document delivery service (DDS) continuously play an important role in assisting patrons obtain information not owned by their home library. The challenge is how to bring a range of technology and services together to provide an ILL/DDS service that is satisfactory to patrons and librarians (Jackson, 1998).

ILL is a well-known activity based on cooperation between libraries and one manifestation of resource sharing. In the past, most libraries made use of ILL as a last resort for supplying materials to its clientele; therefore, insufficient funding and work force was allocated to ILL, and, consequently, the performance of ILL was far from satisfactory. Now, several factors jointly drive libraries change their attitude toward ILL. These factors include the exponential growth in the volumes and varieties of publications available to libraries, the soaring costs of materials, and the reduction of library budgets. It is increasingly impossible for a single library to purchase all the materials relevant to its users; and, as a result, ILL gradually regains its importance to libraries.

As in other countries, Taiwanese libraries have been using interlibrary loan for nearly 30 years. In the traditional ILL process, most patrons mailed or brought paper request forms to the ILL offices of their libraries, and then the ILL offices would mail or FAX the paper request forms to lending libraries. Most lending libraries used FAX or the Taiwan Postal Service for photocopies (non-returnable materials), and the Taiwan Postal Service for returnable materials. In these circumstances, the average turnaround time of ILL requests was long. Furthermore, no national method was available to handle the process of billing and payment.

A domestic investigation (Chou, 1998) stated that the traditional ILL in Taiwan had a number of bottlenecks, to include the following:

(1) Libraries disregarded the importance of ILL; therefore, insufficient budgets and staffs were allocated to the ILL operation.
(2) The subject coverage of each library's holdings did not have distinguishing characteristics.
(3) No nationwide organization coordinated the planning, cooperation, and service of ILL activities.
(4) No comprehensive union catalog for the holdings of Taiwanese libraries was available.
(5) The ILL process did not exploit any computer and network technology, such as using the newly emerging Ariel mechanism to deliver photocopies.
(6) The lending of material was concentrated on a few large libraries, which increased the workload of large libraries, and, as a result, disinclined large libraries from participating in ILL.

The above six bottlenecks can be roughly divided into policy and technology issues: the first three are policy issues and the rest are technology issues. Thorough investigations into the holding strategies of Taiwanese libraries and the evaluation of access versus ownership are necessary to remove these policy bottlenecks, which cannot be achieved in a short period. On the other hand, technology bottlenecks can be alleviated by using computer and network technology, which is the spirit of the electronic library. Furthermore, the removal of technology bottlenecks may encourage the shift in policy.

In view of this, STIC and NCTU Library started developing the *Interlibrary Loan Networking System for Taiwanese Libraries* (the *ILL System*, for short) in September 1998 (Ke & Hwang, 2000). The goals of the ILL System lie in expediting the ILL process, enhancing patron service, and alleviating the workload of librarians by adequately utilizing computer and network technology. In the end, we expect that the ILL System will play an essential role in supporting cooperative collection development among Taiwanese libraries.

The prototype for the ILL system was developed as a result of a project sponsored by MOE. This project included 16 major medical libraries and was coordinated by National Taiwan University Medical Library and the NCTU Library. It aimed at cooperative serial collection development for Taiwanese medical libraries. The participant libraries deemed that the success of cooperative serial collection development could be attributed to two factors. First, the characteristics of the serials collections of participant libraries should be understood comprehensively so that the responsibility for serials acquisition could be shared. Second, a rapid and quality interlibrary loan and document delivery service should be provided for patrons to obtain materials not in their home libraries. Therefore, in order to achieve its goal, the project established a serial union catalog for comprehensively understanding the serial characteristics of participating libraries, and developed an online system for providing fast and quality interlibrary loan. This project lasted from January 1997 through December 1998, and a prototype serial union catalog and online ILL system resulted. When the project ended, STIC took over the prototype and granted NCTU a project for developing the prototype into a system suitable for all Taiwanese libraries. In this project, an *ILL Service Center* was also founded to offer essential services and assistance to participating libraries.

Design Principles and System Features

The ILL System is a user-centered system. In other words, the underlying design principle of this system entails satisfying the ILL-related needs of a variety of users. Three kinds of users are involved in the system operation: patrons (ILL requestors), librarians, and system administrators. The following separately describes the requirements of the three kinds of users.

(1) Patrons: the system should provide them with the mechanisms to

  • Recognize which libraries have the materials they need;

- Place ILL requests online and handily;
- Trace the processing status of their ILL requests;
- Obtain the materials they need rapidly and correctly; and
- Pay ILL fees conveniently.

(2) Librarians:

- Borrowing Librarians: the system should provide them with the mechanisms to
  - Manage patron accounts (add/modify/delete patrons);
  - Review borrowing requests to verify and correct the bibliographic and holding information;
  - Send requests to lending libraries promptly;
  - Track the processing status of each outgoing request; and
  - Inform patrons of related messages.
- Lending Librarians: the system should give them the mechanisms to
  - Accept and review lending requests;
  - Support the photocopying process (for non-returnable materials) and the checking-out process (for returnable materials); and
  - Track the processing status of each lending request.

(3) System Administrator: the system should provide them with the mechanisms to

- Balance ILL billing and payment;
- Invoice participating libraries; and
- Conduct usage statistics and analysis.

Taking these design principles and user requirements into account, the ILL System possesses the following features:

(1) WWW-based working environment and centralized database

The ILL System was designed via the three-tier Client/Server Web architecture. The underlying database management system is Microsoft SQL Server, which stores the serial union catalog, the transactions of all requests, and the information about libraries and patrons. The user interface and internal processing logics are developed by means of the Active Server Page (ASP) programming language. The system is WWW-based. Patrons and librarians do not need to install additional software other than WWW browsers to use it. By connecting to the WWW server of the ILL System, patrons and librarians can perform ILL-related actions from anywhere 24 hours per day and seven days per week (without restrictions based on the

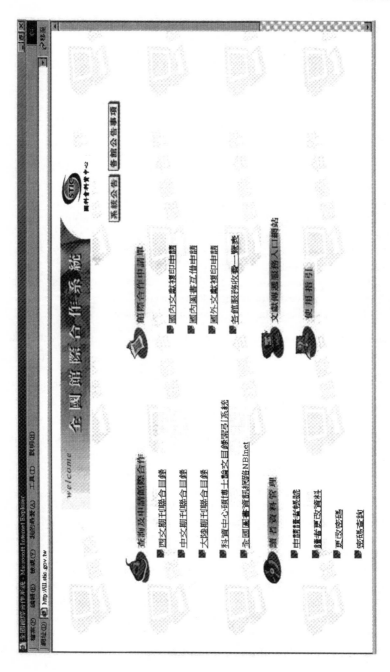

Fig. 2. Home Page of the ILL System.

opening hours of libraries). Figure 2 shows the home page of the ILL System (http://ill.stic.gov.tw).

(2) Integrated union catalogs

Two union catalogs are linked to the ILL System in order that patrons can query them to find the libraries that own the materials they need. The first is a serials union catalog comprising about 30,000 journal titles (foreign, Taiwanese, and Mainland China journals) owned by more than 300 Taiwan libraries; this serials union catalog is compiled by STIC. The second one is NBINET (National Bibliographic Information Network), a book union catalog managed by the National Central Library. NBINET is the achievement of a cooperative cataloging program in which more than 60 Taiwan libraries participated.

(3) Patron-initiated requests

The system permits patrons to submit ILL requests online. When requesting material, a patron may search the union catalogs first to identify the owning libraries of the material. He can then fill out an online form to place his request. When a patron fills out the request form, the system will pass the bibliographic and holding information for the material automatically from the union catalogs, saving patrons time and reducing potential errors that might occur when filling out the form. As the union catalogs are not 100% correct, a patron can also retrieve and fill out a blank request form for materials not found in the catalogs. When placing a request, a patron can choose a suitable delivery method (including Taiwan Postal Service, fax and Ariel) to be used by the lending library to send the material. In addition, a patron may select at most three lending libraries to process his request in sequence. If the first library fails to fulfill the request, it will be forwarded automatically to the succeeding libraries in turn. In case no domestic libraries own the needed material, a patron can still issue an international ILL request by filling out a blank form.

(4) Librarian-mediated ordering

Librarians are involved closely in processing ILL requests. For instance, before an ILL request is sent out to lending libraries, it is reviewed first by borrowing librarians to ensure that the requestor has correctly provided all of the necessary information.

Furthermore, a request will go through a number of transaction states before it is completed whether it succeeds or fails. These states include *Waiting for Review, Waiting for Processing by Lending Library,*

In Processing, Waiting for Pick Up, Request Successful, and *Request Rejected.* Either borrowing or lending librarians are responsible for switching from one state to the next, according to the actual processing status of the request.

(5) Traceable ILL states and statistics

The system keeps track of the states of all ILL requests, providing benefit to librarians and patrons alike by making them aware of the processing status of each request. Additionally, the system regularly generates statistics, including the number of requests, average turnaround time, fill rate, and the number of requests per journal per library. Libraries can exploit these statistics to improve their ILL performance and, in the long run, to refine their collection-development policies.

(6) Centralized billing and payment

Billing and payment for ILL transactions may be the most tedious and time-consuming part of the ILL operation. The traditional billing and payment model is decentralized. In other words, a library has to bill every library borrowing materials from it and pay every library lending materials to it. In this model, librarians, especially the librarians of larger libraries, have to spend a lot of time on the routine process of billing and payment. OCLC's implementation of the ILL Fee Management (IFM) system (http://www.oclc.org/oclc/menu/feeman.htm) in 1995 is a pioneer endeavor to create a centralized billing and payment model. The ILL System incorporates an ILL fee management mechanism similar to OCLC's IFM system. The ILL Service Center takes charge of the process of invoicing and payment.

Figure 3 depicts the operation procedure of the ILL System. Since the system is library to library, each ILL requestor must be a patron of a participating library. The operation procedure consists of eight major stages:

(1) An ILL requestor makes use of the union catalogs to identify which Taiwanese libraries have the material he or she needs. After determining the owning libraries, he or she can issue an ILL request by writing an online ILL request form. If no Taiwan library has the material, the user can issue an international ILL request. After the patron places the ILL request, a transaction with status *Waiting for Review* will be created in the centralized database.

(2) The ILL office of the patron's library reviews the *Waiting for Review* request and then sends it to the lending library. After it is sent to the lending library,

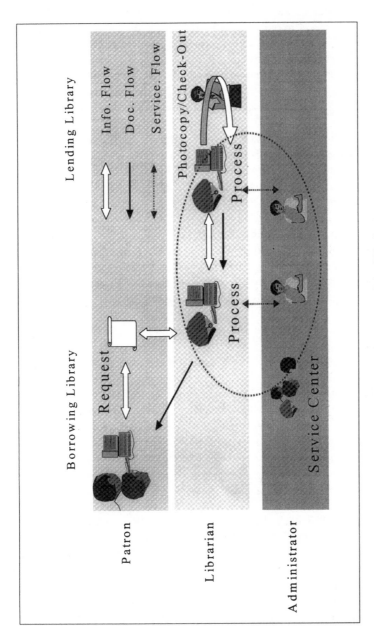

Fig. 3. Operation Procedure of the ILL System.

its status will be switched to *Waiting for Processing by Lending Library*. If the request is international, the ILL office determines to which international document supplier or broker it can be sent. The subsequent processing of an international ILL request is not controlled by the ILL System.

(3) When a lending librarian receives a request with the status *Waiting for Processing by Lending Library*, that person switches the status to *In Processing*, and then fetches the material from the shelf and photocopies it if it is non-returnable.

(4) The lending librarian employs the delivery method specified by the requestor to send the material (or its photocopy) back to the borrowing library. After sending out the material, the librarian changes the status into *Material Sent Back*.

(5) When the borrowing librarian receives the material, changes the status to *Waiting for Pick Up*.

(6) The requestor goes to the ILL office to obtain the material and pay the ILL fee. The borrowing librarian changes the status to *Request Successful*.

(7) The borrowing and lending librarians will reject a request if they cannot fulfill it. At this time, the status is switched to *Request Rejected*.

(8) When librarians have any difficulties in using the system, they can E-mail to or call up the system administrator to help them.

ILL Service Center

Together with the ILL System, STIC and NCTU launched an ILL Service Center located in the NCTU Library. Its primary tasks encompass: (1) developing and debugging system functions, (2) assisting librarians in solving problems encountered when they use the system, (3) conducting centralized billing and payment, (4) regularly generating usage statistics, and (5) hosting training courses and user group meetings. In addition, the Service Center collects and investigates feedbacks from librarians and patrons to enhance the system.

Status Quo

STIC and NCTU launched the ILL System and Service Center in July 1999. The libraries eligible to use the system are members of the *Interlibrary Cooperation Association* (ILCA). We can consider that the members of the ILL System form an implicit consortium. Up to April 2001, ILCA has 450+ member libraries. Of these ILCA libraries, 365 (about 80%) employ the system in their daily ILL operation, and 235 of the libraries using the system participate in the centralized billing and payment system. The libraries not joining the system are mostly public and military libraries, and the primary reasons for not joining the system are: (1) a lack of computer/network infrastructure, and (2) security regulation for connecting to the Internet (for military libraries). Conflicts with the internal accounting procedure of the library represent the major reason why a few libraries do not take part in the centralized billing and payment system.

Evaluation

According to a few investigations in the literature (Arkin, 1998; ARL, 1998, 1997; Fleck, 2000; Kilpatrick & Preece, 1996; Preece & Kilpatrick, 1998), several indicators can be used to measure the effectiveness of interlibrary loan, including: (1) turnaround time, (2) cost, (3) fill rate, and (4) user satisfaction. A preliminary study was conducted to evaluate the effectiveness of Taiwan's ILL System. This study used the requests submitted to the ILL System from 1999/Q3 to 2001/Q1 (21-month period) for analysis. The following reports on the findings of this study.

User Patterns

The first analysis was designed to learn which specific patron categories made use of the ILL System. We expected that faculties and graduate students would use the system heavily. 14,800 patrons submitted requests into the system. Figure 4 shows the percent of users for the four categories: faculty, graduate student, undergraduate student, and others. About one-half users were graduate students and 30% were faculties. Figure 5 shows the percent of requests placed by each category of patrons. While 30% of users were faculty members, they placed 38% of requests; on the other hand, undergraduates accounted for 12% of the total users, but they only requested 6% of materials. Only graduates and other users had a close correlation between the percent of users and requests. This finding conforms to our expectation and is similar to the results of Beam's investigation (1997). This finding could be interpreted as follows. First, most of the materials eligible for interlibrary loan are research oriented, which imply that they are more suitable for faculty members and graduates than undergraduates. Second, most Taiwanese libraries do not subsidize interlibrary loan. Since in most cases undergraduates had to pay the fees by themselves, they might have been reluctant to place requests. In contrast, faculty members and graduates are more likely to pay the fee with their research funding.

In order to have a picture about how heavily patrons rely on interlibrary loan to obtain the materials they need, we gathered statistics about the frequency of ILL requests, as shown in Fig. 6. About 60% of patrons requested materials through the system five or fewer times, 15% requested them six to ten times, and only one quarter of patrons placed requests eleven or more times.

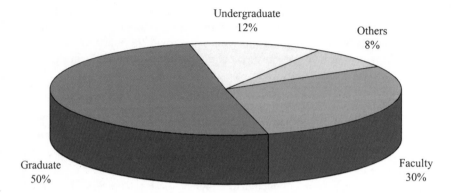

Fig. 4. Percent of User Categories.

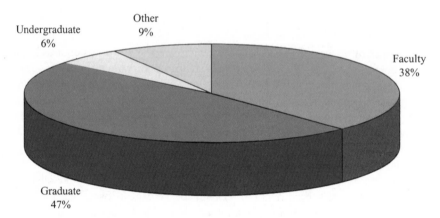

Fig. 5. Percent of ILL Requests Placed by Each Category of Users.

Domestic and International Requests

Patrons can place three kinds of requests via the system: domestic requests for non-returnable and returnable materials, and international requests for non-returnable materials. Table 4 shows the frequency of the three kinds of requests. Figure 7 depicts the percent of the three kinds of requests. As the function of requesting domestic returnable and international non-returnable materials was released in January 2000, the frequency of the two kinds of requests was zero during the third and fourth quarters of 1999. The total number of requests made was 207,166. It can be observed that the majority of the requests (around 94%) were for non-returnable materials.

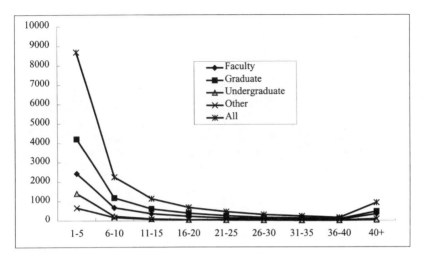

Fig. 6. Frequency of ILL Request by Each Category of Users.

Complete Rate and Fill Rate for Non-Returnable
Table 5 shows the number of requests for non-returnable (domestic and international). A total of 194,173 requests was submitted. Among them, 157,396 were successful, 29,263 failed, and the remaining 7,514 have not yet been completed. Here we define the *Complete Rate* and *Fill Rate* as follows.

$$\text{Complete Rate} = \frac{(\text{Successful\_Requests} + \text{Failed\_Requests})}{\text{Total\_Requests}}$$

$$\text{Fill Rate} = \frac{\text{Successful\_Requests}}{\text{Total\_Requests}}$$

As indicated in Table 5, the complete rate and fill rate were sustained at a high level.

Reason for Unfilled Requests
An analysis was carried out to understand the reasons why requests for serials were unfilled (failed). The analysis result is shown in Fig. 8. "Title not owned" (35%) and "Volume not owned" (26%) were the two main reasons why requests were rejected. From the two reasons, we inferred that the accuracy of the serial

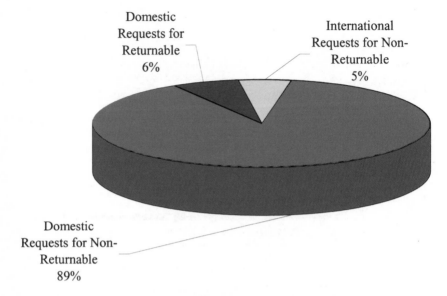

Fig. 7. Percent of Domestic and International Requests.

union catalog is essential to ILL. A further investigation into the necessity of the serial union catalog to ILL is described later.

Turnaround Time & Delivery Method
Figure 9 depicts the average turnaround time. The turnaround time in the system is defined as the time for a successful request to change its status from *Waiting for Review* to *Waiting for Picking Up*. This definition is an upper bound of the

Table 4. Request Frequency of Domestic and International Requests.

	Domestic Requests for Non-Returnable	Domestic Requests for Returnable	International Requests for Non-Returnable
1999/Q3	3196	0	0
1999/Q4	19119	0	0
2000/Q1	24260	1577	1258
2000/Q2	29929	2112	1943
2000/Q3	31246	2358	2118
2000/Q4	38589	3244	2516
2001/Q1	37407	3702	2592

Table 5. Statistics on Requests for Non-returnable Materials.

	Total Requests	Successful Requests	Unfilled Requests	Complete Rate	Fill Rate
1999/Q3	3196	2444	644	96.62%	76.47%
1999/Q4	19119	14982	3694	97.68%	78.36%
2000/Q1	25518	20919	3883	97.19%	81.98%
2000/Q2	31872	25963	4692	96.18%	81.46%
2000/Q3	33364	27102	4981	96.16%	81.23%
2000/Q4	41105	33520	5879	95.85%	81.55%
2001/Q1	39999	32466	5490	94.89%	81.17%

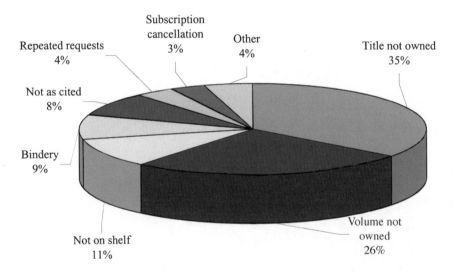

Fig. 8. Reasons for Unfilled Requests.

turnaround time for the ILL System, in that, if librarians do not switch the transaction state according to the real processing status, the turnaround time would lengthen. It can be observed from Fig. 9 that the average turnaround time from the third quarter of 1999 to the first quarter of 2000 was a little longer than that of other periods. The primary reason is that the ILL System had just made its debut and the librarians had not yet gotten used to employing the system in their daily ILL operation. After the initial phase, the turnaround time has improved progressively. Beginning with the second quarter of 2000,

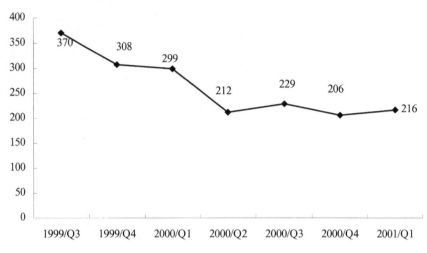

Fig. 9. Average Turnaround Time (Calendar Hour).

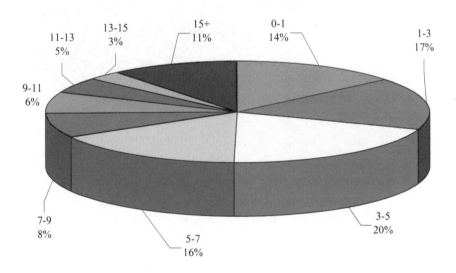

Fig. 10. Distribution of Turnaround Time (Calendar Day).

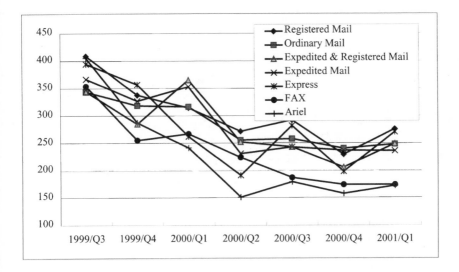

Fig. 11. Average Turnaround Time for Delivery Methods (Calendar Hour).

patrons could obtain the materials they requested within ten calendar days on average.

We also analyzed the distribution of turnaround time. As indicated in Fig. 10, 14% materials arrived within one day and 67% materials arrived in a week or less. This is a significant improvement over the service provided using the traditional ILL process.

A factor influencing the turnaround time relates to the methods employed to deliver materials. In Taiwan, seven kinds of delivery methods are available: registered mail, ordinary mail, expedited and registered mail, expedited mail, express, fax, and Ariel. Figure 11 shows the average turnaround time for each delivery method. Consistent with our thinking, fax and Ariel had the shortest turnaround time.

It is interesting to investigate the actual delivery time required using each method. Figure 12 shows the average delivery time for each. The average delivery time for a specific method is calculated as the time required for a filled request to change its status from *Material Sent Back* to *Waiting for Picking Up*. This definition is an upper bound of the delivery time for the ILL System. Figure 12 gives a general idea about the efficiency of each delivery method (and the efficiency of Taiwan Postal Service). One additional point arises: it may be said that fax and Ariel deliver photocopies instantly; however, approx-

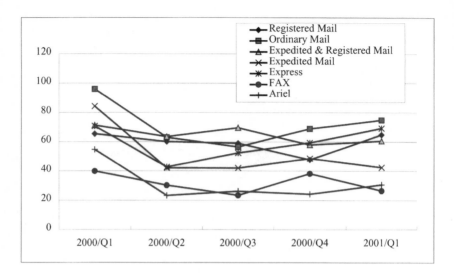

Fig. 12. Average Delivery Duration for Delivery Methods (Calendar Hour).

imately one day was necessary for a request to change from *Material Sent Back to Waiting for Pick Up*. From our understanding of the behavior of librarians, we deduce that the one-day delay results from the fact that librarians usually process (and switch the state of) requests in batch (once or twice per day). The one-day delay may be subtracted from the figures presented in Figs 9–11 to have a closer measurement of average turnaround time.

The final statistic concerning delivery methods is the distribution of requests via different delivery methods. The results are depicted in Fig. 13.

Support for Collection Development
One ultimate goal of the ILL system is to support serial collection development for participating libraries. To accomplish this goal, the ILL system has to provide libraries with the information necessary for evaluating the cost of access versus ownership (Ferguson & Kehoe, 1993). For example, the frequency and total fee of borrowing requests for each serial title can be exploited to answer the question of whether it is more cost effective to pay the cost of subscription price versus paying ILL fees. Table 6 gives the top-ten borrowing serial titles of NCTU, ranked by the total amount of ILL fees collected. The subscription fee of each serial title in Year 2001 is also shown. It can be seen from this table that the subscription price of each title was higher than the cost of ILL.

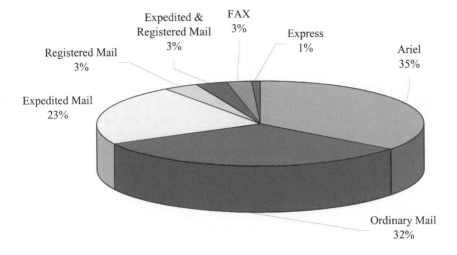

Fig. 13. Distribution of Requests Using Different Delivery Methods.

Table 6. Top-10 Borrowing Serial Titles of NCTU, Ranked by the Total ILL Fee.

Ranking	Serial Title	Total Fee (US$)	Request Frequency	2001 Subscription Fee (US$)
1	SPIE (Journals and Proceedings)	159	12	NA
2	Journal of Luminescence	103	22	2113
3	Journal of the Electrochemical Society	82	78	560
4	Statistics in Medicine	34	25	2495
5	Journal of Microcolumn Separations	27	21	1002
6	Journal / American Water Works Association	26	18	85
7	The Journal of Chemical Physics	21	21	4455
8	Journal of the Patent and Trademark Office Society	22	12	50
9	Journal of Solid State Chemistry	20	19	3499
10	Journal of Applied Physics	19	20	3100

Table 7 shows the distribution of request frequencies for the serials titles requested by the patrons of NCTU. Table 7 indicates that it was very rare for one title to be requested repeatedly. During the twenty-one months covered by this study, NCTU patrons requested articles from 1604 titles. Nearly 70% of these titles were borrowed only once; the majority of the titles (94%) were requested four or fewer times. Beam (1997) conducted a similar analysis of requests for articles ordered from the document delivery supplier Uncover. Forty-eight percent of the journals in her study received only one request within two years, and 85% were requested one to four times. Both indicated a lower percentage than that of the corresponding analysis in this paper. Beam also found fifteen and 4% of the journals received 5+ and 10+ requests, respectively. Both indicated a higher percentage than that of the corresponding analysis in this paper. Since the difference between Beam's and our analysis is significant, it is interesting to investigate further if patrons behaved differently in requesting articles from interlibrary loan and commercial document suppliers.

User Satisfaction
Librarians and patrons are the primary users of the ILL System. Their satisfaction is essential to measure the success of the system. In September 2000, STIC and NCTU jointly conducted a survey of librarian satisfaction. A questionnaire was distributed to 127 librarians at a user group meeting, and 107 librarians responded. Table 8 lists the questions of this survey, and Table 9 gives the survey result.

The questions were partitioned into three categories. The first category concerned the user-centered design principle. In general, librarian satisfaction was high. Of those responding, around 71% indicated that patrons learned the system very easily in training sessions; about 83% indicated that they were pleased with the patron and librarian interfaces.

The second question related to the quality of ILL service after the system was used. Eighty-seven percent of the responding librarians perceived the turn-

Table 7. Serials Titles Requested by NCTU Patrons via the ILL System.

	Number of Serial Titles	Percentage
Total Serials Title Accessed	1604	100%
Title with One Request Only	1096	68%
Title with One to Four Requests	1512	94%
Title with Five or More Requests	92	6%
Title with Ten or More Requests	39	2%

Table 8.   Questions of the Survey of Librarian Satisfaction.

System Functionality and Interface

Q1 Is it easy for patrons to learn the system?

Q2 Is the patron interface (search union catalogs, place requests, check request states) satisfactory?

Q3 Is the librarian interface (review requests, process requests, etc.) satisfactory?

Performance

Q4 Is the turnaround time of the ILL system quicker than that in the traditional ILL age?

Q5 Does the quantity of borrowing requests increase after the ILL system is used?

Q6 Does the quantity of lending requests increase after the ILL system is used?

Q7 Is the service provided by the ILL Service Center satisfactory?

ILL Workflow

Q8 Does the ILL system simplify the ILL process and reduce librarian load?

Q9 Does your library allocate enough manpower to handle the ILL service?

Q10 As a borrowing librarian, do you review the ILL requests placed by your patrons before sending them to lending libraries?

Q11 As a borrowing librarian, if you do not review the ILL requests placed by your patrons, is it acceptable to remove the review mechanism (i.e. a borrowing request could be sent out directly to the lending library without the intervention of borrowing librarians)?

Q12 Should librarians, rather than patrons, make the selection of lending libraries?

Q13 Should the ILL System forward a request automatically to the successive lending library if the current one cannot process it within N days?

Table 9.   Results of the Survey of Librarian Satisfaction.

Questions	Very Positive	Positive	Average	Negative	Very Negative
Q1	75		29	1	
Q2	13	77	18	1	0
Q3	12	75	18	0	0
Q4	89		12	1	
Q5	62		41	2	
Q6	54		39	2	
Q7	21	72	13	0	0
Q8	73		24	6	
Q9	8	41	46	8	2
Q10	84		NA	22	
Q11	26		5	3	
Q12	44		NA	61	
Q13	85		0	11	

around time to be improved. Sixty percent and 57% perceived the quantity of borrowing and lending requests increased respectively. Eighty-eight percent deemed that the service offered by the ILL Service Center was satisfactory.

The third set of questions asked about the impact of the ILL System on the workflow of ILL operations. The first question in this category (Q8) was whether the ILL system simplified the ILL process and reduced librarians workload. Of those responding, 71% made a positive response, and another 23% observed no significant process simplification or load reduction. A few (6%) of librarians responded negatively because: (1) the quantity of requests had been raised; (2) librarians spent a lot of time training patrons to use the system; (3) librarians were very cautious and still kept handwritten records of the requests made; (4) patrons made mistakes very often when filling out the bibliographic and holding information on their requests; and (5) libraries could not participate in the centralized billing and payment process. Most of those problems are common when a new system is in its initial stage of implementation. We believe these problems will be alleviated once the ILL System matures and librarians and patrons get used to it.

Regarding the effort allocated to the ILL service, it can be observed from the responses of Q9 that most libraries (90%) had adequate or average staffing. As mentioned previously, a request has to be reviewed by a borrowing librarian before it is sent to the lending library. But did indeed borrowing libraries check each request? The responses of Q10 revealed that the majority of borrowing libraries (about 79%) reviewed each request, checking the correctness and completeness of the bibliographic and holding information, the delivery method desired, the cancellation date, whether the lending library stopped service, and whether the same patron requested the same material repeatedly. Although 21% of librarians did not review any requests, most of them (26 of the 34 respondents) still thought the review mechanism should remain in force.

Q12 inquired about who, (librarians or patrons), were better at making the selection of lending libraries. Less than half of the respondents thought that librarians were better. These respondents felt that librarians knew the characteristics of the holdings of other libraries more comprehensively than patrons; in addition, librarians knew which libraries provide efficient and quality service. Nevertheless, as Taiwanese libraries had different ILL pricing models and most libraries did not subsidize ILL requests, 58% of the respondents preferred to let patrons themselves make the selection in order to avoid arguing with patrons.

Q13 asked whether librarians wanted the system to automatically forward each request to the successive lending library if it was queued up in the current library for a couple of days. Eighty-nine percent made a positive response because forwarding it could accelerate the turnaround time. In addition, they preferred that the system automatically forward a request if it had been queued up for three or seven days. On the other hand, 11% did not like this function, because sometimes librarians might forget to switch the status of a request even if they had completed the process. In this case, a request would be processed by two or more lending libraries by mistake. Since automatically forwarding requests is indeed a feasible mechanism to shorten the ILL turnaround time, we are pondering how to implement this mechanism while limiting the number of mistakes made.

In short, the above study showed librarian satisfaction to be high. Patron satisfaction is another aspect that is important in measuring the success of the program. An in-depth investigation into patron satisfaction is going to be carried out in the near future.

Experiences

Importance of Union Catalogs to ILL

Analysis of unfilled interlibrary loan serial requests via the ILL System (Fig. 8) showed that "Title not owned" (35%) and "Volume not owned" (26%) were the two main reasons why requests were unfilled. The question is whether an accurate serial union catalog can improve the fill rate of the system. Ryan-Zeugner and Lehman (1999) reported an investigation into the connection between union catalogs and interlibrary loan based on the interlibrary loan at the University of Notre Dame. They found that the project conducted by Notre Dame to maintain a union listing helped their fill rate rise from 55% to 62%. In addition, their survey of unfilled requests showed a dramatic drop in the percentage of request denied because the "Volume not owned". Based on their and other research in the literature, we deem that union catalogs that are accurate and beneficial for improving the fill rate of the ILL System.

Before the method of improving the accuracy of the serial union catalog linking to the ILL System is described, it is important to understand how it is created and maintained. At present, no on-line system for updating the serial union catalog exists. STIC has maintained the serial union catalog in batch for many years. The union catalog is processed once per year. Every year STIC requests that Taiwanese libraries give them the bibliographic and holding records of their serials. Since not all library automation systems in Taiwan can export ISO2709 records, data in ISO2709, and many other formats for the records are acceptable. After STIC receives the records, it corrects errors (such as spelling errors), merges records (A specific title may be owned by many libraries, merges the corresponding records coming from those libraries together), and asks NCTU to make the union catalog available online. This update mechanism has many shortcomings. First, the process of correcting errors and merging records is time consuming and labor intensive. Second, the union catalogs cannot reflect the update in real time. Third, despite STIC's endeavor in correcting errors, STIC does not report the results of error correction to libraries and ask libraries to rectify the corresponding records in their library automation systems; therefore, the same errors recur year after year.

Along with the survey on librarian satisfaction, reported previously, STIC and NCTU conducted a survey about how well the serial union catalog integrated with the ILL System. Ninety-seven out of the 106 respondents (92%) felt that the accuracy of the serial union catalog were satisfactory (52%) or at least acceptable (40%). Others complained that there were too many errors, updating was too slow, there was no real-time updating, and they were unable to add/delete/modify records on-line. Another question asked about librarians' opinions on the mechanisms for updating the union catalog. Thirty percent of the respondents preferred the current mechanism (update the union catalogs in batch once per year). Thirty-nine percent wanted to update their holdings on-line in a record-by-record manner. Twenty-seven percent wanted to import their ISO2709 records into the online union catalog. Some respondents even suggested combining the three mechanisms.

According to the responses from librarians, a redesign of the serial union catalog is under discussion and may be carried out in 2002. The new serial union catalog will be capable of uploading or downloading ISO2709 records, reporting to libraries errors encountered when records are uploaded, and updating individual records online. We expect that the new serial union catalog will not only be beneficial for improving the ILL fill rate, but will also be advantageous in supporting cooperative cataloging for serials. Furthermore, the mechanism for reporting errors that occur in uploading records will help libraries rectify the corresponding records in their local library automation systems.

Essentiality of Core Team

Interlibrary cooperation in Taiwan was once rather loose. Most cooperation programs were restricted to those that did not cost libraries too much extra time and effort beyond their regular duties. However, to conduct a large-scale interlibrary cooperation program like the ILL System, tight collaboration is the key.

The 16 major Taiwanese medical libraries were the core team of the ILL System in the prototyping phase. Due to their similarity in subject coverage and the established strong communications network in their business, it was natural and common for medical libraries to hang together in implementing joint programs. In developing the prototype, these medical libraries and the NCTU Library met almost every month to address issues of policy, implementation and technique. To control the progress of prototyping well, every meeting had a concrete agenda, and checkpoints for the next meeting were determined before the meetings ended.

At present, the *Information Service Division of STIC* and the NCTU Library constitute the core team. The former takes charge of policy decisions, and the latter is responsible for systems development, maintenance and service. A united core team is essential to carry out an interlibrary cooperation program for three reasons. First, it helps the group reach consensus; second, it improves the prospect of making significant progress within a short period; third, it saves the time and effort that must be expended by other libraries.

Governmental Support

Both the prototyping system and the formal ILL System are governmentally supported, and libraries do not pay any money for using them. But, how about the future? Of course, it would be best if the Government will permanently support the operation of the ILL System and Service Center. However, as the directions of the Government are not always consistent with the expectations of libraries, it is possible that the Government will eventually cease adding or supporting new functions advantageous to libraries in the future. In our opinion, Taiwanese libraries should discard the idea of a free lunch and progressively adopt a model that is more self-supporting for the ILL System and Service Center. One possibility is stated as follows: the Government subsidizes the development of the basic ILL System and the operation of the Service Center; and libraries then co-fund the development of value-added functions. But, Taiwanese libraries should not disregard the contribution of the Government to the outstanding achievements of the ILL System, no matter what the future operation model will be; furthermore, we expect that the Government will be able to subsidize pilot projects beneficial for cooperation among libraries.

Strong Interaction between Participant Libraries

The success of an interlibrary cooperation program counts on possessing strong interaction between participant libraries. The Service Center executes many actions to keep close relationship between participant libraries.

(1) Before the system was released formally, 32 major libraries were invited to test the system. The feedbacks from these libraries were used to fine-tune the system.

(2) In 1999, the ILL Service Center held nine training sessions around Taiwan for introducing the system to librarians. Four hundred and thirty librarians from 304 libraries attended the trainings. Through the trainings,

librarians could learn the system quickly and the Service Center could receive suggestions from libraries.

(3) User group meetings take place every year. In the meetings, new functions and policies are introduced, awards are made to the ten libraries with the best service performance record, surveys of librarian satisfaction are conducted, and librarians' experiences in using the system are shared. In addition, suggestions for modifying or adding functionality are received.

(4) Whenever a policy decision has to be made, a number of libraries are called together to look for consensus. For example, in September 2000, because of a few difficulties encountered in implementing the centralized billing and payment system, 20+ libraries gathered to consider alternatives. The wonderful thing is that a new scheme for implementing centralized billing and payment was proposed in the meeting and has since been successfully carried out.

(5) The ILL Service Center exploits E-mail, fax, and telephone to communicate with participant libraries to answer their questions, announce new information, and so on.

Future Perspectives

In the future, NCTU and STIC will keep improving system functions according to the responses of librarians and patrons. Comprehensive statistics will be generated to analyze ILL performance and to support the establishment of collection development policies of participating libraries.

STIC and NCTU plan to further develop this system into Taiwan's ILL/DDS portal site. The idea is to integrate all domestic ILL/DDS sources into the system, as the system owns a well-controlled workflow and centralized billing and payment mechanism. Specifically, a few organizations in Taiwan have already established bibliographic databases for their collections and offered ILL/DDS. However, most of these bibliographic databases and ILL/DDS services are separate or just allow users to write online request forms. We can integrate these databases and ILL/DDS services into the ILL System. In this manner, users will face a unified system for conveniently requesting any kinds of materials, and librarians will have a unified workflow system to process any kinds of ILL/DDS requests and handle the burdensome billing and payment details.

Two tasks are being undertaken to establish the portal site. First, a *WWW-based Information Center for Document Delivery Service* is being created. It is a WWW site that collects abundant information related to document delivery service. It also educates patrons as to how to acquire various kinds of materials they need (http://ddsportal.stic.gov.tw). It also links a variety of bibliographic databases and ILL/DDS services to the ILL System. At present, the *Indexing Database of Doctorate Dissertations and Master Theses in ROC* created by STIC has been linked to the system. Additionally, the integration with National Central Library's *Remote Electronic Access/Delivery of Document Services* ("*READncl*" for short) (Sung & Jeng, 1999) is being undertaken.

The ILL System may adopt the International ILL Standard (ISO, 10160 & 10161)[3,4] for future communicating with other international Systems, like OCLC's ILL System. In this manner, a global ILL/DDS mechanism can be created to suport the users of Taiwanese libraries.

CONCLUSION

The concepts of resource sharing and interlibrary cooperation have long been a tenet of librarianship. Libraries usually put the concepts into practice by means of consortia. Ushering in the era of the electronic library, libraries have to exploit computer and telecommunication technology to redesign their operations and services. Similarly, the electronic library offers libraries opportunities and challenges for handling resource sharing, interlibrary cooperation, and library consortia.

This article has discussed two outstanding programs in Taiwan developed to actualize resource sharing and interlibrary cooperation in the era of electronic library. First, the Consortium on Core Electronic Resources in Taiwan (CONERT) has been established to deal with the issues raised by the emergence of WWW-based electronic resources; the second is the development of the Interlibrary Loan Networking System for Taiwanese Libraries (the ILL System) to improve the performance of interlibrary lending and borrowing.

The emergence of electronic resources raises many new issues that cannot be resolved by any single library. CONCERT was established to deal with these new issues. The core program of CONCERT lies in cost-effectively offering foreign electronic resources by exercising group purchasing power for Taiwanese libraries. To resolve the problem of limited Internet bandwidth, several electronic resources have been made available by means of a mirror-site approach. A number of formal systems have also been introduced into CONCERT for its efficient and proper operation, including systems concerning selection, evaluation, promotion and training.

Interlibrary loan is an important channel for obtaining materials not owned by a library. An efficient and effective interlibrary loan can be achieved by realizing the spirit of the electronic library. With this in mind, STIC and NCTU developed the ILL System. ILCA members have been using the ILL

System for nearly two years. All participating libraries regard this system as
a useful tool to enhance their daily ILL operation and service. According to
the statistics gathered, the ILL performance is improved indeed. In the future,
the ILL System will play an important role in cooperative collection development.

NOTES

1. TANet (Taiwan Academic Network) is the primary network used by schools in
Taiwan. MOE takes charge of the administration and funding of TANet.
2. The systems of CSA, Ei, Elsevier, ISI, and OVID were once maintained by the
InfoSpring Project. Except for CSA, the maintenance of all other systems has been gradually transferred to the current consortium host.
3. ISO/DIS 10160-Information and Documentation – Open System Interconnection
Interlibrary Loan Application Service Definition, 1993.
4. ISO/DIS 10160-Information and Documentation – Open System Interconnection
Interlibrary Loan Application Protocol Specification, 1993.

Web Sites of Related Institutions or Organizations mentioned in the article.

* National Science Council. http://www.nsc.gov.tw.
* Ministry of Education. http://www.moe.gov.tw
* Science and Technology Information Center. http://www.stic.gov.tw.
* National Chiao Tung University. http://www.nctu.edu.tw.
* Interlibrary Cooperation Association. http://www.ilca.org.tw.
* National Central Library. http://www.ncl.edu.tw.
* Consortium on Core Electronic Resources in Taiwan. http://www.stic.gov.tw/fdb.
* Interlibrary Loan Networking System for Taiwanese Libraries. http://ill.stic.gov.tw.
* International Coalition of Library Consortia (ICOLC). http://www.library.yale.edu/consortia

ACKNOWLEDGMENTS

The *NSCDL Project*, the *Interlibrary Loan Networking System for Taiwanese
Libraries* and this article are fully supported by the Science and Technology
Center (STIC) of National Science Council (NSC), under the contract numbers:
88-1-001, 88-1-002, 90-F-001, and 90-R-001.
    The author wants to express his heartfelt thanks to the International Resources
Division, Information Service Division, and Information Technology
Management Division of STIC, for providing valuable information and sugges-
tion in support of this article. The author also acknowledges Ms. Huei-Jen Chen
for her assistance in generating the statistics of the ILL System.

REFERENCES

Allen, B. M., & Hirshon A. (1998). Hanging Together to Avoid Hanging Separately: Opportunities for Academic Libraries and Consortia. *Information Technology and Libraries, 17*(1), 36–44.

Arkin, E. (1998). User Initiated Interlibrary Loan. *Interlending & Document Supply: The Journal of the British Library Lending Division, 26*(3), 119–122.

Association of Research Libraries (ARL) (1998). *ILL/DD Performance Measures Study Executive Summary.* Available at http://www.arl.org/access/illdd/execsum.shtml

Association of Research Libraries (ARL) (1997). Measuring the Performance of Interlibrary Loan and Document Delivery Services. Available at http://www.arl.org/access/illdd-res/articles/illdd-res-measperf9712.shtml

Beam, J. (1997). Document Delivery Via UnCover: Analysis of A Subsidized Service. *Serials Review, 23*(4), 1–14.

Boe, R. (1996). Louisiana Library Network. *Library Hi-Tech, 14*(2–3), 14–20.

Chou (Hu), N. O-L. (1998). Interlibrary Loan Resource Sharing in the Network Era. *Bulletin of Library and Information Science, 24*, 10–16 (In Chinese).

Cleveland, G. (1998). Digital Libraries: Definitions, Issues and Challenges. UDT Occasional paper #8. Available at http://www.ifla.org/VI/5/op/udtop8/udtop8.htm

Ferguson, A. W., & Kehoe, K. (1993). Access vs. Ownership: What Is Most Cost Effective in the Sciences. *Journal of Library Administration, 19*(2), 88–99.

Fleck, N. W. (2000). Interlibrary Loan – A New Frontier. *Library Hi Tech, 18*(2), 172–176.

Hurt, C. (1994). Building the Foundations of Virginia's Virtual Library. *Virginia Librarian, 40*(3), 12–15.

Jackson, M. E. (1998). Loan Stars ILL Comes of Age. *Library Journal, 123*(2), 44–47.

Ke, H. R., & Chang, R. C. (2000). A Case Study of Resource-Sharing Digital Libraries – The InfoSpring Digital Library Project. *Library Collections, Acquisitions, and Technical Services, 24*(3), 371–377.

Ke, H. R., & Hwang, M. J. (2000). Interlibrary Loan in the Digital Era – The Taiwan Serial Union Catalog and Interlibrary Loan System. *Bulletin of Library and Information Science, 33*, 10–25 (In Chinese).

Ke, H. R., & Hwang, M. J. (1999). NSC Digital Library Project: A Case Study of Establishing Web-based Online Electronic Resources. In: C. C. Chen, (Ed.), *IT and Global Digital Library Development* (pp. 225–233). Newton MA: MicroUse Information.

Kilpatrick, T. L., & Preece, B. G (1996). Serial Cuts and Interlibrary Loan: Filling the Gaps. *Interlending & Document Supply: the Journal of the British Library Lending Division, 24*(1), 12–20.

Knigma, B. R. (1997). Interlibrary Loan and Resource Sharing: The Economics of the SUNY Express Consortium. *Library Trends, 45*(3), 518–530.

Kohl, D. F. (1997). Resource Sharing in a Changing Ohio Environment. *Library Trends, 45*(3), 435–447.

Kopp, J. J. (1998). Library Consortia and Information Technology: The Past, the Present, the Promise. *Information Technology and Libraries, 17*(1), 7–12.

ICOLC (1999). Guidelines for Technical Issues in Request for Proposal (RFP) Requirements and Contract Negotiations. Available at http://www.library.yale.edu/consortia/techreq.html

ICOLC (1998a). Guidelines for Statistical Measures of Usage of Web-based Indexed, Abstracted, and Full Text Resources. Available at http://www.library.yale.edu/consortia/webstats.html

ICOLC (1998b). Statement of Current Perspective and Preferred Practices for the selection and purchase of electronic information. Available at http://www.library.yale.edu/consortia/statement.html

Martin, R. S. (1996). Texas: Library Automation and Connectivity: A Land of Contrast and Diversity. *Library Hi-Tech*, *14*(2–3), 291–302.

Okerson, A. (1999). The LIBLICENSE Project and How it Grows. *D-Lib Magazine*, *5*(9). Available at http://www.dlib.org/dlib/september99/okerson/09okerson.html

Perry, K. A. (1995). VIVA's First Year. *Virginia Librarian*, *41*(4), 14–16.

Potter, W. G. (1997). Recent Trends in Statewide Academic Library Consortia. *Library Trends*, *45*(3), 416–434.

Potter, W. G., Russell, R. E., Beard, C. E., Gaumond, G. R., Penson, M. S., & Williams, J. (1996). GALILEO: Georgia's Electronic Library. *Library Hi-Tech*, *14*(2–3), 9–18.

Preece, B. G., & Kilpatrick. T. L. (1998). Cutting Out the Middleman: Patron-Initiated Interlibrary Loans. *Library Trends*, *47*(1), 144–157.

Rooks, D. C. (1996). TexShare: Academic Library Resource Sharing. *Library Hi-Tech*, *14*(2–3), 295–296.

Rusbridge, C. (1998). Towards the Hybrid Library. *The D-Lib Magazine*, (July/August 1998). Available at http://www.dlib.org/dlib/july98/rusbridge/07rusbridge.html

Ryan-Zeugner, K., & Lehman, M. W. (1999). Union Listing and the Interlibrary Loan Connection. *Library Resources & Technical Services*, *42*(4), 313–317.

Sung, C. C., & Jeng, B. M. (1999). National Library in An Electronic Age: The National Central Library's Remote Electronic Access/Delivery of Document Services in the ROC. In: C. C. Chen (Ed.), *IT and Global Digital Library Development* (pp.371–380). Newton MA: MicroUse Information.

Waters, D. J. (1998). What Are Digital Libraries. CLIR (Council on Library and Information Resources) Issues 4. Available at http://www.clir.org/pubs/issues/issues04.html#dlf

Wu, M. D. (1997). Integrated Reference Database of Public and Private Academic in Taiwan. National Taiwan University, Report of a Project Sponsored by the Ministry of Education, Taiwan, R.O.C.

APPENDIX

Assessment Criteria of CONCERT

Table 10. Assessment Criteria of CONCERT.

1. Assessment of Database Systems (See Table 11 for details)	2. Assessment of Electronic Full Text
1.1 Connection/Access Mode	2.1 Integrity of Content (Inclusive of Tables, Figures, Special symbols, etc.)
1.2 Search Interface	2.2 Image Clarity and Readability
1.3 Search Functionality	2.3 (De Facto) Stanford Formats for Full Texts or Images
1.4 Search Result	2.4 Multiplicity of Image Formats
1.5 User Aids	2.5 Inclusion of TOC, Notes, Reference
1.6 Usage Statistics	2.6 Electronic Linkages to Chapter/Section, Reference, Footnote, etc.
3. Assessment of Licensing Agreement	**4. Assessment of Pricing**
3.1 Use restriction	4.1 Comparison with Other Format (like Paper-based, CDROM-based)
3.2 Permission to Interlibrary Loan	4.2 Comparison with Similar Products
3.3 Availability of Archiving/Backfile	4.3 Extra Fee for Future Upgrade
3.4 Permanent Access	4.4 Consortia Special Price
	4.5 One-time or Continuous Charge for Backfile
5. Assessment of Vendors	**6. Overall Assessment**
5.1 Scale and Reputation	___ Exceptional
5.2 Support	___ Excellent
5.3 Customer Service	___ Average
5.4 Free Trial Period	___ No Recommendation
5.5 Training Course	
5.6 Usage Statistics	

Table 11. Criteria to Assess Database Systems.

Connection/Access Mode	
Transmission Speed	___ Excellent (____ bps) ___ Fair (____ bps) ___ Bad (____ bps)
System Stability	___ Stable ___ System Down Occasionally ___ System Down Very Often
Authentication Method	___ IP Control ___ ID/Password ___ Both
Local Mirror Site	___ Yes ___ No
Z39.50	___ Yes ___ No
CGI	___ Ready ___ Have to Be Developed by CONCERT
Search Interface	
Easy or Difficult to Use	___ Easy for Novice User ___ Difficult for Novice User ___ Easy for Advanced User ___ Difficult for Advanced User
Search Mode	___ Basic Mode Only ___ Basic/Advanced Modes ___ Basic/Advanced/Professional Modes
Year Search	___ Search All Years Simultaneously ___ Search Each Year Separately
Linking between Interfaces	___ Good ___ Bad
Design of Interface	___ Appearance ___ Color ___ Browsing Functions
Search Functionality	
Search Mode	___ Boolean Search ___ Natural Language Search ___ Relevant Search
Index	___ Basic Index (___ Abstract ___ Full Text) ___ Browsing Capability (___ Good ___ Fair ___ Bad)
Search Specific Fields	___ No ___ Yes (___ Fields Enough ___ Fields Not Enough)
Search History	___ Able to Combine Previous Searches ___ Able to Modify Previous Searches ___ Able to Delete Previous Searches
Range Limitation	___ Language ___ Year ___ Document Type (Journal, Conference, etc.) ___ Full Text ___ Holdings ___ Other
Exact (Phrase) Search	___ Yes ___ No
Stemming	___ Yes ___ No
Truncation	___ Suffix Search ___ Prefix Search ___ Imbedded String Search
Search Across Databases	___ Re-run Previous Searches in The New Database ___ Search Multiple Databases Simultaneously

Table 11. Continued.

Search Strategy	___ Yes (___ Searchable by Users in the Future ___ Searchable Automatically (AutoSDI)) ___ No
Search Response Time	___ Quick (1-2 Seconds) ___ Slow (Over 10 Seconds)
Search Result	
Display Format	___ Brief ___ Complete ___ Customizable by Users
Sort Order	___ By Publication Date, Author, Title, Source, etc. ___ By Relevance
Electronic Linkage	___ To Other Search Results ___ To Local Holdings ___ To Other Databases of The Same Vendor ___ To Other Databases of Other Vendors
Marked Records	___ Mark All ___ Mark Records Set
Number of Records for Display and/or Download	___ Too Few ___ Reasonable ___ No Limitation
E-mail Function	___ Page by Page ___ Page Sets ___ Whole Document
Print Function	___ Page by Page ___ Page Sets ___ Whole Document
Print Quality	___ Normal Line-Feed, Row-Spacing Without the Interruption of Control Codes ___ Clear and Readable Special Symbols, Fonts, Graphs and Tables ___ Clear and Readable Images ___ Images With the Same Flavor of the Paper Counterpart
Download Function	___ Page by Page ___ Page Sets ___ Whole Document
User Aids	
On-Line Help	___ Context Sensitive ___ Context Insensitive ___ Contents (___ Clear ___ Acceptable ___ Too Simple)
User Manual	___ Can Download from The System ___ Cannot Download from The System
On-Line Tutorial	___ Yes ___ No
Error Message	___ Helpful ___ Not Helpful
On-Line Vocabulary List or Thesaurus	___ Yes ___ No

On-Line Source List	___ Yes (___ Integrated in The Search Interface
	       ___ Another Interface
	       ___ Including the Year Period Available in the
	       System
	       ___ Correctness)
	___ No

Table 11.   Contined.

Usage Statistics	

Provision of Usage
  Statistics
	___ Yes ___ No
	___ On-Line (___ Accessible by Librarians Only
	              ___ Accessible by Anyone)

Update Frequency	___ Day ___ Month ___ Season ___ Year ___ On Time ___ Delay
Statistics Items	___ Detail ___ Acceptable ___ Too Simple ___ Article Level ___ Journal Level
Consortia Usage Analysis	___ Yes ___ No

ABOUT THE AUTHORS

Mark Brogan is a lecturer in the School of Computer and Information Science with teaching responsibilities in End User computing, Internet Computing, Applied Communications and Electronic Recordkeeping. His research interests include preserving digital memory, virtual communities, knowledge management, E-business and public policy for communications and information technology.

Elizabeth Buchanan is Assistant Professor and Co-Director of the Center for Information Policy Research at the University of Wisconsin-Milwaukee. She teaches and conducts research in the areas of information ethics, information policy, research methods, and in particular, qualitative research in virtual space, and distance education pedagogy and administration. She serves as a technology consultant to the Center for the Study of Bioethics at the Medical College of Wisconsin and serves on the Institutional Review Board at the University of Wisconsin-Milwaukee.

Diana Chlebek is an Associate Professor of Bibliography and the Fine Arts, Language, and Literature Bibliographer at the University of Akron. Dr. Chlebek earned her B.A. and M.A. in French Language and Literature from the University of Toronto; M.A. in Library Science from the University of Chicago; and, M.A. and Ph.D. in Comparative Literature from Cornell University. She is an active member of the Western European Specialists Section of the ACRL. Her research interests include comparative librarianship and instruction.

Roger Durbin is Associate Dean, University Libraries and Head of Collections at The University of Akron. He received his BA in English and History and an MA in English from Youngstown State University, and his MLS and Ph.D. from Kent State University. He has been active in statewide collection activities as part of OhioLink's committee structure, and has spoken at local, national, and international meetings on collection and service issues.

William Dworaczyk is currently Director of the Norwick Center for Media and Instructional Technology and Chief Personnel Officer, Central University Libraries at southern Methodist University in Dallas. He holds a Ph.D. in Higher

Education from the University of North Texas with an emphasis on counseling and organizational development.

Philip Hingston has published research in knowledge management, machine learning, information retrieval, neural networks and evolutionary algorithms. In industry he was a senior research scientist and program manager in projects ranging through the development of neural network solutions, advanced planning and scheduling systems, creating and running a global intranet, to introducing knowledge management as a business improvement strategy. As an academic, his main research interest is in Artificial Intelligence, related areas and their applications.

Hao-Ren Ke is the Head of the Digital Library and Information Division of Library of National Chiao Tung University. He has been playing an important role in the sharing of electronic resources in Taiwan. As the technical director of the InfoSpring Project, he installed mirror sites of several electronic resources. Conducting the NSCDL project, he transfers the skills and experiences obtained in the InfoSpring Project to CONCERT. He has developed the Interlibrary Loan Networking System for Taiwanese Libraries which has significantly expedited the interlibrary loan process in Taiwan. By using his technical expertise, he devotes himself to helping libraries in Taiwan move toward electronic libraries.

Diana Kingston is currently Dentistry Librarian at the University of Sydney. Her previous positions include Information Services Librarian at the Medical Library and Circulation Librarian. Diana Kingston's professional interests range from library management to the development of national and international infrastructures in the area of information literacy. Diana Kingston holds a Ph.D. in library and information management from the University of New South Wales.

Jean Mulhern has been the director of the Rembert E. Stokes Library at Wilberforce University in Ohio since 1982. She also is the coordinator of her institution's regional accreditation self-study processes and has been an instructor in its adult degree completion program. She currently is enrolled in the doctoral program in Educational Leadership at the University of Dayton.

James Nalen is an Assistant Professor of Bibliography and Social Science Librarian and Bibliographer at the University of Akron. He received his B.A. from the University of Massachusetts Amherst; M.S.L.I.S. from Simmons College; and, M.S.P.A. from the University of Massachusetts Boston. He previously worked for the Boston Public Library.

Anne Pierce is Assistant Professor, Department of Educaiton, Hampton University, Hampton, VA. Pierce joined the Hampton University faculty in January 2001 after many years in higher education administration. A former Special Libraries Association Chapter President in Connecticut, she recognized early that distance learning would drive educational reform. Her first experiences with undergraduate Internet use were through the NASA National Space Grant College and Fellowship Program. She continues to promote the importance of digital imaging technology and maintains that visual communication is critical to the success of a wide variety of science education activities in both formal and informal online interactions.

Nancy Pitre is an Associate Librarian at Syracuse University. She earned a Diploma of Collegial Studies from the Collège de l'Outaouais and a Bachelor's degree in Business Management from the Université du Québec à Hull, before earning her M.L.I.S. from McGill University. She previously worked for the University of Akron.

Kathy Schulz has been a librarian at Wittenberg since 1987. She worked as a Reference and Instruction Librarian from 1987 to 1995, became acting director in 1995, and was named Director of Thomas Library in 1997. She has a B.S. in Education from The Ohio State University, an M.L.S. from Kent State University, and an M.Hum. from Wright State University.

Victoria Wilson coordinates the Master of Information Services programmes at ECU and lectures on the management aspects of information technology and services. Her research interests include leadership theory and practice, knowledge and information management theory and practice and online learning environments for distance education.

SUBJECT INDEX